Southern Civil Religions

ARTHUR REMILLARD

Southern Civil Religions

Imagining the Good Society in the Post-Reconstruction Era

The University of Georgia Press | Athens and London

© 2011 by the University of Georgia Press

Athens, Georgia 30602

www.ugapress.org

All rights reserved

Designed by Walton Harris

Set in 10/14 New Baskerville

Printed digitally in the United States of America

Library of Congress Cataloging-in-Publication Data

Remillard, Arthur.
Southern civil religions : imagining the good society
in the post-Reconstruction Era / Arthur Remillard.
        p.   cm. — (The new Southern studies)
Includes bibliographical references (p.   ) and index.
ISBN-13: 978-0-8203-3685-5 (hardcover : alk. paper)
ISBN-10: 0-8203-3685-8 (hardcover : alk. paper)
ISBN-13: 978-0-8203-4139-2 (pbk. : alk. paper)
ISBN-10: 0-8203-4139-8 (pbk. : alk. paper)
1. Civil religion—Southern States—History—19th century.
2. Southern States—Religion—History—19th century.
3. Religion and sociology—Southern States—History—
19th century. 4. Religion and politics—Southern States—
History—19th century. I. Title.
BL2527.S67R46 2011
201'.7097509034—dc22   2011012915

British Library Cataloging-in-Publication Data available

To Kate

CONTENTS

ACKNOWLEDGMENTS

MY INTRODUCTION to southern religious history and civil religion came by way of Charles Reagan Wilson's *Baptized in Blood*. To say that I was apprehensive when I asked him to read an earlier draft of this book would be an understatement. Yet, Charles not only gave his seal of approval; he also provided invaluable feedback and guided me through the publication process. Similarly, I came to know Paul Harvey through his scholarship before he twice read my manuscript, passing along priceless critiques each time. Throughout the researching, writing, and revision, John Corrigan could not have been a more ideal mentor. I would not be where I am today without him. To Charles, Paul, and John, I am eternally grateful for your brilliant scholarship and boundless generosity.

I wish also to thank those friends and colleagues who have given of their time, insights, and kindness, in particular Kelly Baker, Joseph Williams, Howell Williams, Michael Gueno, Jordan Smith, Matt Sayers, Kevin Vaccarella, and Dawn Hutchinson. Rhys Williams, Katie Oxx, Patrick Hayes, and Sharon Davies helped me to think through some of the finer points in this book, while Amy Koehlinger, Amanda Porterfield, and Elna Green helped me in framing the "big picture." I am grateful to the many archivists and librarians who have assisted me, especially Dale Couch, Kathy Shoemaker, Elisa Baldwin, Boyd Murphree, and Jim Cusick. A special thanks to Dean DeBolt for pointing me to material on Sidney Catts; to Richard Chastang for supplying me with information on Bishop Allen and the Father Coyle affair; and to John Wright for sending me copies of his research on the Coyle murder and trial.

Much of my understanding of southern religion, history, and culture has come through extended conversations with Lee Willis and Mike Pasquier. Thus, I often called on them to read chapters, sometimes on a moment's notice. And, to my good fortune, they always came through with just the right mix of criticism and praise. I have also relied on Lee and Mike for a good laugh, a challenging long run, and an in-depth discussion about very pressing matters—such as the latest college football polls.

The students, administration, staff, and faculty at Saint Francis University have made it a perfect place to write, teach, and work. I thank Stephen Baker, Rosemary Bertocci, James Gerraughty, Grant Julin, Julia Levin, Chuck Olson, Gabriel Zeis, Denise Damico, Lindsay Ross-Stewart, Mike McKale, Kirk Weixel, Gordon Thomson, Wayne Powel, Andy McKee, Lisa Moser, and the recently deceased Steve Neeley. I am thankful to Tim Whisler, Brent Ottaway, Robin Cadwallader, and the School of Arts and Letters for granting me release time to finish this book. Dan Fredricks read each chapter with great care and gave outstanding stylistic advice. So too did my parents, Vince and Joyce Remillard, to whom I am also indebted for encouraging me to pursue the charmed life that I now live.

For their tireless work, painstaking attentiveness, and willing patience I am grateful to the good people at the University of Georgia Press, in particular Nancy Grayson, John McLeod, Jon Davies, and Beth Snead. M. J. Devaney's copyediting skills are nothing short of superb. Any errors that might remain are my own.

Of course, my most trusted editor, motivator, advocate, and friend has been my wife, Kate. Her intellect is exceeded only by her selflessness and compassion. So it is to Kate, with love, that I dedicate this book.

Southern Civil Religions

You cannot step twice into the same river, for
other waters and yet others go ever flowing on.

— HERACLITUS

INTRODUCTION

Competing Visions of the Good Society

THIS BOOK IS ABOUT the diverse and competing ideal visions of society existing in the post-Reconstruction South (ca. 1877–1920). Blacks,
whites, men, women, northerners, southerners, Democrats, Republicans,
Catholics, Protestants, and Jews all spoke of social unity, peace, and prosperity. Their preferred means for achieving these ends, however, often
differed. When articulating these differences, people drew ideological
lines between those who they believed were good for society and those
they believed were not. The good society of the southern "redeemer"
politician, for example, lacked the supposedly debauched influence of
northern "carpetbaggers." Similarly, southern Catholics living in the
1910s cast nativists as "untrue Americans," whose presumed contempt
for religious freedom ran contrary to democratic ideals. Whether redeemers or northerners, Catholics or nativists, each side's moral vision
for society took shape through mutual opposition, making it all the
more important for us to understand both perspectives.

This book situates itself at the nexus of religion and public life, where
social values, beliefs, and symbols assume a transcendent status. From
blacks describing emancipation as a divine gift, to prohibitionists equat-
ing alcohol consumption with a defiance of God's law, the rhetoric of

1

faith saturated the southern landscape. More, this language often punc-
tuated a given speaker's assertion that his or her vision for society was
righteous, going beyond individual interests and serving a higher good.
Other historians of the South have similarly used the idea of civil religion as an interpretive tool in their work. Chief among this body of
literature is Charles Reagan Wilson's *Baptized in Blood.* "Without the Lost
Cause," Wilson remarks, "no civil religion would have existed. The two
were virtually the same." From Virginia in the east to Texas in the west,
monuments devoted to Confederate heroes such as Stonewall Jackson,
Robert E. Lee, and Jefferson Davis represented stone manifestations of a
southern white civil religion. This common faith created from "the heritage of the Southern past," explains Wilson, became a defining feature
of the era and region.[1]

While *Baptized in Blood* details the civil religious mind of the South's
white Protestant power elite, this book has a more varied focus, looking
beyond the white majority—as well as within it—to uncover the competing moral codes of the era. It breathes new life into an established
subject, making the Lost Cause one civil religious topic among many.
Some groups had more political influence, economic strength, or numbers than others did. Still, the politically disfranchised, the economically
alienated, and the numerically diminutive had the will and imagination
necessary to envision on their own terms what society *ought* to be. These
social ideologies interacted with others, agreeing on some points and
differing on others. Accordingly, this book is a comparative, nonlinear,
decentered history of southern civil religious discourse.

From Lumpers to Splitters

The fractured approach of this book draws from trends influencing both
southern religious history and civil religion theory. Scholars in these
fields have begun looking beyond majority groups and focusing instead
on the contributions of those formerly left on the periphery. In his overview of southern religious history, Paul Harvey explains how the "splitter" historians of the 1980s and 1990s upended the accounts of their
"lumper" forbearers.[2] Samuel S. Hill, one of the "lumpers" Harvey cites,
had argued in *Southern Churches in Crisis* that the revival culture of the

early nineteenth century came to define southern evangelicalism for generations. Practitioners of the faith, Hill had lamented, became overly concerned with conversion and ignored social matters.[3] *Crisis* influenced a generation of "lumpers," who, Harvey summarizes, "understood southern evangelicalism as a solid and singular formation." By contrast, the contemporary "splitter" historians, such as Beth Barton Schweiger, have redirected attention to the "contrasting layers and individually interesting pebbles" of the South's faith patterns.[4] The preachers depicted by "lumpers" were ignorant, backward, and concerned only with converting the unconverted. In contrast, Schweiger's ministers were erudite, ambitious, modern, and decidedly progressive.[5]

For Harvey, the writing of southern religious history has undergone a transition from emphasizing singularity to detailing diversity. Accordingly, he explains, Wilson's *Baptized in Blood* "contrasts with much of the newer 'splitter' scholarship." This is less of a rebuke and more of a call for a new direction.[6] While some have taken steps toward rethinking Wilson's thesis, emphasizing the influence of progressivism, for example, no study has looked beyond the southern white sphere of influence for the content of civil religion.[7] This task rests at the center this book.

Similar to southern religious history, civil religion theory has also undergone a "splittering." In his 1967 essay "Civil Religion in America," sociologist Robert Bellah launched an effort to describe *the* national civil religion. In America, he wrote, "there actually exists alongside of and rather clearly differentiated from the churches an elaborate and well-institutionalized civil religion." The "American way of life," according to Bellah, has a religious dimension, derived from a common history and institutionalized through national myths (George Washington crossing the Delaware), symbols (the Statue of Liberty), and rituals (Memorial Day ceremonies).[8]

Following Bellah's lead, a wave of civil religion scholars endeavored to describe how a religiously pluralistic society could coexist in relative harmony.[9] Many echoed C. Conrad Cherry, who called civil religion "a national faith made up of images and beliefs that Americans can hold in common."[10] Alternatively, sociologists N. J. Demerath and Rhys Williams encouraged scholars to examine the plural realities of civil religious discourse. They suggested that scholars take up "the contexts and uses of civil-religious language and symbols, noting how specific groups and subcultures use versions of civil religion to frame, articulate, and legitimate their own particular political or moral visions."[11] Some have accepted this challenge. Randi Jones Walker references the Demerath/Williams thesis in her analysis of speeches delivered in 1832 by Antonio Jose Martinez, in Taos, New Mexico, and Francis Gray, in Boston. Both speeches were about political independence. Walker carefully notes, however, that the speakers' "myths of origin" reflected their respective cultural backgrounds, political agendas, and geographic locations. "The society of the United States," Walker concludes, "is too complex to be understood in terms of a single myth of origin, no matter how dominant." She beckons civil religion scholars to democratize their studies and embrace "the complexities of American experience."[12]

Despite the work of Walker and others, many have continued echoing Bellah, writing about *the* American civil religion that integrates different voices into one national worldview.[13] Such a tendency has drawn the decided disapproval of Ira Chernus. For civil religion to remain relevant, he explains, scholars would need to "claim no supposed consensus but allow 'us' to speak in all our diversity."[14] The present study accomplishes this end, emphasizing the many moral visions of the post-Reconstruction era. Public devotions to the Confederacy were clearly a significant part of southern white identity. And this population occupied the seat of power in politics, law, society, and industry. There were, though, other groups in the South with unique moral visions for society. If there was one civil religion after Reconstruction, it had many forms, and even the smallest populations influenced the most powerful groups.

From Civil Religion to the Good Society

In referring to "civil religion" and "civil religious discourse" at the same time that I invoke the "good society," the "social ideal," the "public good," the "common good," and "moral vision," I hope to avoid debates over civil religion's definition and focus instead on the content of the category. Others have taken a similar approach. In *Habits of the Heart*, Robert Bellah abstains from referencing civil religion. "I . . . grew weary of the whole definitional debate," Bellah explains, "since I was always interested in the substantive issues, not the definitions." *Habits*, he continues, is "very much concerned with the same substantive issues as my writings on civil religion."[15] Likewise, sociologist Phillip Hammond recognizes that a "conceptual fog" hovers over civil religion, hindering its conceptual viability. He favors the term "legitimizing myth" to examine the "stuff" of civil religion.[16] And in his recent writings, Rhys Williams has not mentioned civil religion but instead has framed his work as a consideration of "how religious ideas undergird the cultural themes that inform how Americans think and talk about public politics."[17]

Bellah, Hammond, and Williams—all prominent voices in the civil religion discussion—stopped using the term "civil religion." Interestingly, though, the "good society" has appeared in each scholar's post–civil religion writings. Philosophers use this phrase to describe an ideal state that maximizes unity, peace, and prosperity while minimizing conflict and strife.[18] *The Good Society* is Bellah's follow-up to *Habits*, in which he and his coauthors examine "the patterned ways Americans have developed for living together."[19] Hammond, for his part, has described civil religion as "a religion not of salvation but of the good society," while Williams has published an article entitled "Visions of the Good Society and the Religious Roots of American Political Culture."[20] Following this well-trodden path, this book identifies the many perceived good societies of the post-Reconstruction South. The qualifier "perceived" is important to note. The following chapters do not seek to determine whether any one perceived good society was, or was not, truly "good." Rather, they echo Williams: "Everyone is for the public good but what that means, or more accurately *whose* vision of the public good is predominant, is very much contested."[21]

In many respects, the "good society" is another way of talking about American exceptionalism. In "A Model of Christian Charity," John Winthrop imagined that Puritans shared a special covenant with God, one that he pledged to protect by enforcing biblical codes of belief and behavior. This new society, he believed, would be a "city upon a hill" for the entire world to emulate. In the post-Reconstruction South, advocates of the Lost Cause used similar language. They announced that God had not abandoned the South but was chastening southerners and challenging them to fulfill the region's ultimate destiny and purpose.[22]

But the language of southern exceptionalism did not always link back to the Lost Cause. In 1877, a Tallahassee newspaper warned lazy people to stay away from Florida. The state instead demanded "[intelligent] and industrious men," who would "develop our resources and make it the Eden of America."[23] Florida was the least populated state in the former Confederacy. But it was growing. And as tourist locations, farmable lands, and abundant resources started to attract people from all over the nation, some Floridians began envisioning how these changes would work to make the state exceptional. They identified certain values as being essential to the common good and used these standards to measure the righteousness of people, places, ideas, and policies.

Indeed, in the forthcoming chapters, social values and their relationship to an envisioned good society occupy a central role. Bellah's mentor, Talcott Parsons, had defined social values as the "normative judgments held by the members of the society which define with specific reference to their own society, what to them is a good society." Similarly, Bellah proposes that social values "indicate what is a good society, what is good social action, what are good social relations, what is a good person as a member of society."[24] Following Parsons and Bellah, this book recognizes social values as the metaphorical bricks in the boundary walls enclosing group perceptions of the good society. For example, many southern whites depicted white supremacy as an indispensable social value, particularly as it related to prosperity. For scores of blacks, however, voting, office holding, and owning property became practices of a freedom they believed God granted and emancipation confirmed. In each race's direct and indirect confrontations, blacks and whites identified their values as superior while casting their opposition's values as undermining the public good. This book endeavors to identify and contextualize these sorts of differences and to show how there was no consensus view in the South on the region's ultimate purpose and destiny.

The Wiregrass Gulf South

In 1907, Professor H. E. Stockbridge of Florida's State Agricultural College addressed members of the Southeastern Stock Growers' Association. "From biblical days the cry of the herdsman has been for cheap lands," he proclaimed. Where, though, could one find cheap land in America? Certainly not the Corn Belt, he observed, which was once inexpensive but was no longer. Stockbridge's answer was the "denuded forest lands of the 'wire-grass' South"—in northwest and middle Florida and the surrounding portions of Georgia and Alabama. The timber industry had done the work of clearing the land. Now millions of acres of cheap land sat waiting, all "perfectly adapted to grazing and the growing of abundant crops."[25]

This book is set within this Deep South subregion, which I refer to as the Wiregrass Gulf South or simply the Wiregrass South.[26] The towns and cities I most frequently mention are Tallahassee and Pensacola in Florida, Mobile in Alabama, and Thomasville and Albany in Georgia. Encompassing inland locations, coastal ports, and a state capital, the Wiregrass Gulf South offers a suitable cross-section of the American South in the post-Reconstruction era. Here the social, political, cultural, and religious developments and tensions that characterized the New South unfolded just as they did elsewhere in Dixie but always in unique ways.[27] Consider Stockbridge's plea to stockmen. He was a prototypical voice of the New South, an optimist who found redeeming power in agriculture. But for every progressive Stockbridge, there was a counter-voice warning against growth and expansion. Writing to a Tallahassee newspaper, one cattle farmer claimed that an "evil" new tax on beef had resulted in local butchers drawing their beef from thirty miles away in Georgia. He fumed that while the Georgia farmer has no stake in the community, a local farmer "has a good name to make." Quality beef from closer locations, he speculated, "will mean more for Tallahassee than a cotton mill or a new railroad."[28]

Growth and migration had moral meaning in the Wiregrass Gulf South, as these social forces had become very much a part of the region's identity. Prior to the war, however, the Wiregrass South was known principally for its cotton plantations and meager ports. It saw only minor conflicts during the Civil War, mostly near the port cities of Mobile and Pensacola, that usually resulted in Union victories.[29] In March 1864, the Confederacy's fortune changed at a battle just south of Tallahassee. Union general John Newton received reconnaissance that the Confederate soldiers in Tallahassee were leaving to defend south Florida. In response,

Newton deployed approximately one thousand troops to Saint Mark's hoping to take the last Confederate capital not under Union control. Word of the Union's arrival soon reached Tallahassee, where militia members and cadets from the West Florida Seminary gathered and marched south. The hastily assembled Confederate forces succeeded in repelling Union troops at Natural Bridge. This victory became a proud moment for many southern whites of the region. "God has been good to us," wrote Tallahassee's Susan Bradford Eppes after the battle, "and the enemy was completely routed." But with Confederate loss looming, Eppes would later recall, "our rejoicing over victory was short-lived . . . and the South entered upon that awful period known as the days of Reconstruction."[30]

In the Wiregrass Gulf South during the Civil War, North and South stood apart in ceaseless tension. Bullets rarely flew, but their fingers were always on the trigger. After the war, the tension remained, albeit without the threat of full-blown warfare. Instead, there was ambiguity. Railroads aided the growth and development of the Wiregrass South, but these railroads often had northern connections. An insufficient prewar railroad system combined with forests, marshes, and swamps to make traveling through states like Florida nearly impossible. Following Reconstruction, Florida legislators relaxed railroad regulations in hopes of attracting developers. Henry Plant and Henry Flagler, both northerners, managed to forge amicable relationships with many members of Florida's Democratic legislature. Between 1879 and 1901, Plant and Flagler received eleven million acres of state land. The "Plant System" consisted of railroads and hotels along the central Gulf Coast. Similarly, Flagler's railroads and hotels extended along Florida's east coast and by 1912 connected to Key West. Both railroad systems expedited trade and provided the means for northern tourists to visit Florida and prospective landowners to relocate there. The state's entrepreneurs sent travel books and brochures north that touted the scenery, rich soil, and "healthful" air and water. Such efforts to populate Florida had positive results. The population increased 42 percent between 1900 and 1910 and 29 percent in the following ten years. Florida's growth rate was twice as high as the national average. Despite the potential economic advantages, the state's rural white majority remained wary. In 1900, approximately 80 percent of Florida's population lived outside of major towns and cities. These "wool hat" Floridians harbored a deep distrust of the urban, progressive "silk hat" agenda. The state's successful politicians, therefore, had to strike a balance, embracing progressive reforms but assuring rural Floridians that "corporate interests" and "outsiders" like Plant and Flagler would not overtake the state.[31]

Despite wool hat protestations, the railroads extended throughout the state, facilitating growth in Florida and the Wiregrass Gulf South. The population gains in this region were prolific compared to those of the rest of the former Confederacy.[32] Between 1885 and 1905, Alabama's total railroad mileage more than doubled. Cotton, lumber, iron ore, coal, coke, and pig iron all traveled these railways and eventually were funneled to Pensacola, until federal grants helped modernize Mobile's port. As a result, between 1880 and 1901 the value of Mobile's exports grew 142.7 percent.[33] For inland locales like Thomasville and Albany, new railways provided farmers with an efficient means of sending goods to outlying ports. Prior to the war, south Georgians shipped cotton and other crops to Florida's Gulf ports via circuitous railways and inefficient roads. After the war, Thomasville became the final stop for the Atlantic and Gulf Railroad, which gave farmers direct access to Savannah. In addition to moving material goods out, this railway ushered wealthy tourists southward to Thomasville, who enjoyed vacationing in the town's various extravagant hotels. Prospective landowners and farmers from the North and South also relocated, hoping the region's "rich soil" and cheap land would lead to positive crop yields and material prosperity.[34]

No doubt, railways made this region and its resources more accessible. But as was the case elsewhere in the South, blacks rarely saw the fruits of these developments. In 1900, blacks represented roughly 43 percent of Florida's population; this number dropped 34 percent by 1920. As whites from the North and South flooded the region, they soon came to share the opinion that blacks merited neither fair wages nor legal protection. Between 1882 and 1930, there were 226 lynchings in Florida alone, giving it the highest lynching percentage in the South.[35] Ironically, railways—that symbol of prosperity and positive change for so many—carried spectators and participants alike to the 1893 lynching of Henry Boggs in Fort White.[36] The rails also brought blacks North during the "Great Migration," many of whom left the South in the hope of better wages and fairer treatment.[37]

As the physical territory of the Wiregrass Gulf South developed, so too did its moral territory. Mapping the moral landscape, however, was an ongoing task, subject to change depending on the speaker, topic, and time. Relocated northern tourists, industrialists, and settlers interacted not only with southern blacks and whites but also with the established and vocal Catholic and Jewish populations. By taking all voices into account, we come to see just how chaotic and unfinished the civil religious discourse of this era and region was. All groups, no matter their size or power, criticized certain social values while cherishing others and produced an image of the good society. The Wiregrass Gulf South was an unfinished South, where questions of society's teleology were a work-in-progress.

The Many Voices of the Many Souths

In 1941, journalist Wilbur J. Cash theorized that "if it can be said that there are many Souths, the fact remains that there is also one South," which essentially for him was the property of whites.[38] This study appropriates and redefines Cash's idea of "many Souths," using it to emphasize the diverse social values and moral visions of the Wiregrass Gulf South. There was no single way that people envisioned the South; rather, their social ideologies manifested a constant tension between the way things were and the way they wanted them to be.[39]

Chapter 1 introduces the southern white "redemption narrative," which described Reconstruction as an era of profound disorder and political redemption as a moment of divine liberation. With the South in southern white hands, the narrative proclaimed, an era of "true progress" ensued. Railroads, education, agricultural advancements, and sectional reunification were all proofs to southern whites that the redeemed South was a blessed land. While cherished for some, these symbols of progress risked provoking an antinorthern ire. In west Florida, Charles W. Jones and William D. Chipley balanced progress and tradition and became civic saints. Jones, an Irish Catholic immigrant, secured civil religious consensus with the Protestant majority by becoming a redeemer politician who facilitated west Florida's post-Reconstruction growth. Chipley was a Civil War veteran, industrialist, and Democratic politician, whose railroad through west Florida made Pensacola's port more accessible to outlying areas. In death, admirers erected a monument to this booster of West Florida to celebrate his progressive spirit.

Chapter 2 conceptualizes the "race problem" as a civil religious "place problem," characterized by the dueling values of white supremacy and black freedom. After Reconstruction, whites held closely to the belief that the South's destiny was dependent on white domination. They prescribed a social and physical "place" to blacks, a boundary that, when transgressed, drew immediate and sometimes violent responses. Meanwhile, blacks envisioned their own place in society, not only accommodating or resisting the code of white supremacy but also producing a vision for society that grew out of their definition of freedom. Catholics were also contributing to this place problem, developing separate churches, hospitals, and fraternal organizations. Some black priests pressed against racial prejudice, confronting a white hierarchy that had absorbed the South's racial status quo. No doubt, the southern white majority willingly mobilized its killing energy to maintain the boundaries separating the races. In 1904, rumors of "Before Day clubs" sent the Wiregrass Gulf South into a panic. The clubs supposedly met in churches and plotted to overthrow white society. Even though most whites eventually dismissed the rumors, the image of the clubs represented the ultimate spatial transgression in the minds of many whites.

Chapter 3 describes the civil religious significance of "true womanhood" and female devotion. In this era of rapid change, the Lost Cause gave nostalgic white southerners a stable "true history" of the Old South and the Civil War. Women became principal facilitators of the Lost Cause, raising funds for statues, hosting Confederate memorial days, and "educating" the public. Sympathetic male observers frequently commended the devotion of these "Daughters of the South." Men also praised women engaged in progressive reforms, such as prohibition, although they sometimes expressed caution, emphasizing that the true woman avoided all activity bearing resemblance to "woman's rights" advocacy. Within Catholic circles, a similar tension characterized exchanges between Mobile's Bishop Edward Allen and Mother Austin Carroll. While supportive in public, in private settings Allen expressed reservations about Mother Austin's forthrightness. He even actively worked for her transfer from his diocese. Mother Austin, though, was admired by Catholics and non-Catholics alike. Such high regard for women religious figures by the 1910s was rare, as nativism swept the region. Conversely, Jewish women fit more seamlessly into the mainstream, developing their own organizations that advocated benevolence and religious unity. The differing response to Catholics and Jews was part of a broader pattern in the Wiregrass Gulf South, whereby Jews paved roads into public life that Catholics never could.

Chapter 4 considers the civil religious worldviews of Jewish men in the Wiregrass region. While white Protestants and Jews differed in their institutional religious practices, many shared a similar moral vision. Religious devotion, philanthropic work, civic involvement, military service, and Democratic Party politics were each key features in their respective good societies. As a result, Jews thrived in many areas of southern life, such as business, politics, and fraternal orders. Still, prejudice loomed in the background. From stereotyped stage images to the lynching of a pencil factory owner in Atlanta, Jews saw the face of anti-Semitism firsthand. Even in the nativist 1910s, however, Jews in the Wiregrass region like Mobile's Leon Schwarz served in elected offices and voiced their public opinions. Moreover, they cast anti-Semitism as a perversion of the American ideal, which they believed Jews shared and helped to create.

Chapter 5 examines the civil religious conflict between Catholics and Protestants during the era of nativism. In 1916, Sidney J. Catts won the governorship of Florida largely because of his anti-Catholic platform. Letters sent to Catts praised his stance against "political Rome" and labeled him a "true patriot." For Catholics, however, Catts's apparent disregard for religious freedom threatened the fabric of social life. Tensions between Catholics and Protestants escalated in the following years, eventuating in the murder of Birmingham's Father James Coyle in 1921. Throughout the affair, arguments over who was, and was not, a "true" American came to the fore. Coyle's murderer was acquitted, dealing a decided loss to Catholics. Nevertheless, their voices influenced what had become a ubiquitous discussion about the Catholic place in southern society.

The Coyle affair is a fitting emblem for this book. Here, two civil religious discourses competed and defended a particular vision of society marked by who counted as truly American. In this symbolic, rhetorical, and legal tug-of-war, the majority had more strength and pulled the Catholics into a proverbial muddy pit. But in those moments of mutual resistance, we find two sides struggling to actualize their good society. Power, in other words, could not strip away from Catholics the will to imagine, create, and project an inclusive social ideal. A similar dynamic characterized exchanges between blacks and whites, northerners and southerners, Republicans and Democrats, progressives and traditionalists, and all different combinations therein.

My exploration of voices from the numerical and ideological periphery is not a simple exercise of forcing anomalies into the center of the story. Nor does it discount the fact that the central powers of the Wiregrass South were (broadly speaking) white Protestant Democrats from the middle and upper classes. Rather, I seek to emphasize how even the smallest groups in the Wiregrass South shaped the social values of those in power. The members of the majority did not create their vision of the public good in isolation. Nor did they act without opposition. Instead, even though they were a dominant force in the public square, they too were compelled to state and defended their values and to disclaim and invalidate values they believed would bring the South into chaos. Understanding any vision of the good society requires an inspection of the complex and competing forces that have shaped it.

Because this book frequently turns attention to the edges of southern society, it omits mention of or downplays some undeniably powerful forces. One obvious example is the Southern Baptist Convention (sbc), which became the largest single denomination in the South by the 1890s. "Whether in manning the front lines in the battle for white supremacy, combating threats such as Populism, or fighting the demon rum," writes Paul Harvey, the Southern Baptist Convention "in the late nineteenth century defended the conservative, hierarchical social order of the South."[40] I do not dispute that the sbc placed an evangelical stamp on the white "Southern way of life." As Harvey emphasizes, however, members did not always speak with one voice. They occasionally disagreed on the importance of progress, racial matters, the legitimacy of liberal theology, and the social gospel. Nevertheless, while not completely solid, the s b c was an important group after Reconstruction that receives little attention in the following pages. Instead, I look to the underrepresented voices of the era, endeavoring to show how they shaped the civil religious discussion.

In his *Upon the Altar of a Nation*, Harry S. Stout uses the idea of civil religion to frame his "moral history" of the Civil War. He describes how, throughout the conflict, North and South remained certain that their cause was objectively right, true, and divinely ordained.[41] Similarly, what follows is a "moral history" of the post-Reconstruction South. In each chapter, religious figures, language, allusions, and institutions appear forthrightly. But this book is not about revealed religion. It is about the key values that people used to define, idealize, and defend their vision for how society *ought* to be and about how even the smallest social groups (Jews and Catholics) and the most marginalized (blacks and "carpetbaggers") were part of this discussion. In other words, the many voices of the many Souths all worked to make their good society become *the* good society.

CHAPTER ONE

Progressive Voices, Traditional Voices

Reconstruction, Redemption, and the "Gospel of Material Progress"

THE LOST CAUSE LOOMED LARGE in the white Wiregrass South's social identity, physical landscape, and daily discussions. But as a civil religious force, it stood neither alone nor without opposition. "Mr. Pollard, in his history *The Lost Cause*, talks pathetically about the people's grief and lament over the downfall of the Confederacy," charged John Crary of Bluff Springs, Florida. "Nothing could give a more false coloring of the fact." Crary assured readers that Confederates fought with honor and courage and that their chivalry was unmatched. But by the war's conclusion, he contended that most were relieved. "It is and was a very easy matter for men like Mr. Pollard, who were constantly surrounded by and mixed with Confederate officials, to be fully deceived and ignorant of the true inward feeling and sentiment of the people." In Crary's view, people were more interested with moving forward, in securing a home and a livelihood. He wanted to help. Crary was a brickmaker and a northern transplant to west Florida, having moved from Ohio before the war. While opposed to secession, he supported the southern effort. After the war, his brick business flourished. Crary believed he had a biblical responsibility to treat his employees fairly by paying just wages and limiting the workday to eight hours. He also encouraged more northerners to settle in Florida, certain that this would make places like Pensacola great seaports.[1]

To borrow Will Campbell's characterization of his iconoclast grandfather, John Crary "was not the Southerner one reads about in books."[2] The relocated Yankee admired the South but criticized the Confederacy. Like his contemporaries, however, Crary preached the "gospel of material progress." As a brickmaker, Crary described his chosen building material as the source of potential greatness in the South and nation. "A great, wise, healthy, good people, must have good buildings, public and private." Thus, "good bricks" were, for Crary, a necessity for a thriving society, and so too was responsible leadership. According to the brickmaker, a good businessperson needed to be a good American. A king, he explained, lived by the motto "Ourselves first; God and country last." But the "true, loyal American" would retort, "God and country first, ourselves last." Crary loathed America's "supremely selfish" millionaires and celebrated the "poor inventors," who were, for him, "the true source of our great material wealth, and moral force of character."[3]

John Crary's bricks built both buildings and a civil religious discourse characterized by a blend of Christian idealism and American exceptionalism. Similarly, whites throughout the growing Wiregrass region idealized other markers of progress such as railroads, public schools, and modern farming methods.[4] In contrast to Crary, though, most Wiregrassers developed a narrative identity grounded in an assumption that Reconstruction's end marked the South's liberation from "radical rule" and beginning of a better and blessed time. These troubadours of material progress sang the praises of political redemption while also demonizing northern carpetbaggers, turncoat scalawags, and incompetent freedmen. While all such people were contemptible, the carpetbagger occupied a central place in the redeemer's symbolic universe as a morally bankrupt political opportunist, the embodiment of Reconstruction's social upheaval.

As Crary's example reminds us, however, the Wiregrass Gulf South was defined by people flowing in and out of the region, often bearing competing visions of the good society. For a northerner like Congressman William D. Kelley, the region's material progress was the result of southerners forgetting their "misguided" past and, ultimately, becoming more northern. Many southern whites held the opposite view, developed from their own sense of time and place. Committed to sustaining a relationship with the Old South, many southern progressives credited their heritage with enabling a new era of prosperity—a prosperity that would have come sooner had Reconstruction never happened.

As more northerners traveled to the Wiregrass region, some were welcomed by the white establishment as able assistants in the spurring of growth in the region. Others were seen as invaders, lingering agents of Reconstruction who sought only to exploit the Wiregrass region for their own personal gain. Politicians, then, had the challenging task of balancing progress and tradition, of finding a middle ground between growth and southern independence. In west Florida, Senator Charles W. Jones adeptly balanced these concerns. In death, admirers apotheosized his memory, heralding his progressive reforms and forgetting his inglorious demise. William D. Chipley, also from the western part of the state, earned civic sainthood when, following his death, admirers constructed a monument celebrating him.

While monuments to Robert E. Lee, Stonewall Jackson, and Jefferson Davis littered the South, Chipley's monument symbolized another, future-oriented, social ideal. It was an ideal heralded by the likes of John Crary, whose business ventures in west Florida helped bring new people and prosperity to the region. Progress was a contested value, however, bearing a range of meanings that shifted along with the rapidly developing social and physical landscape of the Wiregrass Gulf South.

The Redemption Narrative

As Reconstruction came to an end, southern white politicians developed, deployed, and repeated the rhetoric of "restoration." These Democratic "redeemers" envisioned a postwar South that maintained its prewar political and social structures. Yet the South's planter-dominated past was no more. In its place was a new order of middle- and upper-class white leaders preaching what Dewey Grantham calls the "gospel of material progress." Their Edenic "New South" was materially prosperous and forward looking yet cloaked in a pious reverence of tradition. Public education, railroad reform, agricultural modernization, and reunification were all part of a "New South creed," which forged an ambiguous place between past and future.[5]

Political redemption brought not only political power to the southern white majority but also narrative power. In their stories of the New South's rise, they intentionally used the language of sin and redemption to frame the region's supposed resurrection from the ashes of Reconstruction. A central character in this story was the imagined northern carpetbagger. Rarely if ever named, the carpetbagger was a practitioner of "Yankee faith," an advocate of racial equality, and the ultimate embodiment of disorder. Conversely, southern Democratic redeemers made "home rule" a reality, launching an era of progress and prosperity. This "redemption narrative," as I call it, appeared throughout the Wiregrass Gulf South, elevating to sacred status Democratic politics and progressive landscapes such as buildings, roads, schools, and farm fields.[6]

Redemption narratives often began with a dour description of Reconstruction, with the depraved carpetbagger standing in the middle of the chaos. In Mobile, Episcopalian bishop Richard Wilmer blasted the "more violent members of the 'Republican party,'" who during Reconstruction considered the American Constitution a "'covenant with Hell'" because "it protected the South in their property." In contrast, the Democrats in the South, according to Wilmer, had always taken the Constitution as a "solemn compact between the States, and the sole guaranty under which the Southern States held their institutions." Even after Reconstruction, the North had clung to its un-Constitutional ways, he claimed, and the South would need to remain wary of greedy politicians whose covetous eyes looked to exploit the southland and its people.[7]

The equation of carpetbagger with social evil had become dogma in the moral calculus of southern whites who relayed the story of Reconstruction. In his diary, attorney Stephens Croom bewailed that Mobile in Reconstruction was a shadow of its Old South self. Once cotton had flowed through its ports, citizens had enjoyed "wealth and luxury," and the whole city had been filled with "activity and hope." Then the carpetbagger arrived and, Croom fumed, left nothing behind but a demoralized population with only a faint memory of its prosperous past. The cumulative sense of "despair" in Mobile, Croom concluded, "makes me heartily wish I had lived in some land where there was promise."[8]

The religious tone of Croom's ruminations, unlike those of Bishop Wilmer, remained under the surface, buried in the rhetoric of despair and hope. But both Mobilians blamed carpetbaggers, self-interested northerners who had no concern for the South, for the city's industrial and moral degradation. And both agreed that the only remedy was "home rule," a critical part of their good society.[9] The longing for home rule fueled not only antipathy toward the North but also made heroes of southern obstructionists who stood in the way of Reconstruction politics. As Edward Ayers explains, redeemers "defined themselves, in large part, by what they were not."[10]

In 1868, Georgia legislators called for a convention to incorporate the Fourteenth Amendment into the state's constitution. The mostly Republican conventioneers decided to hold the convention in Atlanta and requested funding from Georgia's Democratic governor, Charles J. Jenkins. Jenkins refused. In response, federal officials ordered Jenkins's removal from office. Before leaving, however, the former governor took possession of Georgia's official seal, an assortment of records, and $400,000 of state money. In 1871, southern Democrats regained control of the governorship and the state legislature. To celebrate the victory, Jenkins returned Georgia's official seal.[11] Shortly after Georgia's political redemption, Florida's former Reconstruction governor, David S. Walker, praised Jenkins in a commencement address to graduates of Young's Female College in Thomasville.[12] He informed the crowd that Jenkins was a great patriot who kept the state seal "unpolluted from the touch of the usurper." Georgia's subsequent political victories were surely the product of providential will, he suggested. The state had broken free of its "shackles," while Florida, he mourned, was "still in the house of bondage."[13]

The civil religious content of Walker's rhetoric identified the present exceptionalism of Georgia and the potential exceptionalism of Florida by contrasting home rule with "occupation." For many in the Wiregrass Gulf South, proof that political redemption was a divine mandate came in the form of material progress. In 1892, Mobile's Kate Cummings recalled that Reconstruction had brought "troubles too numerous to mention" and filled Mobile's heart with "apathy and despair." Then, with political redemption, Mobile's desolation "passed away forever." The author applauded the fact that the city had since become "one of the most favored spots on this beautiful earth," in large part because of industrial development. Railroads and thriving ports, Cummings believed, demonstrated that "God is indeed showering his blessings upon this sunny land."[14]

For Cummings, Mobile was her good society. Ordinary places and ordinary activities, now free from northern intrusion, stood in her view as extraordinary signs that political redemption had been a success. Like Cummings, Wiregrassers frequently localized southern exceptionalism, highlighting the unique character of their hometown or state. "The future of Florida can not be estimated," announced one newspaper, "so great are its possibilities and present capabilities."[15] Caroline Mays Brevard expressed a similar optimism when assessing Tallahassee's future but not before painting a grim picture of its past. During Reconstruction, she remembered, the city had lacked all of the features of a stable society, including "commerce," "currency," "legal status," "system of labor," and "certainty of the peaceable possessions of homes and lands." Worse in her mind were the apparent restrictions on religious freedom. "In a land where the separation of church and state was supposed to exist, clergymen were ordered to pray for the President of the United States, under penalty of imprisonment and the closing of the churches." In one instance of forced prayer, Brevard remembered church members departing in protest, defying convention and "leaving none to say 'amen' but the troops who were present to enforce order." At the church, federal officials arrested one man, Brevard sardonically noted, for his "too free expression of opinion."[16]

A church, for Brevard, served as a stage on which white southerners did the moral work of regaining their dignity by inverting the power structure and refusing to pray. This process, in her mind, showed how those who resisted were the true inheritors of the Constitution. Similarly, Bishop Wilmer alleged that during Reconstruction, the North "had abrogated all the sanctions of our former legislative, judicial, and executive government." Wilmer told his congregation to express "more earnest prayers unto God that He would give grace to these soldiers who held us under the bayonet, to 'execute justice, and maintain truth.'" The bishop decreed it inconceivable that they should pray for the "'health, prosperity, and long life'" of the president. When "officers with swords at their sides" demanded that Wilmer offer such a prayer, the bishop claimed he and his "brethren" refused. Moreover, he directed fellow clergymen to do the same, calling the prayer "out of place and utterly incongruous."[17]

Churches became a location for protest in the accounts of Brevard and Wilmer. Their memories restored dignity to the white South while delegitimizing the authority of carpetbaggers, who, they implied, violated the principles of America's sacred documents. But Brevard and Wilmer assured that not all northerners were evil. Their redemption narratives erected solid walls between North and South, on the one hand, and left doors open for a certain type of northerner to enter, on the other. As Brevard described the redeemed South, she extolled all of the symbols of "progress" such as railroads, public education, and industry. Such developments had continued well into the twentieth century, she theorized, precisely because Floridians carefully combined "elements of both south and north" to develop the state's vast resources. Brevard predicted that the state's future would "be as glorious as the past has been — perhaps more glorious."[18] Bishop Wilmer made similar remarks. There was a "large body of people" from the North "whose culture, refinement, and large-hearted generosity" were worthy of "admiration" and "gratitude." There were only a few fanatics, and they were the ones who "waged a destructive war," "laid waste to our territory," "revolutionized our domestic and political life," and "persistently [aimed] at our humiliation."[19] In the accounts of Brevard and Wilmer, northerners are sometimes the intrusive carpetbagger of Reconstruction, and other times the benevolent assistant in rebuilding the South.

This rhetoric of the "large-hearted" northerner grew out of a broader effort in the New South to rebuild relations with the North. In the Wiregrass Gulf South this was particularly important, since a developing tourism industry relied on wealthy northerners to travel southward. Travel pamphlets assured potential visitors that southerners would welcome their presence. One pamphlet reproduced a letter supposedly penned by a northerner visiting Thomasville in 1876. "Northern people are treated with much respect and courtesy and welcomed as citizens; and contrary to a too prevalent Northern notion, ladies will be welcomed into good society. . . . I like Georgia, her government and her people, and only regret that I did not come here at an earlier date."[20]

Hospitality had replaced animosity, and pamphlets like these advertised a southern social ideal that embraced northerners. Redemption narratives, then, often traversed an uneasy ground between the two images of the northerner. Some Wiregrass southerners invoked the region's attractiveness to northerners as proof of its exceptional role in healing wartime wounds. In a speech to the United Daughters of the Confederacy, Tallahassee's Susan Bradford Eppes left little doubt that home rule was a necessity for social stability. After Reconstruction, the South, like "Sampson of old," "rose in her might and broke the shackles that bound her." Having secured home rule, Eppes claimed, the South had been "vindicated in the eyes of the World," and "none now deny the Constitutional right of secession, and the fact remains that the South was absolutely within her rights in leaving the Union."[21] While critical of the North and Reconstruction, Eppes also remarked on the fruits of business collaboration between the North and the South in Florida and suggested that Florida had become the "peacemaker" state. "Florida has done much to heal the wounds of the War Between the States; today, there is less of bitterness on the part of the Floridian than in other States, the settlers coming in from the frozen North meet with nothing but kindness and welcome from the friendly hand of the Floridian." Eppes then speculated that this cooperation proved that Florida was "Blessed of God."[22]

Part of Florida's destiny, for Eppes, was fulfilling a divine mandate to restore peace. Correspondingly, a combination of peace, prosperity, sectional reunification, and regional exceptionalism characterized the rhetoric of Pensacola's John B. Jones. Reconstruction for him was nothing but a "reign of debauchery and terror" overseen by northern "political vampires." He insisted that carpetbaggers corrupted every sector of civic life in west Florida. Then political redemption arrived and Jones's heroes, southern Democrats, joined forces with "some Northern immigrants who composed the better class of the white inhabitants." Together, they revived Pensacola's "civic pride" and "moral stamina" to make it "among the most progressive cities in the South." For Jones, "real progress and prosperity" appeared in the form of paved streets, buildings, parks, and churches.[23]

Jones's words did the civil religious task of inscribing sacred meaning onto physical structures. Ordinary places, for him, told the story of Reconstruction, redemption, sectional cooperation, and progress. For likeminded citizens of Pensacola, another noted landmark on the city's sacred map was the public school. As Dewey Grantham explained, "the school was almost always regarded by the reformers as a redemptive force in the development of a better South."[24] When a Pensacola public school opened in 1887, the local newspaper celebrated it as a clear sign of the city's progressive rise.[25] In her dedication address, Elma MaClay envisioned children coming to the building "with willing feet and glad hearts to meet their teachers, knowing they will find a pleasant smile and a gentle hand to lead them up to all that will make life good and noble." The new schools being built differed substantially from the "charity institutions" of Reconstruction, which had "thrust upon us northern ideas and systems." She assured her audience that the new school would teach "southern education, southern culture and [southern] refinement."[26] Inscribed on the bricks and mortar of this place, then, was a civil religious discourse that narrated a moral message about northern despotism and the redemptive power of home rule.

From built environments to the very soil of the South, the language of progress influenced how southern whites remembered the difficulties of the past and envisioned the future. In the inland locations of the Wiregrass Gulf South in particular, modern agriculture came to embody the endless possibilities of progress.[27] In 1876, Thomas Janes, Georgia's commissioner of agriculture, published the "Handbook of Georgia," which aimed to convince farmers that recent technological advances would help them produce larger crop yields. Janes implored fellow Georgians to "look forward" and recognize that "the future of the state is full of hope." It was a hope born not from political circumstances or material development but rather from the people of the state. "The best inheritance of the New South from the Old South is the Southern people" whose "progressive energy," he predicted, would transform Georgia through agriculture.[28] Janes handled the Old South with a gentle hand, making certain not to offend the sensibilities of traditionalists as he tried to push farmers in new directions.

Like Janes, other advocates of agricultural progress in the Wiregrass South looked optimistically at their home soil and envisioned farmers as redemptive agents. In 1878, Lucius C. Bryan of Thomasville launched a short-lived monthly periodical, the *South Georgia Agriculturalist,* bearing the motto "Devoted to Agricultural, Literary and Scientific Knowledge."[29] In his first issue, Bryan told readers that he hoped the periodical would become "a storehouse" of agricultural knowledge and a documenter of south Georgia's progress. He pointed out that the *Agriculturalist* was not only for farmers but for anyone with an "intelligent progressive mind." Farmers were central to human existence, he continued, and everyone had a duty to understand and support their "great work."[30] Both the people of Thomas County and the land itself were exceptional in Bryan's view. The "garden spot of the South," he observed happily, had developed a noteworthy reputation for farming. "The truth is, that when the people of Thomas county determine upon a success, they never fail to achieve it. The reason is, that they have all the material in hand. They have the climate, soil and variety of productions for the best fair in the South, and they have men of intelligence, enterprise and vim to 'put things together right.'" Bryan speculated that new agricultural advances, combined with the "vim" of the people, would result in more wealth and prosperity for everyone in the region.[31]

Both Janes and Bryan made farmers into "redeemers of the soil" whose progressive spirit was critical to southern advancement.[32] Not every account of the rural South and its people was this affectionate. In a Thomasville newspaper, one native southerner who had relocated to the region for the farming recalled feeling "sick and faint" when he arrived. Facing a potentially "blank future," he described the "very kind-hearted people" of Thomas County as being "very ignorant as to the ways of the outside world, or the laws of God or the country." But railroad expansion, roads, crop development, and Sunday schools were addressing this supposed disparity. All of these markers of progress indicated to him that Thomas County had finally forgotten its undistinguished past.[33]

Bryan portrayed the people of Thomas County in the 1870s as progressive, enlightened, and industrious, while in the 1880s, the relocated southerner described the locals as backwards. Even within the southern white circle, then, material progress was an unfinished project. The perspective of northerners complicated matters. The imagined carpetbagger of the southern white redemption narrative symbolized all things evil and chaotic. But the carpetbaggers themselves saw things differently. In 1876, Pennsylvania congressman William D. Kelley visited the Wiregrass South and delivered a series of lectures expressing his hope that Reconstruction would hasten industrial expansion and racial harmony. Much to his disappointment, he discovered that southern whites were not receptive to his message. One of his lectures in Mobile ended in a race riot.[34]

Recalling his travel through the Wiregrass South, Kelley portrayed the Old South as "a land of desolation" wrought by a single-crop economy; here "fields were fenceless and uncultivated, and . . . people were without reproductive stock." He confessed that Reconstruction had made things worse, in large part because of the North's "record of blundering egotism." Political redemption, Kelley admitted, marked a major turning point, but even then, it took time for the region to advance. Florida, in his view, had been particularly slow. By the late 1880s, however, the state had embraced "the progressive life" that had elsewhere been "animating, illuminating, and blessing the New South." Kelley further explained that this New South mirrored the "modern" leanings of Christianity, which resulted in "the advance of civilization, [and] the progress of wealth and refinement." For the Pennsylvanian, Florida's greatest assets were its diverse resources and warm climate. In exploiting these resources, he concluded, Floridians had broken "from the thralldom of a misguided past" and embraced the divine impulses of progress.[35]

Kelley's definition of progress was filtered through a northern Christian lens. He bundled notions of northern Protestantism and northern progressivism and identified Florida as being a deficient society until it embraced the northern-inflected New South. Southern white redemption narratives sought to crush that lens into a million pieces, casting the northerner as responsible for holding the region back. The northerner was a lonely voice, for sure. But he was part of the region's civil religious discourse, a swirling sea of competing values battling for supremacy and making distinctive claims for how society ought to function.

Visions of the good society in the Wiregrass South, whether they emanated from the North or the South, always had an appropriate counter. By the 1910s, public figures in the Wiregrass region developed a new social pariah, the Catholic. Yet in the immediate years after Reconstruction, this same region made an Irish Catholic a civic saint. While differing in his denominational ties, this public figure preached from the gospel of material progress, demonized the North, and won the public's favor in the process.

Senator Charles W. Jones and "the Purity of His Political Reputation"

Commenting on the postwar South, a Union officer remarked, "Every community has its great man, or its little great man, around whom his fellow citizens gather when they want information, and to whose monologues they listen with respect akin to humility."[36] For many white west Floridians, Senator Charles W. Jones of Pensacola was a "little great man." A Democrat and an Irish Catholic immigrant, Jones earned a reputation as an agent of material progress after Reconstruction. In death, white citizens remembered him as a politician who always stood "for the people."[37] In 1874, Jones won a tightly contested race for a federal Senate seat. The first Florida Democrat to hold this position, he aligned with conservative southerners and worked to end Reconstruction.[38] After 1877, Jones used his political status to acquire federal monies for Pensacola's naval base, fund the construction of numerous public buildings in Pensacola, and redirect postal routes through more sections of Florida. A Pensacola newspaper cheered his reelection in 1881, proclaiming that it "was demanded by the people, who appreciated the ability and faithfulness [with] which he served his state."[39] A newspaper in Montgomery, Alabama, agreed. "No member of the Senate has achieved a wider or more deserved reputation which, we may say, is coexistive with the limits of the Union."[40]

In his reelection speech, Jones echoed the southern white redemption narrative, stressing the importance of political freedom. The political systems of Reconstruction, he charged, were simply the mouthpieces of corrupt northern Republicans. "[Rejoice] and be thankful to heaven," Jones advised the crowd, that this era had passed and they were free to express their political will. Through "the providence of God," the senator elaborated, citizens could now restore government and make it "a creation in their own 'image and likeness.'" Throughout the South, Democrats were winning elections, but Jones warned that Republicans had malevolent plans. "After trampling under foot every sacred right and maxim which was cherished among the jewels of freedom of the South," Jones contended, Republicans were plotting a return. He feared that if not stopped, northern domination could again trickle southward.[41] The Catholic Jones differed with his majority Protestant audience on religious doctrine. But he found a common language, rooted in a redemption narrative, which found a shared enemy in the northern politician.

The strength of Jones's bond with west Florida would be tested when, shortly after his reelection, a strange sequence of events threatened to tarnish his reputation. Following the spring session of 1885, an exhausted Jones retreated to Canada and then to Detroit. His vacation ran longer than expected, and the senator missed the December session. Rumors in the media claimed that Jones had been unsuccessfully pursuing a thirty-five-year-old love interest, Clothilde Palms. Throughout the spring of 1886, numerous senators—both Democrat and Republican—along with Florida's governor, Edward Perry, tried to convince Jones to return for the next session. Jones refused. Meanwhile, he lost his committee seats, and Governor Perry temporarily replaced him with General Jesse J. Finley. In 1888, Florida elected Samuel Pasco to Jones's seat. Though homeless and broke, the unstable Jones ignored his family's pleas to return to Florida, choosing instead to follow his wealthy mistress. Reports also said that Jones worried that some mysterious "enemies" sought his demise and that Detroit was his only safe haven.[42] An Alabama newspaper speculated that Jones had a "brain disease," at the same time recalling his "lovable, genial, almost boyish temperament." An anonymous senator likewise relayed that "Jones is crazy on several subjects—on religion, on women, on liquor, and on the Constitution. It is a sad case."[43] In May 1890, Jones's son John committed his father to the Saint Joseph's Retreat, an insane asylum in Dearborn, Michigan. The former Florida senator remained there until his death on October 11, 1897.[44]

John Jones wrote a gleaming obituary for his father. The elder Jones, he proclaimed, fought continually for "the rights of common people" and rejected bribes promising "great wealth" in exchange for political favors. "Senator Jones remained without even the shadow of suspicion to darken the purity of his political reputation." His father's "public life was distinguished by the strictest integrity and honesty as his private life has been by the utmost purity." Attempting to turn attention away from his father's dishonorable demise, John reported on his death and potential afterlife: "His faith was most beautiful. Although having a strong desire to live, he resigned himself to the holy will of God. After receiving all the consolation of his holy religion, he died a most beautiful death."[45] John Jones's obituary notably affected William Blount, an attorney in Pensacola who had opened a law office with Charles Jones in 1875. Blount wrote, "What you have is the record of a great man and one which should be distributed as much as possible."[46] One Pensacola newspaper called the Catholic burial of Jones "touchingly eloquent and comforting." In summation of the service, the author exclaimed: "Thus endeth the last chapter of the life of a great and distinguished Floridian. When in years to come the roll of our state's distinguished men shall have been called none will shine more radiantly to her credit or her fame than the name of Chas. W. Jones, patriot, senator and Statesman. Fare thee well."[47]

Controversy marked the final days of Jones's life, yet admirers memorialized what they believed was his "pure" political and personal reputation. He was an ideal leader in their good society. The *Pensacola Daily Times*, which tended to view Jones favorably during his political career, did not immediately run an obituary. One Pensacola resident found this to be "positively shameful." "No man was more of a democrat than Ex-Senator Jones: no man served Florida in the federal senate more brilliantly than he, and no city could boast of achievements by one of its citizens which it could be more proud of than those accomplished by the late Ex-Senator Jones." The editor, L. Hilton Green, responded that he personally attended the funeral but had not the time to compose a suitable obituary. Regarding the specific criticism, the editor countered, "I would hardly take notice of your correspondent X's letter were it not that I am quite sure that all the city authorities hold in deep respect the memory of the late ex-Senator Jones."[48]

Admirers of Jones remembered him as a gleaming light of public nobility, keeping his peculiar end in the background. The *New York Times* made no such omission. After noting Jones's Senate career, the paper recounted with gritty detail the story of his abandonment of politics and his unrequited love.[49] For those who admired Jones, his supposed "for the people" Democratic politics made him a respected figure, worthy of a heavenly afterlife. In what was a Protestant South, this Irish Catholic earned two election victories, a demonstration of his ability to speak the region's civil religious language. His Catholicism, in this section of the Wiregrass South, was not a barrier. But this would change. By the 1910s, many white Protestants in this area became profoundly distrustful of Catholic politicians. Florida elected Sidney J. Catts to the governor's seat in 1916, and anti-Catholicism was his central campaign theme.[50] But Senator Jones lived in a different time. Then, political redemption and material progress registered as signs of a good society. Admirers looked past his religious commitment and chose instead to apotheosize his memory as a redeemer and ignore his foibles as a lovesick madman. The same year Jones died, west Florida lost another admired white political and industrial leader. Credited with the "upbuilding of West Florida," William D. Chipley became another icon of progress.[51]

The "Sacred Charge" of William D. Chipley

Soon after his death, Pensacola citizens erected a monument to Chipley, which read:

> Soldier—Statesman—Public Benefactor. On the battlefield he was without fear and without reproach; in the council of state he was wise and sagacious; and in his public and private benefactions he was ever alert and tireless. The history of his life is the history of the upbuilding of West Florida; and its every material advancement, for two decades, bears the impress of his genius and his labor.
>
> He fought for the Confederacy . . . bled for her at Shiloh and Chickamauga. He was creator and builder of the Pensacola and Atlantic Railroad, President of the Board of Trustees of the Confederate Memorial Institute, Vice-President of the Board of Trustees of the Florida State Agricultural College, member of the Board of Trustees of Stetson University and

Tallahassee Seminary, chairman of the State Democratic Executive Committee of Florida, Mayor of Pensacola, and State Senator of Escambia
County. In all, he did his duty thoroughly and well.[52]

During the late nineteenth century, granite and marble statues to the
heroes of the "Lost Cause" captured, for many southern whites, a set of
social values rooted in memories of the Old South and Confederacy. In
contrast, Chipley's monument recognized this value system alongside
a New South value system, wherein railroads, schools, and Democratic
Party politics held sacred status. In the minds of many west Floridians,
Chipley was a "true" son of the South because his progressivism was
suitably southern. Chipley had critics. Political enemies inverted all of
Chipley's accomplishments to portray him as an inauthentic southern
Democrat who put money and status ahead of people. But these voices
would fade when Chipley died, and Pensacola would only remember his
contributions to the region's growth. All told, a glance at Chipley's life
offers some ground-level insight into the complexities of the Wiregrass
South's civil religious discourse as it related to progress. Change was
rapid, opinions were diverse, and a memory of war and Reconstruction
still informed everyday actions and thoughts.

Born in 1840 in Columbus, Georgia, Chipley, the grandson of a Baptist
minister, attended the Kentucky Military Institute and Transylvania
University before enlisting in the Confederate army at the age of twenty-
one. He served with the Ninth Kentucky Infantry and rose quickly, earning the rank of captain. Chipley's career as a soldier was a difficult one.
He sustained injuries at Shiloh, Chickamauga, and Peachtree Creek,
where he also became a prisoner of war. By the war's conclusion, Chipley
had returned to Columbus and became a successful corn and bacon
merchant. His business suffered, however, owing to an unlikely sequence
of events born from the tensions of Reconstruction.[53]

Between midnight and one in the morning on March 31, 1868, five
armed and hooded men stormed a black brothel in Columbus and drew
aim on a disoriented George W. Ashburn, a white man who lived there.
Rising from his bed and grabbing a pistol, Ashburn tried in vain to defend
himself. The mysterious men quickly overpowered Ashburn and shot
him several times. In the days following, rumors swirled as to the gang's

membership. Most of Columbus's citizens believed that the perpetrators were part of the newly formed Ku Klux Klan. Ashburn was a former slaveholder and an established citizen of Columbus before the war. After the war, however, he aligned with northern Republicans, served as a delegate at the 1868 Reconstruction Constitution Convention in Atlanta, heralded "radical" Republicanism, and vehemently criticized the area's Democrats. As if this were not enough, the "scalawag" Ashburn also shared a bed with Hannah Flourney, the mulatto owner of Columbus's lone black brothel.[54]

Federal authorities launched an investigation targeting anyone who was either near the brothel that night who possessed a mask. Ironically, on the evening of Ashburn's shooting, Chipley had hosted a masquerade ball for Columbus's white socialites. This coincidence resulted in the arrest of Chipley and eleven of his guests. At the July trial at Fort Pulaski, former Georgia governor Joe E. Brown served as the prosecuting attorney. Alexander Stephens, former vice president of the Confederacy, argued on behalf of the defense. Before the trial, Brown sent Stephens a letter offering to release Chipley on the grounds of insufficient evidence. Chipley demurred and chose instead to stand trial with his fellow defendants.[55] The trial drew national attention. Each day reporters detailed the drama between the defense and the prosecution. Charges of prisoner abuse soon emerged, adding more intrigue to the story. In spite of all the excitement, however, when the Fourteenth Amendment passed, General Meade sent orders from Atlanta to suspend the trial. With no verdict delivered, all of the accused were set free.[56]

Chipley's merchant business deteriorated in his absence and he declared bankruptcy in 1872. This proved fortuitous, as he began working with Georgia's booming railroad industry. In 1876, Chipley relocated to west Florida, where he served as the general manager for the Pensacola Railroad. He quickly gained the confidence of the state's legislature, and, in 1881, he led a twenty-two-hundred-person workforce that cleared the way for a railroad connecting Pensacola to River Junction, just outside of Tallahassee. A Pensacola newspaper commented favorably on Chipley's endeavors: "Capt. Chipley is among the most enterprising liberal and public-spirited citizens of Pensacola and if the benefits derivable from our railroad lines were in his hands alone . . . our city would be the main terminal and principal depot of these railroads."[57] The author's hope that Pensacola would become a central railroad depot soon materialized. On January 1, 1885, the Louisville and Nashville line—which played a critical role in rebuilding the South during and after Reconstruction—incorporated Chipley's independent railway.[58] The merger connected what was an isolated west Florida port with Jacksonville and Saint Augustine to the east and Mobile and New Orleans to the west.[59]

This remote portion of the Wiregrass South became a bit more developed with Chipley's railway. Locals were not oblivious to this fact. As one journalist summarized, "Without the name of William Dudley Chipley the history of Pensacola could not be written."[60] He became known as "Mr. Railroad of West Florida" as his transpanhandle line enabled the mass transport of commerce and travelers in and out of west Florida. Prior to this, cotton growers floated crops on the Chattahoochee River to Columbus and risked losing goods when the river was low. Additionally, sawmills opened along the new railroad, which gave the region a new lumber and turpentine industry.

For their part in connecting the Wiregrass region to the nation, railroads became powerful symbols of the redemptive side of New South progress. Writing in 1879, for example, General Henry Morgan of Albany, Georgia, claimed that emancipation and Reconstruction brought a sudden "shock" that "paralyzed the whole Southern country." The South began recovering, claimed Morgan, when southern white Democrats "recuperated the almost desolate country." The new leadership facilitated the completion of the South Georgia and Florida Railroad. Accordingly, the region began growing, "[businesses] began to revive, and Albany, like other Southern towns and cities, soon took a new start in the stride of progress and improvement."[61] Critics, however, were less enthusiastic. Many southern lines were northern owned, fueling the suspicion of southern traditionalists wary of outside intrusion. Moreover, railroads sometimes instigated intra- and interstate rivalries. In the Wiregrass South after Reconstruction, politicians from Florida's panhandle threatened to secede to Alabama unless Florida met the region's rail needs. Conversely, Mobile officials criticized businesses in central Alabama for sending goods through Pensacola's port.[62]

In Pensacola, Chipley faced his share of critics. The *Commercial*, a newspaper that favored Chipley early in his career, began feuding with the builder, calling him "the little octopus" who had "a slender following in this county."[63] Rival politicians, like west Florida's Wilkinson Call, a leading voice in the state's growing populist movement, charged that Chipley's railroad dealings were less than honorable. In southern white circles, not all progress was good progress, and not all Democrats were good Democrats.[64] But Chipley would be remembered for his contributions to west Florida. After he died, a Pensacola newspaper recalled that when Chipley was planning his railroad, pioneer folk in the region were angry. It was "their" country, and Chipley was an intruder. One day when surveying the area, he met an elderly woman who, not knowing who she was talking to, lambasted "old Chipley's railroad." Chipley patiently listened and then asked if she had documents for her property. She did not. Chipley loaned her $15 to purchase a homestead entry and then told her who he was. Ten years later, Chipley met the granddaughter of the old woman. She thanked him for his generosity and explained that she attended school on the profits made from selling the property. When Chipley died, the author surmised, the young woman was among legions of others who "[cherished] his name in sacred memory."[65]

Criticized by some, Chipley's railroad was respected by others. Railroads not only fueled west Florida's industrial expansion but also gave northern tourists an expedient means of traveling southward. Pulling them in this direction was Chipley's chautauqua, founded in 1885. During the late nineteenth century, the chautauqua movement spread rapidly through the North and Midwest. Many southern whites, however, remained wary of the organization's liberal Protestant underpinnings. The movement began through the efforts of Ohioan Lewis Miller, a Methodist layperson, and John H. Vincent, a Methodist minister and former circuit rider from Illinois, who worried that Sunday school instructors lacked a proper education.[66] On August 4, 1874, at Lake Chautauqua, New York, they organized the first Sunday School Normal Assembly of Methodists, a two-week-long educational forum for Sunday school instructors. The following year's meeting adopted the name of its location and drew national attention when General Ulysses S. Grant attended. Reporting to newspapers that he enjoyed the peaceful setting and opportunities for learning and reflection, Grant thrust the chautauqua into the national spotlight. Chautauquas soon appeared elsewhere in the nation. Attendees were mostly white and middle class. Chautauquas were not tied to any denomination, but liberal Protestantism informed the social message of the meetings. Sessions addressed everything from fine arts, music, dance, and self-improvement to suffrage, racial equality, and public school reform.[67]

Not surprisingly, then, the chautauqua movement made little headway in the conservative South. By 1900, 101 chautauquas existed nationwide, only 10 of which were in the former Confederacy. The movement's "liberal creed," Andrew C. Rieser notes, put the chautauqua in line with U. S. Grant, the Republican Party, and the Grand Army of the Republic. The southern chautauquas borrowed from the northern format but avoided topics considered off limits by locals. Southern chautauquas, like their northern counterparts, appeared in bucolic settings. Attendees stayed in extravagant hotels, and university professors led sessions. Unlike in the North, southern meetings did not hold sessions addressing racial equality, female suffrage, and the social gospel, favoring instead issues like sectional reunification.[68] Vincent himself hoped the chautauqua movement would "mitigate sectional antipathies," and New South advocates like Atlanta's Henry Grady felt the same.[69] In 1886, Grady delivered his infamous "New South" speech in New York, assuring audience members that the South had "wiped out the line where the Mason Dixon's line used to be."[70] Two years later, using the same conciliatory tone, he invited northerners to a chautauqua near Atlanta. Those who attended witnessed in Grady's built landscape the ideals and values of his New South. It was the product of southern progress, a value that emphasized reconciliation with the North. But the chautauqua also brought visitors into contact with southern white notions of regional pride. At the meeting, Grady hosted a Confederate memorial day celebration and displayed a fifteen-foot portrait of Jefferson Davis for the Fourth of July.[71]

The South's handful of chautauquas had become a chapter in the southern progressive "gospel of union," which encouraged sectional collaboration for the purpose of achieving greater material prosperity.[72] Preaching this gospel meant reaching out to the North but also appeasing southern audiences when necessary. Florida's chautauqua no doubt walked this fine line. In August 1884, the Reverend Dr. August H. Gillet of Cincinnati journeyed to Jacksonville, Florida, in search of a location for a winter chautauqua. When word reached west Florida, Chipley promptly dispatched a representative, who convinced Gillet to visit Lake DeFuniak. The site having been deemed ideal for a meeting, Chipley proceeded to use his legislative skills to incorporate the Florida chautauqua.[73] He began advertising the 1885 meeting, sending promotional pamphlets throughout the South and North, offering everyone convenient transportation on his railroad. Chipley also set aside two hundred acres of land on which the extravagant Hotel Chautauqua would be constructed.[74]

The northern-based chautauqua movement thus found a new home in a region that for decades had been wary of the carpetbagger. Florida's physical map was expanding alongside its moral map, which made reunification part of its progressive territory. This was a theme written into Lake DeFuniak's geographic identity. The town sat just east of Pensacola and was the product of Chipley's Pensacola and Atlantic Railroad. In May 1881, while traveling through the then vacant Walton County, Chipley and a surveying party came upon a circular lake one mile in diameter. According to one highly stylized account, Chipley "seemed to have unbounded faith in the future prospects of the place." One of Chipley's traveling partners, Colonel T. T. Wright, had a revelation while staring at the lake. He reportedly urged Chipley to build a "tabernacle . . . for the gathering of the clans, for the mingling and intermingling of people from all over this great country of ours, so as to . . . bring about better political, moral and social relations between the people at large." The account concluded that Chipley's chautauqua accomplished just this. "There is not a town south of this fading, imaginary 'Mason and Dixon' line in which there is a broader, a more catholic spirit, especially among the veterans of the two armies of the late war." Accordingly, when one of the town's oldest Union soldiers died, three Union soldiers and three Confederates served as pallbearers. "This spirit of faith in our founders seemed to take hold on people from its incipiency."[75]

For some southern whites, the chautauqua and Lake DeFuniak had become prime locations for realizing the progressive aim of reunifying the sections. Their words drew on a broader southern rhetoric but made west Florida exceptional in achieving this end. More than being *just* a story of reunification, though, it also testified to the moral value of railroads and land development. Behind this transition from wilderness to settled landscape was a New South visionary, William D. Chipley. But his brand of progress had limits—limits that spoke to the concerns of fellow southerners. At a chautauqua meeting, organizers assured attendees that the meetings would remain "conservative" on matters pertaining to the Sabbath. "The tendency in many parts of our country," the program read, "is toward the entire destruction of sacredness hitherto belonging to the Sabbath day." It was a perceived moral shortcoming that organizers maintained would not infest the Florida meeting. Put simply, they intended to respect "Christian ideas concerning the observance of the [Sabbath]."[76]

Sabbath observance had become a paramount concern for southern reformers after the war. Ministers worried that violating it would lead to the degradation of church and society.[77] A Methodist minister in Tallahassee called Sabbath desecration a "national sin, threatening the existence of the Republic itself."[78] In Pensacola, a Presbyterian minister warned that anyone who violated the Sabbath was "no patriot," the Sabbath being "linked with the well-being of the state, and the purity and welfare of the nation."[79] The Florida chautauqua's call to distinguish itself from a supposed national trend of ignoring the Sabbath dropped an anchor of tradition in the flowing waters of change. At the same time, though, that chautauqua promoters were trying to calm southern nerves, they were also busy appealing to northern desires for nature, wilderness, solitude, and learning.

In January 1886, August Gillet published the first monthly edition of the *Florida Chautauqua* from his hometown of Cincinnati. The publication labeled DeFuniak Springs a veritable paradise.[80] Methodist bishop W. F. Mallalieu wrote: "The grand old pines are here, tall and straight. The Winter sun makes brilliant their long, green leaves; the balmy odor exhaled from every tree fills all the air with soothing, health-giving influence. . . . The soil of this locality is open, sandy, porous loam, so that, rain as it may, mud is an unknown thing; and what lovely rides and walks along these winding paths and noiseless woods." Mallalieu described the chautauqua as "a haven of repose for the weary. It is a scene of heavenly activities for the strong and vigorous. . . . It has kindled pure, holy, manly, womanly aspirations in scores of thousands whom without it life would continue to be as it has been, a ceaseless, round of duties and drudgeries."[81] The 1886 assembly bore the fruits of these promotional efforts. The five-week meeting drew record numbers, as Chipley offered reduced train rates to Florida's schoolteachers and administrators and convinced the state to pay their salaries while attending the meeting. In addition to using the chautauqua to draw northerners to the region, then, Chipley also used it to benefit the educational development of Florida.[82]

As the Florida chautauqua grew, reunification remained a principal subject. In 1896, General George B. Loud, a former Union soldier from New York City, infused the "gospel of union" into yet another stylized account of Chipley's discovery of DeFuniak Springs. "After his days of weary tramping through a semi-tropical forest, Mr. Chipley, as he gazed up at the dark, graceful pines waving high above his head, and looked into the crystal waters of the lake flashing back the deep azure of the vaulted heavens, as they lapped the white sands at his feet exclaimed, 'Here a town shall be built.'" In this rugged "garden of the gods," Chipley and his fellow laborers cleared the land and prepared it to become a meeting place to "stimulate thought and to cultivate a desire for a higher and better civilization." Armed with new knowledge and insights, attendees then returned home better able to advance humanity. For this, Loud proclaimed, "loud hosannas" have resonated throughout the nation for Chipley.[83]

The Florida chautauqua had become means by which southern whites did the civil religious work of developing a new relationship with the North. The voice of a Union officer commending the work of the southerner Chipley indicates that there was common ground on this objective. Chipley and the chautauqua both represented a form of progress that welcomed the northerner and placated the southern white majority. Chipley's ability to navigate the line between progress and tradition no doubt was a political asset. During Reconstruction, Chipley had served as the chair of the Democratic executive committee in Muscogee County, Georgia. In Pensacola, he held the office of mayor and city commissioner.[84] In 1887, the city commission elected Chipley as its president. The *Pensacola Advance-Gazette* praised the decision, predicting that he would "proceed to use his utmost endeavors to put the city affairs in the best condition possible." Likewise, a Tallahassee newspaper announced, "He is eminently the right man in the right place as his administration will prove, and the record of his long usefulness to Pensacola will be enlarged by what he will accomplish for her advancement." Chipley himself expressed humility when commencing his "sacred charge." He assured his constituents that he would conduct business "without fear or favor." Moreover, if empowered with the trust of the people, he pledged to work tirelessly for the "advancement of Pensacola."[85]

For those who benefited from his work, Chipley was an ideal leader in their good society. For his political enemies, however, he was anything but. In October 1895, Chipley, then the state senator for Escambia County, announced his intention to run for the U.S. Senate. He sought to replace fellow Democrat and political rival Wilkinson Call, a strong voice in the state's populist movement. Chipley tried to win over critics by voicing support for the presidential campaign of William Jennings Bryan. At the May caucus, Chipley initially garnered forty-nine votes to fellow Pensacola resident Stephen R. Mallory's forty-seven. However, after a series of political maneuverings, senators Rawls, Morgan, and Barber changed their votes, thus giving the victory to Mallory.[86] Afterward, the defeated Chipley refused to shake hands with Rawls. As far as Chipley was concerned, Rawls was a "traitor" whose first initial, J., stood for "Judas."[87]

A political charlatan to some, Chipley was a hero in the eyes of many west Floridians. On his train ride through west Florida, Chipley met sympathetic crowds in many of the towns that he had founded. In DeFuniak Springs, devotees held a sign reading "Hon. W. D. Chipley. Honor to whom honor is due." The cheering community of Bonifay flooded the train station to see their defeated hero. According to a Pensacola newspaper, men in the crowd reached out to touch Chipley, only to "give way to their emotions and weep." Thousands packed the streets of Pensacola waiting for Chipley, who was met by a veritable parade complete with exploding fireworks, his namesake, the Chipley Light Infantry, firing volleys into the air, and Pensacola's Third Battalion band playing a victory tune. Observing the scene, the reporter noted that "no defeated candidate in any state ever received such an exhibition of loyalty."[88]

Chipley addressed the crowd from Pensacola's opera house. Grateful for the support, he called himself "the proudest man within the limits of Florida" and said that he felt amazingly content despite the loss. He retold the story of the caucus and the "treachery" of his foes and paused to wonder why specifically Senator Rawls changed his vote. Rawls, Chipley puzzled, had been a Christian with such high character "that he quit his church because no organ was introduced into its sacred precincts." Alas, his vote switch along with that of the others counted as a great sin for Chipley, who discounted the white, Christian, Democratic credentials of all of them. In a dismissive tone, he assured the audience that he bore "no resentment" toward them — even Senator Mallory, with whom Chipley had a longstanding rivalry. "I only mention them because I am reciting history; they are unworthy of mention in any other connection." What he hoped for was peace within the Democratic Party. "I do not mean the peace that characterizes the lion and the lamb when they lie down together, with the lamb inside the lion, but honest harmony, with mutual respect, mutual recognition and forbearance." Chipley believed that such peace was possible, with God's assistance. The reporter covering the event called Chipley "an inspiration to all men in public life," who despite the "treachery" of his opponents, maintained his honor and "redeemed Florida."[89]

The political contest grew out of a civil religious conflict within the southern white Democratic ranks. Recall that the southern white redemption narrative placed a premium on "home rule" and assumed that after Reconstruction, stability and normalcy had returned to the South. Yet there was no shortage of political contests in the years following Reconstruction, and feeding these differences were competing civil religious discourses. Ten years after Chipley's loss, a political observer referred to the caucus as a battle between Florida's "corporation, and anti-corporation crowds."[90] Populist Democrats looked at Chipley as a classic land grabber, a self-interested industrialist whose allegiance was to personal gain.[91] Chipley, in contrast, claimed his opponents were neither proper Democrats nor proper Christians, the line between these categories not being distinct in his mind. Both Chipley and his opponents had developed an image of the good society, a vision that was informed by their own idea of what progress looked like in Florida, the South, and the nation.

Still, in west Florida, Chipley had a devoted following who even when he lost treated him as a conqueror returning from battle. When Chipley died in Washington, D.C., on December 1, 1897, the ensuing lamentations solidified his sainted image for many west Floridians. The *Daily News* wrote a somber description of Chipley's funeral in his hometown of Columbus. Many placed flower arrangements on his tomb, which emitted a "fragrance seeming to exhale the sweet incense of love that prompted the givers."[92] Dr. J. William Jones, a Baptist minister, presided over the funeral. He opened by noting that usually his eulogies were brief but because of Chipley's extraordinary life, this eulogy would be longer. Jones noted that Chipley came of age right when the Civil War began. The young man could have avoided service, the minister suggested, but Chipley's sense of honor and devotion to "his beloved South" would not permit it. When the war finished, Chipley returned to his home, which rested in ruin, causing many to lose hope. Rather than raking "the ashes of the dead past," Jones proclaimed, Chipley set forth to "make a glorious future for his beloved South." Thus, the eulogy wrote Chipley into a redemption narrative, a description of war, Reconstruction chaos, and post-Reconstruction progress. It was a narrative developed through explicit Christian references. Jones emphasized this point by claiming that during Chipley's final moments "he did not speak of the victories that he had won, but simply breathed the simple prayer of his childhood 'Now I lay me down to sleep, I pray the Lord my soul to keep; If I should die before I wake, I pray the Lord my soul to take.'" Pausing, Jones turned to the crowd and asked, "Can you doubt that its incense ascended to Heaven?" The minister then addressed the Confederate veterans in attendance and empathized with them and their wartime loss. With their numbers dwindling, Jones challenged each of them to ask themselves if they would be ready, as Chipley was, "when the summons of death" arrived. In Chipley, Jones saw an ideal Christian leader for the New South, someone both devoted to faith and devoted to the rebuilding of a crumbling nation.[93]

Others mourning Chipley's death echoed these conclusions and emphasized his contributions to Florida's material development. On the day of Chipley's passing, Mr. A. Stoddard of New York sent Pensacola a letter of condolence. He mourned the passing of one of "Florida's greatest citizens," a man who had accomplished "more by a hundred-fold to develop the resources of the state." Stoddard was sure that Chipley's "unusually great brain power and wonderful executive ability" would be missed greatly by Floridians. The "best and most lasting monument [to Chipley]" are "the great public improvements which he brought about during his lifetime."[94] The material developments that Chipley's progressive spirit enabled carried positive moral weight for Stoddard. Officers with Florida's chautauqua felt similarly. "To his keen foresight, contagious enthusiasm, and inspiring generosity, DeFuniak and her chautauqua owes everything." They called Chipley "true, honest, devoted and fearless" and stated that they planned to build a monument in Chipley's honor. While a monument was perhaps insufficient to his greatness, the authors remained confident that Chipley's "enduring" goodness would remain "in the hearts" of those who remembered him.[95]

Chipley's political colleagues also remembered Chipley in death, drafting a resolution in which they called him "a man who had employed every effort, and used every influence, to secure the prosperity of this State, by the up-building of its agricultural, mineral, and [manufacturing] industries, and its charitable and educational institutions." Individual state senators also eulogized Chipley. Senator O'Brien recalled Chipley's "Southern patriotism" during the Civil War and "active part in the political, financial and agricultural upbuilding" of Georgia during Reconstruction. Florida needed someone like Chipley, O'Brien continued, since he used the state's "many undeveloped resources" to create widespread prosperity. Doing this was no simple task. Chipley had to contend with the remnants of "the barbaric system of reconstruction that had been left as a legacy to the oppressed people of the South." But Chipley was "in every sense a man of progress" who overcame such obstacles. He also clung to tradition. According to O'Brien, Chipley had led an effort to erect a monument to Confederate soldiers in Pensacola. This, he claimed, was a testament to Chipley's "belief in the justice of their cause, and his love and admiration of the Southern soldier." While committed to the South and proud of his service, O'Brien assured his colleagues that Chipley was no hostile partisan. Instead, the former Confederate had devoted himself to healing "the scars of war" and unifying "the whole country in peace, concord and prosperity."[96]

O'Brien's eulogy traversed the difficult ground separating past, present, and future. In remembering his colleague, the senator lauded the Confederacy, criticized Reconstruction, paid reverence to the Lost Cause, and referenced material advancements as proof of Chipley's civic sainthood. Senator Myers spoke similarly. The "marvelous growth and development of that section of our State," he opened, had become an "imperishable monument to [Chipley's] broad philanthropy and enlightened public spirit." He then recalled Chipley's senatorial run, using it to portray Chipley as a person with remarkable composure. "I [have never] known a man to conduct himself, under trying circumstances, with more dignity and consideration." Myers contended that Chipley was "goaded in debate" by his adversaries but refused to sacrifice his dignity in the process.[97]

Chipley's progressive spirit was also memorialized by Senator Gillard, whose poem read:

> His deeds become his monument
> Better than brass or stone,
> They bore his name on glory's roll
> Unrivalled and alone.[98]

While Gillard and many others pointed to the very landscape of Florida as Chipley's monument, the citizens of Pensacola decided to build a stone one. On July 12, 1899, a committee in Pensacola paid $3,000 to the Muldoon Monument Company in Louisville for a nearly forty-foot granite monument dedicated to Chipley's "upbuilding of West Florida."[99]

Memorializing the "Spirit of Progress"

The redemption narrative of whites in the Wiregrass Gulf South did the civil religious work of repairing a damaged public identity and projecting

a progressive social ideal. It redefined the region in light of what southern whites believed was the disruptive occurrences of Reconstruction.
Carpetbaggers, depicted as heartless propagators of "Yankee faith," were
everything that the redeemers believed they were not. Political redemption took power from the North and reasserted home rule, the narrative
announced. The good society of the post-Reconstruction South was a
place of progress, where railroads, schools, agricultural advancements,
and the like each symbolized the bounties of home rule. The South,
in this vision of society, was even adept at repairing old wounds. Still,
the redemption narrative carefully identified a "better class" of northerner who supposedly helped the region rebuild both materially and
ideologically.

Thus the redemption narrative gave white southerners a new sense of
time and place and a new list of sinners and saints. As the Wiregrass region grew and developed new landscapes, nostalgic storytellers credited
their heritage with enabling this progress. And carpetbaggers too would
leave an indelible mark, becoming a synonym for political corruption in
both their past and present. But northerners were more than imagined
foils. They were real people in the Wiregrass South whose interpretations
of the war, Reconstruction, and material progress sometimes drifted
from the majority's script. Both northerners and southerners lived in
the region and traveled through it. Their respective visions of the good
society interacted directly and indirectly in the public sphere, agreeing
on points and differing elsewhere about the region's raison d'être. Civil
religious competition also existed within the white South. No doubt, the
story arc of the redemption narrative belies the complexities of southern
white political life. William D. Chipley was a hero to some but a "little
octopus" to others. Chipley himself had categorized his Democratic foes
as "unworthy" members of his party.

Republicans and Democrats, northerners and southerners, Lost
Causers and progressives all lived in the Wiregrass Gulf South, and they
all articulated their most cherished social values. Many of these values
related to race, a consuming topic after Reconstruction. "The Road to
redemption is under the white banner," a Mobile newspaper proclaimed
in 1871, warning fellow Democrats to avoid courting black votes.[100]

Nothing—not political redemption, material progress, or promises of riches—could trump the southern white necessity to maintain racial supremacy. Race became arguably the preeminent topic of the era, and interactions between blacks and whites would produce new layers of civil religious diversity and conflict all throughout the Wiregrass Gulf South.

CHAPTER TWO

Black Voices, White Voices

The Race Problem as a Place Problem

BENJAMIN JEFFERSON DAVIS called his hometown of Dawson, Georgia, a "peaceful" place but qualified that assertion by noting that "it was the peace of the master's domination over the slave; a kind of peace that white supremacists say is disturbed when Negroes become restless for their rights." To maintain this peace, Davis continued, blacks avoided mentioning voting, office holding, just wages, and functioning schools. And the Constitution? "The Negroes knew very well that the U.S. Constitution had no bearing on Georgia. They knew that the law was what the 'white folks' said it was." At times, whites announced their "law" through public performances, like when the sheriff processed through the black part of town to apprehend a man who had "sassed" a white woman. The scene, Davis observed, "looked like a parade, on the one hand, and a funeral on the other." Everyone recognized that the accused would not find justice in a white court and that his future life on the chain gang would push him to the brink of death. The setting for this procession was a black neighborhood, a dirty, treeless "slum," according to Davis. The white side of Dawson, however, was "clean" and "the sidewalks planted with cool trees; the dirt streets were smooth and well-groomed." A railroad track separated the sides, as did the evolving rule of white supremacy.[1]

The railroad track of Davis's memory stands as a powerful image of the moral implications of spatial organization. In Dawson and elsewhere in the Wiregrass region, blacks rarely saw the terminus of the New South's prosperity train. Instead, they operated within a white vision of the good society, one that promised stability so long as blacks stayed "in their place." The specifics of this place were often vague, only becoming clear when a black person did something that the white majority deemed "out of place."[2] Indeed, the "race problem" was also a "place problem." Reconstruction's end left white southerners struggling to order society in light of war, emancipation, and occupation. Certainly, this involved coming to grips with industry, northern tourism, immigration, and the like. But nothing was quite like race, a topic that managed to influence all corners of white civil religious discourse.

But Wiregrass blacks too were engaged in defining their place, one drawn by the freedom they believed God granted and emancipation confirmed. Their civil religious discourse drew freely from the quarries of black history, Christianity, and American democracy. It resisted the white status quo at times, and placated the white majority others. But blacks were not merely responding to whites. Rather, black civil religious discourse aimed to create a society where members of the race prospered and thrived. Catholics also were involved in this conversation. In the Wiregrass Gulf South, white Catholics developed a racial ideology that localized social forces pulsating in the South, Northeast, and Europe. Ultimately, black Catholics discovered that their "place" in the church was little different than it was in the Jim Crow South.

No doubt, whites held the balance of power in the Wiregrass region, a fact that should not be denied or brushed aside. When a place violation occurred, whites could manipulate the law or mobilize their killing energies. In 1904, unsubstantiated rumors of black-led murder clubs swirled in the Wiregrass Gulf South. In response, the white power structure pressed its authority onto black communities and firmly asserted the black "place" in society. Meanwhile, blacks once again confronted the reality that the freedom they imagined was still a long way from coming.

The "Creed of the People"

In 1908, pugilist Jack Johnson knocked out Tommy Burns to become the first black heavyweight champion. Despite the victory, many whites were unconvinced of his legitimacy. Instead, they favored Jim Jefferies, the white former champion who had refused to fight Johnson, believing it beneath him.[3] But public pressure and the promise of a payoff was too much to resist. Jefferies conceded to a bout. On July 4, 1910, Johnson soundly defeated the white boxing legend, and race riots erupted throughout the nation. In response, U.S. representative Seaborne A. Roddenberry from Thomasville drafted a bill restricting interstate shipment of Johnson's fight tapes, hoping this would avert any future riots. In 1912, Congress passed the bill after Johnson defeated the "white hope," "Fireman" Jim Flynn. At the debate, Roddenberry declared that "no man descendent from the old Saxon race can look upon that kind of contest without abhorrence and disgust."[4] When Johnson married a white woman, Roddenberry continued his campaign against the boxer, proposing a Constitutional ban on interracial marriage. "We can do no greater injustice to the negro," he warned, "than to let our statutes permit him to entertain the hope that at some future time he or his offspring may be married with a woman of the white race. . . . The consequences will bring annihilation to that race which we have protected in our land for all these years."[5] Roddenberry would later elaborate on just what these "consequences" would be. "It is destructive to moral supremacy, and ultimately this slavery of white women to black beasts will bring this nation a conflict as fatal and as bloody as ever reddened the soil of Virginia or crimsoned the mountain paths of Pennsylvania. . . . Let us uproot and exterminate now this debasing, ultra-demoralizing, un-American and inhuman leprosy."[6]

For Roddenberry, Jack Johnson's athletic prowess and sexual liaisons symbolized an extreme act of transgression, one that the white politician used to mobilize legal opposition to interracial marriage. Speaking from the Wiregrass South, Roddenberry echoed common white southern civil religious sentiment that viewed racial intermixing and racial equality as sure signs of social decay.[7] In 1914, Thomas P. Bailey of the University of Mississippi wrote that the "creed of the people" dictated that blacks

were "inferior" and that whites "must dominate." His creed emphasized
also that white supremacy was not the will of humans but rather developed from "the leadings of Providence."[8] Segregation, then, had a
strong religious dimension. It also had an intellectual edge. In his 1898
Essays on the Civil War and Reconstruction, Columbia professor William A.
Dunning invoked racial theories derived from social Darwinism and eu-
genics, sometimes referred to as "scientific racism," to support it. At its
core, scientific racism reasoned that blacks had not progressed along the
evolutionary path as far as whites had.[9] Dunning used this methodology
to argue that blacks were intellectually unable to understand and exercise the rights and duties that "radical Republicans" had conferred on
them. Northern meddling, he concluded, was the final reason for the
"disaster" of Reconstruction.[10]

White supremacy rested on assumptions that God had willed it for
social order or on the idea that racial separation was a self-evident
truth. Both perspectives influenced white redemption narratives in the
Wiregrass Gulf South, stories of the region's supposed Phoenix-like rise
from the ashes of Reconstruction. Often, freed people were seen as a
source of social instability. Mobile newspaperman Erwin Craighead recalled that Reconstruction left the town in a "chaotic state": the "white
men of the South [were] disfranchised because of their participation in
the conflict—and the negroes, recently freed, [were] crowding into the
cities, to exercise and enjoy the privileges of citizenship newly conferred
upon them." Whites, he continued, were unraveled because the "service class" suddenly occupied "the position of power" and was exercising
"political control over more intelligent people." Whites trembled with a
"fear of the unknown," recalled Craighead, wondering if blacks would
"concert together" and stage a revolt and overrun the town.[11]

For Craighead, the chaos of Reconstruction was a direct result of unrestricted black freedom. Other redemption narratives in the Wiregrass
Gulf South repeated this theme while also laying added blame on carpetbaggers for "corrupting" blacks. In Mobile, Kate Cummings remembered that emancipation caused a "revolution in the social customs."
The "suddenly enfranchised" freed person, she explained, had "no
idea of freedom, excepting that it would give him a life of idleness and
pleasure." To illustrate this, Cummings recalled returning home from

church with her niece one Sunday, only to find the route crowded with "gaily dressed" blacks. Maneuvering through the sidewalks, Cummings's anger grew. When she confronted a group of black children and politely asked them to move, one replied, "The middle of the road is for you and the sidewalk is for us." The confrontation, which got her blood boiling, was for Cummings an emblem of Reconstruction. Blacks had been emboldened enough to disregard white social boundaries and profane the territory outside their assigned "place." Cummings, however, relieved blacks of sole responsibility for Reconstruction, choosing to also castigate "carpetbaggers." These "unscrupulous men," she charged, won political posts by soliciting votes from blacks, whose blind allegiance to the northerners brought further peril to the South. Cummings conjectured that if white southerners had been in control after the war, blacks "could have been molded to our interest." While Mobile had become more "progressive" since political redemption, she lamented the racial legacy of Reconstruction, which in her view remained an ongoing problem.[12]

Blacks consorting with northern carpetbaggers formed the backdrop against which many redemption narratives bespeaking an ethic of white supremacy would emerge. In the Wiregrass Gulf South, northerners living in the region occasionally suffered the consequences of this image. In 1877, a Tallahassee newspaper claimed that northern businesspeople had been facing social alienation, something that was "universal through the South." The reason, theorized the author, was the "deep-seated and undying hostility" toward the North for its role in Reconstruction and, in particular, for organizing black votes for northern causes.[13] For some southerners, there certainly was an "undying hostility" toward the North. Nearly fifty years after this newspaper account, Tallahassee's Susan Bradford Eppes described carpetbaggers as swarming "like a flock of vultures" southward after the war, intent on pitting blacks against their former owners.[14]

Eppes's redemption narrative predictably depicted blacks as unprepared for emancipation and carpetbaggers as having exploited the black vote. But for her, another culprit of Reconstruction chaos was Africa itself, a continent where "superstitious" societies practiced improper forms of worship such as "Voo-Doo." In her view, the slave trade rescued "these heathen souls" from the pitfalls of the "dark continent."

But emancipation came too soon, long before the "civilization" process could be completed and Africa could be extinguished from these former Africans. As evidence, she described a typical black church service. Blacks streamed to rustic buildings where they sang, danced, and wailed uncontrollably—in her mind, these physical gestures of black religious practice were all inauthentic. "[Negroes] will stay up night after night at the 'distrac-tid meetin's,' making noise enough to really distract everybody in the vicinity, then go to their work the next morning and drowse over it all day, truly not earning the salt in their bread."[15]

For Eppes, most blacks were "shiftless, untruthful, unreliable," and devoid of feelings of "moral obligation." But there were exceptions. To adjudicate these differences, she identified blacks who had discarded their "emotional religion." This "better class" of blacks had transcended the patterns of their racial kin and achieved material gain as a result. Turning this minority into a majority, Eppes reasoned, would require the commitment of young men imbued with a (white) Christian spirit who were ready to enter the mission fields of the black South. Such a spiritual army, she suggested, could very well dismantle the "tottering structure of emotional religion" that had been built by blacks and construct "a foundation of truth, honesty, purity and love."[16]

With paternalism in no short supply, Eppes was at least slightly optimistic about racial harmony. Others had less hope. John Crary of Bluff Springs, Florida, advocated the mass deportation of blacks to Africa. Like Eppes, he recounted a history of slavery that started in Africa, a continent distinguished by "over thirty centuries" of "hopeless savage barbarism." He insisted that slavery served the divine purpose of civilizing blacks, but unlike Eppes, he argued that the "hand of Providence" had granted emancipation at the proper time in history. More work, however, was needed. The political freedoms granted by emancipation, Crary theorized, would eventually translate to political power. This violated his normative sense of how politics ought to function; namely, as a white-led institution. If blacks held political power over whites, chaos and rioting would result. So Crary looked to Liberia, depicting it as a black Eden where the race could finally enjoy "freedom, civilization, true religion, arts of peace, commerce, and the grand and noble work of transforming . . . the most naturally favored quarter of the earth."[17]

Crary's deportation solution echoed with whites elsewhere in the South who were worried about a new generation of "headstrong" blacks who might demand more freedom.[18] This response to the race problem saw no hope for blacks in America and looked to the physical place of Africa as a solution. Others were not so pessimistic, believing that racial discord would cease if white Christians colonized black communities and churches. Sometimes whites wrote the "race problem" into seemingly unrelated social causes, such as prohibition. "Run the saloons out of the South and the race problem will be practically solved," snapped a Pensacola editorialist. He imagined a community with two churches, one black and one white. "Let them hold the same kind of services, sing the same songs, and preach from the same texts, and a race problem is the last thing in the world that either thinks about." But if these churches are bars, he continued, "you have a race problem inside of twenty minutes." Blacks were not inherently bad, in his mind. A hard-working black man who avoided trouble was "trusted and respected by his white neighbors and they live side by side, each in his respective sphere." Whiskey unsettled this harmonious vision of society, since it produced a "shiftless, worthless negro" who would "spread terror through the community." If society were to stand and blacks and whites were to keep to their respective "places," then, the editor argued, white men in the region would have to put an end to alcohol sale and consumption.[19]

Similar calls, grounded in an assumption that alcohol corrupted blacks, who then would threaten the "purity" of white women or amplify racial discord, sounded throughout the South.[20] Prohibitionist voices joined a civil religious discussion on the race problem, while other voices warned of a looming racial apocalypse or called on white Christians to colonize black communities. For New South entrepreneurs courting northern audiences, there was no race problem.[21] In 1886, speaking to an audience in New York, Atlanta newsperson Henry Grady backhandedly admonished Alexander Stephens's "Cornerstone Speech" of 1861, in which Stephens located slavery at the center of southern life. Stephens's kind, Grady assured, no longer inhabited the New South, "a perfect democracy": "a social system compact and closely knitted, less splendid on the surface, but stronger at the core." In his New South, blacks enjoyed "the fullest protection of our laws and the friendship of our people."[22] His sanguine portrayal of the South was intended to assuage northern fears of racial unrest. Similar pronouncements emerged from the Wiregrass Gulf South. In 1877, Pensacola's William D. Chipley composed a travel pamphlet labeling Florida "the Italy of America." Northerners would not find hostility from locals or racial strife in the state, he averred. "The people are pleasant, refined, and intelligent, and the stranger is surprised at the cordial hospitality extended from every quarter."[23] A Thomasville pamphlet devoted an entire section to race relations, claiming that any suggestion of racial discord in the region was the product of misinformed politicians. A visitor to Thomasville would quickly recognize that interactions between blacks and whites were "perfectly kindly." "Every man, white or black, is free to think and act for himself, so he does not violate the law. And that law is made to apply to all without distinction of race, color or previous condition." In fact, the pamphlet continued, blacks in Thomasville, who were "orderly, law-abiding and contented" and who were "availing themselves of the opportunities afforded to obtain information and an education" were positively prospering.[24] A pamphlet advertising Tallahassee proudly announced that the Civil War had "swept negro slavery away," leaving behind only farmable land and social stability.[25]

Efforts to attract northerners proved successful in the Wiregrass South. But northern tourists and transplants would see something quite different from what the pamphlets described. While Henry Grady spoke optimistically about harmonious relations between the races to his northern audience, he changed his tone when speaking to southerners. "The supremacy of the white race of the South must be maintained forever," he averred, "and the domination of the negro resisted at all points and all hazards—because the white race is the superior race. This is the declaration of no new truth. It has abided forever in the marrow of our bones, and shall run forever with the blood that feeds Anglo-Saxon hearts." Unity, peace, and prosperity, for Grady, required that the code of white supremacy "must be maintained."[26]

Writing in his diary from Thomasville in 1895, visiting northerner G. B. Zimmerman witnessed what white domination had done to black communities. At a church service, he listened to a sermon from a Baptist minister, visiting from Mercer University, who was "a good sensible, spiritual, [and] practicable talking" preacher. The minister told stories about the abundant black poverty in the region, including one about a black boy headed to school with hardly any food for lunch. Zimmerman wondered how any child could learn on an empty stomach. "His talk was good," he reflected, "and should do the community good, in the way of creating more interest in schools in this community, for they are very deficient."[27]

Zimmerman's visit to the Wiregrass South opened his eyes to a white social system that offered little opportunity to blacks. While he showed a measure of empathy for the black condition, other northerners found common ground with their white counterparts.[28] Leaving during the winter of 1877, Chicago's Erastus Hill traveled southward by rail to Macon. He initially thought this would be a "delightful trip for this season of the year." But his gleeful disposition turned sour when he discovered the absence of sleeping cars. Hill rued the thought of "sitting up with niggers and crackers all night." The former, he complained, "don't know as much as a good intelligent mule." With contempt brewing, Hill talked politics with his southern white travel companions and found that he agreed with them on many matters. He wrote that like southerners, northerners also were "tired of this continual wrangle" over Reconstruction. Both sections wanted peace, prosperity, and an end to political agitation. If the "niggers in this state" would vote for Democrats, Hill postulated, the South's problems would be no more. He criticized northern "carpetbaggers," claiming they "lied to and cheated" blacks during Reconstruction, while southern whites had been the "real friends" of blacks. Sitting on the train, Hill understood why the "decent" white southerners were Democrats. Republicans had "forced" on the South a "diabolical set of rascals" who plundered the region after the war. With a new political worldview, the northerner declared, "my mind has changed wonderfully."[29]

Hill's moral and political conversion involved his adopting a civil religious discourse that made white supremacy a value necessary for the public good. William George Bruce of Wisconsin had a similar revelation when he traveled to Florida intent on desegregating the schools. "Their law was inhuman, unjust and un-American, and we the people of the North would boldly tell the southerners what was what." When reaching his destination, Bruce confronted school officials in Florida, who explained "the danger of exposing little white girls to contact with negro children who knew no sense of modesty and who came from families utterly lacking in morality." Convinced, Bruce and his fellow protesters tore apart their resolutions, admitted to the wisdom of segregating schools, and confessed that if placed in a similar situation they would have done the same. Racial segregation, Bruce concluded, was not in fact "un-American."[30]

The moral codes of northerners traveling southward were subject to change, but not all of them spoke with the white South's civil religious accent. In 1907, a Pensacola newspaper interviewed J. E. Callahan. The seventy-year-old Maine native owned a mill in Pensacola and described himself as a Reconstruction "carpetbagger." Callahan recounted a very different history of war and Reconstruction than his southern neighbors did. During the Civil War, he explained, northerners fought "in the defense of their Country and in the cause of Human Freedom." This same spirit carried into Reconstruction; in this era northerners had been anything but "a band of heartless wretches, plundering the helpless." Instead, they were patriotic Americans committed to a "holy cause." Born in Ireland, Callahan speculated that his early experiences with oppression there made him sympathetic to the black cause in the South. Additionally, his immigration to America and subsequent rise to wealth taught him that anyone who worked hard could prosper. "I believed, as many others of my associates did, that the Negro if he had his freedom, with his acquaintance with the agricultural and mechanical labor of the South, well acclimated, and a powerful physique, would become an important factor in the development of the resources of the country." Callahan would be disappointed. Emancipation gave blacks everything they needed to prosper, he claimed, but they lacked the "character," "responsibility," and "earnestness of purpose" to succeed. In final analysis, Callahan found "little in the negro character to be admired." None of this was the North's fault, he added. The southern effort to reenslave blacks hindered any progress that northerners could have made. But Callahan saw hope in the rising generation of southerners, less easily persuaded by "designing politicians whose whole motive was to hold up the 'nigger and carpetbagger' to scare white men into

Democratic ranks." Callahan was a critic of the white South, but he made it clear that neither he nor his fellow Republicans favored racial equality. "No Northern man invited a colored man to his table, or to his family circle."[31]

Neither bashful nor apologetic about being a carpetbagger, Callahan lauded his cause despite the outcome. The Wiregrass Gulf South's growth and development drew people like him into the civil religious conversation, and their views took the majority's vision of the good society to new places and sometimes inverted their value system. Just as northerners' voices were small but significant, Catholics' were also. A decided religious minority, black and white Catholics entered the civil religious fray on matters of race, just as they did in the prewar era. Some French missionary priests in Maryland, Kentucky, and Louisiana owned enslaved people, and others articulated a proslavery ideology. When Pope Gregory XVI denounced the slave trade in 1839, the missionaries scrambled to assure the faithful that domestic slavery remained acceptable. While similar to their southern Protestant counterparts, Catholics defended slavery through the lens of a Catholic theology born in Europe. They essentially reasoned that in certain settings, slavery guaranteed social order. The same reasoning would apply to segregation.[32]

In 1908, Father Patrick Bresnahan traveled through Florida on mission work. Before his trip, the priest believed that blacks had been improperly treated in the South. On seeing the region for himself, however, Bresnahan admitted that "the Southern gentleman understands what is best for his colored neighbor and accordingly does treat him justly." In Tallahassee, he found prosperous black communities "ever and always keeping in their place." Enabling this were the wise and noble "captains and colonels of Dixie land." Although Bresnahan commended the work ethic of these black communities, he lamented the state of black Catholic life. He blamed secret fraternities and non-Catholic black churches for the problem, both of which did not properly teach "Christian morality."[33]

Father Bresnahan, like other visiting northerners, saw wisdom in the ruling order's subordination of blacks. Unique, though, was his Catholic angle. The out-of-place black person, for the priest, joined a fraternity or joined a non-Catholic church. Catholics elsewhere in the Wiregrass Gulf

South shared these concerns and developed solutions that they believed walked the line between including blacks in the church and maintaining segregation. In 1909, Father Conrad Rebesher, a black pastor in Mobile, organized the Knights of Peter Claver, a black Catholic fraternal organization. Black men, he lamented, showed "great negligence, and little interest" in Catholicism, due in part to secret fraternities.[34] The Knights promised to combat this, he proclaimed, and show blacks "the beauty of the Catholic doctrine."[35]

Rebesher used the Knights of Columbus as a model but recognized that black men could not join the all-white fraternity. In Mobile, the racial lines of the South did not stop at the doors of the church. The geography of the Catholic South looked similar to the Protestant South, with separate parishes, hospitals, and schools. Each place had a function that won praise from the hierarchy when it operated within the realm of acceptability. Mobile's Bishop Edward Allen supported the Knights of Peter Claver and attended their first initiation ceremony. He often expressed genuine interest in ministering to the region's blacks. Allen once commended Montgomery's Father Thomas Donovan for his work with Saint Joseph's College for Negro Catechists. "May God bless this most laudable enterprise which you have undertaken purely for the honor and glory of God and the extension of his kingdom among men!" The college, Allen hoped, would remedy the "moral and social degradation" plaguing "a large portion of our colored brethren." Once they had some "sound religious principles" in their hearts and minds, the bishop expected positive changes for "these often well meaning but sadly misguided people."[36]

For Allen, Saint Joseph's served the positive purpose of educating blacks. But when a black priest was assigned to live there, Allen objected, viewing it as a supreme racial transgression. Soon after his ordination in 1902, Father John Dorsey traveled south on a public ministry aimed at drawing blacks into the Catholic Church. A native of Baltimore and the second black Josephite priest ordained in America, Dorsey became a southern phenomenon, as blacks flocked to hear him preach. "Their enthusiasm knew no bounds," wrote one observer. "Some wept openly."[37] But white priests in Montgomery vociferously objected to Dorsey's assignment to Saint Joseph's. Father Thomas Donovan was an exception. After publicly criticizing his fellow priests for their bigotry, Bishop Allen rebuked Donovan. "If priests are opposed to Fr. Dorsey coming to Montgomery," Allen explained, "it is not from personal antagonism to him but it is because they understand and fully realize how deep seated the prejudices of the white people of Alabama are." To see a black priest living among white priests would antagonize locals who were already suspicious of Catholics. Allen emphasized that he had no prejudices against Dorsey, but he agreed with those who opposed Dorsey's appointment to the college.[38]

Allen saw a South divided by race and adapted the church accordingly. While giving some indication that he was submitting to the racial culture of Alabama, he ultimately fell into line with fellow southern Catholics, operating on the basis of a theological architecture that favored social order over individual freedom.[39] Father Dorsey would spend his career resisting segregation and proposing an alternate theological framework. He stayed at Saint Joseph's briefly and went on to do mission work in the South. Meanwhile, the white Josephite leadership worried that the black priest's position of authority would feed a growing anti-Catholic sentiment in the region. So the Josephites scaled back their black presence in the region. In response, an infuriated Dorsey announced that "prejudice in the Church has kept pace with prejudice in the state." He argued that the church now had "a God-given mission" to eliminate this prejudice from both places.[40] Dorsey had allies including fellow Josephite John Plantevigne. In 1909, Archbishop James Blenk denied Plantevigne permission to participate in a mission in New Orleans. Stunned, Plantevigne pleaded with the bishop that during his mission in Mobile he "met no objection from . . . bishops, priests, nor laymen white or colored." Blenk would not reconsider, resolving that the black priest would unsettle the city's white inhabitants. In response, Plantevigne let loose with a forceful rebuke. "The blood of the Negro boils in resentment of a 'Jim-Crow' system in the Catholic Church," he exclaimed to a gathering of missionaries. "The doors of the Church must be opened full width, not a side entrance."[41]

The racial and spatial conflicts occurring within the Catholic Church reflected a common pattern in the South. The black priests protested, but ultimately the white hierarchy had its way. Still, the priests continued to imagine a society marked by equality and justice. The black majority in the South did the same. Their civil religious discourse had freedom at its core, a freedom that they believed God had granted and emancipation had delivered. As Reconstruction unfolded, freed blacks entered southern society with a new sense of agency, secure in the belief that their freedom was a divine mandate and American promise. Some tried to improve their education or economic status. Others forcefully resisted the white status quo by demanding equal treatment in law, business, and society. But all had to function within a South where white supremacy cast a long shadow.

Black Freedom and the "Good of the Community"

When Albany's Frank W. White died in 1899, Rev. William D. Johnson of the AME church commended area whites for attending his funeral and sharing their tears and sympathy with the deceased's family. For the preacher, their presence proved that any black person could earn respect "when he properly respects others." Johnson encouraged Albany's black community to follow White's example, since his "manhood and Christian citizenship" had earned the admiration of the white community.[42] The funeral both expressed a ritualized mourning of an individual loss and provided a site for announcing a vision of the good society, one that emphasized the redemptive quality of mutual progress. As blacks and whites stood together, Johnson seized the opportunity to project an idealized future marked by prosperity and racial harmony. He moreover called directly on blacks to work toward this vision, hoping, just as Booker T. Washington and others of the era did, that if blacks embraced the ethic of self-help, an era of "mutual progress" would come.[43]

For many blacks in positions of authority within their community, progress was a powerful social force written into their idea of the good society. Its ultimate promise rested in a hope that hard work would translate into white respect. A black newspaper in Waycross, Georgia, speculated that if "intelligent" black leaders stepped forward, blacks and whites would develop a relationship of respectful cooperation. The "law of progressiveness" dictated that people would advance only as far as their leaders would permit. Thus, black leaders needed to be "the most able, worthy, and in short the best men and women, in every sense of the word." The article claimed that elsewhere in the nation black men and women had become "a tower of strength" for the race. A "better day" awaited blacks if motivated leaders would commit to "the progress of the race."[44]

Elsewhere, optimistic black Wiregrassers took a more bottom-up approach, seeing progress as emerging from the daily labors of ordinary people. In west Florida, railroads and a timber boom brought new prosperity to the region, and blacks experienced a moderate level of financial gain as a result.[45] Describing this to a white readership, Pensacola's F. E. Washington wrote that ever since "the shackles of American slavery" had been broken, freed blacks in west Florida had been "contributing our share towards its progress" and advancing on the ladder "that leads to enlightenment and civilization of mankind." As an example, he told of one Baptist preacher, who he described as "a fair example of what the colored people attain when imbued with a progressive spirit." According to Washington, the minister attended Roger Williams University, the University of Raleigh, and the Richmond Institute. In Pensacola, he shared this education with his flock, all of whom benefited as a result. Progressive minds like these, Washington concluded, helped produce "friendly relations" between the races, who both shared a "hopefulness of a new era of commercial advancement for Pensacola."[46]

For Washington, Pensacola was exceptional because it was both mutually prosperous and relatively free of prejudice. Similarly, Booker T. Washington took notice of Pensacola in his 1907 *Negro in Business*, which addressed black progress broadly but made an "intimate study" of Pensacola. Washington found in Pensacola "that healthy progressive communal spirit, so necessary to our people." He cited Pensacola's black advancements in organized religion, labor, education, professional work, newspapers, and political life. The businesspeople in particular, Washington marveled, showed that "in the more progressive colored communities in the South, members of the Negro race are learning to do their own business and direct their own affairs." Like F. E. Washington, Booker T. Washington linked material progress with racial harmony, celebrating the "relations of helpful co-operation" existing between the races.[47] Pensacola became their model of their good society, where blacks were prosperous and whites cooperated as a result.

As a black civil religious value, progress performed the significant function of advancing the race in society. Often, blacks articulated this message in a nonconfrontational manner, avoiding mention of racial violence and focusing instead on an idealized "friendly" relationship between blacks and whites. Thomasville's Rev. Emanuel K. Love, for instance, dwelled on this theme and won white praise in the process. A graduate of the Augusta Institute, Love became the pastor of Thomasville's African Baptist Church in 1879. In the following two years, he baptized 450 people and raised roughly $1,000 to improve the physical condition of his church.[48] So impressive was Love's ministry that Thomasville's white newspaper concluded that "the colored churches are better here than are the white churches." In 1881, Love left Thomasville to assist the missionary efforts of the American Baptist Publication Society. In his resignation letter, Love explained that the effective pastor worked always for "the good of the community." This meant not only preaching but also "rebuking sin and wickedness" such as alcohol consumption as well as working for improved education.[49] A white newspaper bade Love a pleasant farewell. "Rev. E. K. Love has the entire confidence and respect of the citizens of Thomasville, white and black. He has stayed here long enough for them to know his sterling worth. Georgia is a big field, but if there is a man who can work it up, that man is E. K. Love."[50] In 1885, after working the mission fields in Florida and Georgia, Love assumed the pastorate at the First African Baptist Church in Savannah. Whites in Savannah and Georgia generally had a high opinion of the church and its pastors. On his appointment, a white newspaper just north of Thomasville exclaimed, "He is indeed a very intelligent and able man and the church has done well to secure his services. Withal he is pious and devoted to his work. We congratulate all parties."[51]

No matter how many white papers complimented his "sterling worth," and no matter how much whites respected his church, Love still lived in a South where whites did not tolerate an out-of-place black person. In 1889, he and a number of Georgia delegates traveled to the Black Foreign Missionary Convention in Indianapolis. By the 1880s, most major railroads had segregated cars and refused to sell blacks first-class tickets.[52] But an agent from the East Tennessee, Virginia, and Georgia Railroad assured Love that he and his travel companions would have a segregated first-class car. However, it turned out that the train had only one first-class car and one smoking car. The delegates—who were opposed to smoking and drinking—seated themselves in the first-class car. As the train departed, white passengers and rail conductors began to murmur. A black porter quietly informed Love that a telegram had reached the next stop announcing the desegregated train's arrival.[53] According to Love, once the train stopped, "a dozen rough looking men boarded the train and ordered us out of the car. We didn't go, and we were assaulted." The mob drew revolvers, beat the delegates, and forced them off the train. Without the "interference of the conductor," Love speculated, "I think some of us would have been killed."[54]

Love was one of five battered delegates who forged ahead to Indianapolis. They published an article describing the event and expressing their disgust with white America. "We look to God and ask what are we to do? What is the use of appealing to the Government? Our suffering and inhuman outrages are known. The crimes are not committed in a corner—the men were not masked." "The glory of American citizenship," the authors concluded, "means no glory for us."[55] Love preached the gospel of self-help and mutual progress, but he also found deficiencies in a white system that he believed betrayed the very foundation of American freedom. Love's good society pressed against social ideologies developed by whites while also creating a place for blacks that was decidedly more inclusive and just.

In entering the first-class car and writing an article, Love and the others knowingly violated a racial boundary generated by a white civil religious discourse that demanded segregation at all costs. They also produced their own civil religious discourse, one marked not only by resistance but also by an understanding of freedom developed from black history and Christian theology. Love would continue repeating these civil religious themes. In one sermon on emancipation, Love denounced slavery as "the most cruel and diabolical system . . . that ever disgraced this or any other country." With emancipation, he proclaimed, "the mighty arm of Jehovah was moved in our defense." The future of blacks was, he insisted, a future of prosperity, and he assured his audience that God's wrath awaited the Henry Gradys of the South.

Love had no lack of admiration for the members of his race, praising their "moral courage, sweetness of disposition, loving spirit of forgiveness, meekness, humbleness, tenderness of heart, devotion to God and physical discipline." He labeled these qualities "heaven's idea of greatness." In any other nation, the black race would be a cherished asset. But in America, "ignorant" whites refuse to recognize its strengths. Love was still hopeful, reasoning that "ignorance is weakness" and that "God's plan" for America found "righteous intelligence" rising to the seat of power. So for Love, it was only a matter of time before blacks would have full freedom and equality. God had imbued them with an exemplary character, one that America's destiny relied on. But he warned that realizing this vision of society would require hard work. Love implored blacks to educate themselves and create a vibrant press to rally support for civil rights. Still, in his eyes, the blame rested mostly with whites, whose destructive mind-set threatened to undermine the very foundations of America.[56]

Interestingly, while Love's civil religious discourse called for greater justice and inclusion, he did not advocate desegregation, maintaining that "every race should recognize its racial distinction." Love's inversion of white segregation grew out of his own racial pride. "I would rather be with a Negro than with any body else on earth, and I believe no white man when he tells me that he prefers to be with Negroes to being with his own race."[57] In turning the logic of white supremacy on its head, Love pushed whites away from black places while also expanding the social map within which blacks could exercise their freedom. Love was one of many black voices in the Wiregrass region, some of which were more forceful than others in demanding rights. Because whites held the balance of power, advocating too forcibly for civil rights was a risky affair.

Freedom's "Terrain of Conflict"

In his 1913 history of Reconstruction in Florida, William Watson Davis, a native of Pensacola, wrote:

The criminal demoralization of the Reconstruction period was frightful. Men formed the habit of defying the law and resorting to violence to attain their ends. The Southerner was certainly face to face with negro domination foisted upon him by Federal law. He arose to protect his own unwritten laws in order that his property, his self-respect, and his family might not be injured or destroyed. He resorted to physical violence under cover, in one of the most sinister and interesting contests of modern times. And in this contest for a very necessary supremacy many a foul crime was committed by white against black. Innocent people suffered. There is no mercy and scant justice in social adjustment. The negro was first freed, then enfranchised, then launched in practical politics, and then mercilessly beaten into subjection.[58]

Davis divided Florida into black and white—calling the latter a "southerner" but not the former—in an effort to emphasize that without racial boundaries, chaos reigned supreme and necessitated acts of lawless retribution. Racial violence did not end with Reconstruction. From 1882 to 1930, Florida had the highest percentage of lynchings in the South.[59] So while Booker T. Washington and others idealized Pensacola as a racial Zion, residents of the region wrote another story. In 1887, S. D. Jackson of Pensacola explained, "I will tell you [what] they are doing with us down South. They are shooting us down as so many partridges; don't allow editors to speak the truth always through their papers to the people; kicking us off trains whenever they see fit to do so; distribute the school funds as their conscience directs, charging us very often as high as 24 per cent per annum for money when we are compelled to borrow it from them, and thousands of other things too numerous to mention."[60]

West Florida, in Jackson's view, was an unstable and deadly place, the consequence of an oppressive white system that valued racial domination. Emancipation promised freedom to blacks, but as Eric Foner explains, "'Freedom' became a terrain of conflict, its substance open to different and sometimes contradictory interpretations, its content changing for whites as well as blacks."[61] This sense of unsettledness fueled racial violence, which had a clear civil religious dimension. In their examination of civil religion and violence, Carolyn Marvin and

David W. Ingle discuss how nations sometimes mobilize the "killing energy" of citizens for the sake of protecting group unity. A "totem crisis," they explain, refers to a collective "uncertainty about the essential borders that demarcate [a] group."[62] In the New South, lynchings and other acts of vigilante justice did the civil religious work of reasserting boundaries and assuaging white fears over unrestricted black freedom. Thus, performances of ritualized violence in the Wiregrass region were manifestations of a broader southern trend.[63]

In November 1876, a northern governmental agent traveled through Florida investigating cases of voter fraud. Everywhere he went, he saw blacks fearing for their lives. In Hernando County, he charged Arthur Saint Clair, the county commissioner and a black Baptist minister and farmer, with delivering election results to Tallahassee. Saint Clair refused, worried that he would end up like a fellow black politician who "had his back filled with buckshot from a shot-gun in the hands of a Democrat." Saint Clair knew the murderer but refused to tell the government agent who it was.[64] Saint Clair had good reason to be wary. In late June 1877, he and fellow congregant Henry Loyd were set to travel from Hernando County to Tallahassee to meet with an assembly of black Republicans. Convened by Simon B. Conover, a white Republican senator, the assembly intended to address issues of importance facing blacks in the wake of Reconstruction. Saint Clair and Loyd never made it to the meeting. On June 26, two white men assassinated the travelers before they even left Hernando County.[65]

Black leaders promptly denounced the murders. A gathering of black ministers met in Key West and issued a statement announcing their "solemn protest and unqualified condemnation of so dastard and inhumane an act." Saint Clair and Loyd, they proclaimed, were "martyrs of our race."[66] Rev. W. G. Stewart of Tallahassee's AME Church echoed this sentiment in a local newspaper. Stewart, a former slave who aligned with Republicans after the war, became a leading black politician in middle Florida.[67] His letter demanded immediate justice, charging that the victims were killed for their skin color and Republicanism. Stewart further insisted that the murders were part and parcel of a white Democratic effort to abolish all black "rights" and dominate the race as they had done in slavery. Black communities were responding to this attempt to hold them back, he explained, through a series of intense revivals, which kept them "alive in Christ Jesus." But their prayers grew out of fear, not joy, Stewart added, since political redemption had "ruined" their hopes for "future prosperity."[68]

Stewart's letter mourned two deaths and represented white supremacy as a corrupt ethic that would strip from blacks all political, economic, and legal freedom. While whites saw stability in political redemption, Stewart foresaw only chaos. His reversal of the white redemption narrative was not well received by his white audience. Instead, Stewart's historical perspective and faith practices became the subject of ridicule at the hands of the newspaper's editor, C. E. Dyke. The editor belittled Stewart's "religio-political blast" and called it a "curious mosaic" of untruths. Dyke informed readers that Stewart was Tallahassee's postmaster—a position, the editor claimed, that afforded Stewart a $2,600 annual salary. How could someone with this position, he wondered, complain about the lack of prosperity for blacks?

Dyke then turned to black revivals, arguing that their "happy effect" as described by the "Reverent Post-master" contradicted his claim that blacks were in dire need of justice. "Instead of vexing his righteous soul over an 'adversity' that has 'gloriously prospered' [in] his Church, and laying schemes for thwarting the designs of providence, he should, like the apostle, 'thank God and take courage' and pray for a little more of the same sort." But Dyke doubted this would happen. Stewart, in the editor's view, was the product of the "political adventurers" of Reconstruction, who for years fed blacks "false ideas." He claimed that carpetbaggers did not understand how the "naturally excitable" black person had no "true" concept of religion or politics. In politics, Dyke charged, a black person "becomes a fanatic." And in religion, he is "an enthusiast." Dyke stated that blacks would keep their "rights." The murders of Saint Clair and Loyd were, he admitted, "horrible [crimes]." However, "it is not just to attribute that murder to a Democratic victory or to cite it as proof that the rights of the negro are less secure than formerly."[69]

Here, in freedom's "terrain of conflict," stood one black voice struggling to maintain his freedom and a southern white Democrat determined to preserve the rule of white supremacy. The editor got the final word, describing the ideal black person as subservient, passive, and accepting of Democratic rule. Stewart did not fit this ideal. But Stewart's perspective still made its presence known in the Wiregrass Gulf South, depicting white supremacy as inherently contradictory to both Christianity and American democracy.[70] While Stewart was seen as out of place in this instance, other white Tallahasseeans had a higher opinion of him. In 1882, Stewart asked Ellen Call Long to relate the condition of Florida's blacks to a congressional delegation in Washington. Long, a wealthy white member of Tallahassee's elite, agreed. When a friend questioned her decision, Long responded that "it is a conviction of mine that when a negro proves himself worthy morally and capable intellectually of the rewards of citizenship by the practice of honesty, soberness and discretion, he is entitled to enter the list for competitive places of preferment."[71]

For Long, Stewart had made himself "worthy" of recognition through his intellectual and moral uprightness. While she willingly defended her actions to her disapproving friend, Long was by no means an advocate of racial equality. She too carried the banner of white supremacy into the battlefields of the region's dueling social ideals. "Slavery is a necessity to the negro," Long affirmed, "and the negro is a necessity to the South. A labor that can be controlled must work here. A power that can control must civilize the negro. Slavery and the South is the school in which the negro is restrained from vice, and trained in the ways of men and humanity."[72] Like many others, the author equated black freedom with social decay and maintained that only the authority of whites could lead the region to its ultimate destiny.

However, in their quest to establish the boundaries separating black from white, whites exercised forms of vigilante justice that, for many blacks, ran contrary to the foundation of American democracy. To a crowd of over fifteen hundred people in Savannah, Rev. E. K. Love called out to "good people everywhere" to condemn lynching. Lynching, he argued, contradicted the nation's "law of reason." Love hoped that members of both races could work together to end the violent epidemic. But alas, there were too many "ambitious, wicked, designing politicians," politicians who kept "the fire of dissention and race hatred in an everlasting blaze." Combating this required "virtue-loving" people to advocate "open law." Until this happened, Love warned, the sins of America's past—namely slavery—would continue to plague the nation. For the minister, the road toward fulfilling the nation's destiny traveled through the black community, where damage done would have to be repaired and the rights promised through emancipation would have to be granted.[73] But for whites, lynching and other acts of racial violence had become a ritual means for preserving what they believed was essential in society. A Pensacola newspaper explained that all communities accept "certain social ideas" that, when violated by a major felony, call for justice the written law is not designed to correct. Lynching, the author continued, allows a community to "emphasize its abhorrence of crime of a specific character."[74] Since white authority ruled the South, the message of Love and others would go largely unheard, and something as menial as a rumor would continue to excite the deepest fears of whites that blacks were venturing outside their "place."

Before Day Clubs

In the summer and fall months of 1904, rumors of Before Day clubs circulated throughout the Wiregrass South. The stories generally claimed that militant blacks led the clubs, which met in churches and plotted the murders of prominent whites. Most southern whites eventually admitted that these clubs did not exist. But the rumors still stoked the fires of racial discord, since the image of Before Day clubs inverted the white moral order in a manner similar to that of the slave revolts of the Old South. In 1800, Gabriel Prosser, known as "Black Sampson," led one thousand slaves in a failed attack on Richmond. In 1822, Denmark Vesey, an ex-slave and African Methodist, modeled his plan to overrun Charleston, South Carolina, after the story of Joshua and the battle of Jericho. City officials exposed the plan and executed Vessey. And in 1831, Nat Turner staged his slave revolt, the bloodiest in history. A Baptist preacher, Turner led an insurrection that left sixty white men, women, and children dead. In the years that followed, whites remembered the revolts as the worst symbols of an ill-informed black theology. White missionaries on plantations emphasized the biblical mandate for slaves to obey their masters.[75]

After Reconstruction, black schools taught children that Turner was a misguided malcontent who murdered innocent whites for no good reason. The pedagogy reflected an abiding white fear of black domination and a corresponding dismissal of black religion. The Before Day club rumors fit within this story. As the rumors flourished, a Richmond newspaper used the clubs to recall the "awful work" of Turner's "insurrection."[76] But New South fears merited a new chapter. The 1890s saw the first generation of freed blacks come to maturity. Whites worried that these blacks had become too assertive and willing to violate social boundaries. One white manifestation of this fear was the insistence on categorizing blacks as either orderly or disorderly citizens, as those who stayed in their place and those who did not.[77] A Pensacola editor chastened Chicago journalist Ray Stannard Baker, who, after touring the South, proposed that the solution to the race problem was to ignore skin color and treat blacks as human beings. The editor rebutted that Baker's "academic" solution would only work with the "exceptional negro" or the one who had "education and morals." The "criminal negro," however, did not merit human status. It was this "black beast whose baleful shadow" rested on "the whole South."[78]

White reactions to Before Day club rumors were also reactions to the "black beast," a caricature of unrestricted black freedom. So powerful was this image that mobs formed to defend white supremacy. On July 28, 1904, in Statesboro, Georgia, "Boss" Woodrum and Tom Woodcock investigated the burning house of a white farmer, Henry Hodges. Amid the flickering flames, the investigators found Hodges and his family charred and murdered. Statesboro officials promptly arrested approximately a dozen blacks before formally charging Paul Reed and Will Cato. In a statement to the police, Reed's wife, Harriet, implicated both men in the murder. After the arrests, newspapers claimed that Reed confessed to having belonged to a Before Day club. Two black ministers, Reed reported, organized the club with the intent of murdering more whites in Bulloch County. Reed also named other members living in the area. Meanwhile, another rumor claimed Hodges's daughter offered a nickel in exchange for mercy just moments prior to having her head caved in. No proof ever surfaced to validate the story. But it made the angry white population even angrier, and racial conflicts raged in Statesboro's streets.[79]

The threat of lynching prompted Statesboro officials to transport Cato and Reed to Savannah. Even with this measure, a Savannah newspaper morbidly speculated, "the chances of the murderers being legally hung are very slim."[80] In mid-August, the trials proceeded in Statesboro, as Captain Robert M. Hitch's Light Infantry division guarded the courthouse with unloaded rifles. The all-white jury quickly found Cato and Reed guilty and sentenced them to hang. After hearing the case, Judge Daley decided to return the prisoners to Savannah in hopes of avoiding a lynching. This angered an already rowdy, drunken, and armed crowd of approximately a thousand convened outside the courthouse. Despite the pleas of Rev. H. H. Hodges—the murdered farmer's brother—the crowd overpowered Hitch's troops and dragged Reed and Cato out of their cell and through town. The mob settled on a location, poured ten gallons of oil over the convicted, snapped photographs, and set them ablaze. Reed and Cato begged to be shot as the crowed watched the two die slow deaths. After the fire calmed, the mob dispersed with relics of the lynched. Statesboro's white residents soon bought prints of the gruesome lynching photographs for twenty-five cents.[81]

After the lynchings, racial tension in Statesboro remained high. Rumors of Before Day clubs continued to spread, causing many area blacks to flee the town. Officials conducted a perfunctory investigation into the lynchings but indicted no one. A black newspaper in Savannah expressed regret over the "unfortunate" murders of the farmer and his family yet refused to "forgive the lynchers." Statesboro's white officials, the paper scolded, "are opposed to doing anything that looks like protection to the dangerous Negro element and prefer for them to see what is likely to happen if they attempt assault and wholesale murder."[82] Accepting that Reed and Cato were guilty, the paper nevertheless denounced the lawlessness and immorality of the lynchings. In other words, for the author, a truly good society did not permit vigilantism when the rule of law would suffice.

By September's end, the *Statesboro News*, a publication largely responsible for stirring the pot of paranoia, admitted that a Before Day club likely did not exist in the town.[83] When rumors appeared elsewhere, admissions of falsity soon followed. In September 1904, a newspaper in Milledgeville, Georgia, claimed that an area black man was planning to organize a "murder club." An anonymous source cited in the article claimed that he saw "suspicious Negroes going to a certain church in this county." Additionally, the article reported that a merchant sold firearms to the unknown blacks who attended this church meeting. After receiving word of the rumors, AME ministers C. J. Jones and F. L. Fleming convened a meeting of area ministers to investigate the matter. The gathering soon issued a public message. "We found no such order existing," they assured. One pastor theorized that one of his more troublesome members had sparked the rumor. "It is our intention," the statement concluded, "to give the white people our cooperation in running all such lawlessness down and uphold the law at all times."[84] The ministers stressed their willingness to assist, calming the fears of whites. They spoke directly to a white civil religious yearning for black subservience. Wanting harmony rather than disunity, the ministers sought to avoid the ritualized violence that often accompanied such rumors.

Also in September 1904, officials briefly detained five suspected Before Day club members in Talbotton, Georgia. The group allegedly planned to murder two white citizens in nearby Poplar. A judge ruled that the accusations were unjustified and released the prisoners. Soon after, a small gang of mounted riders murdered two members of the group. Talbotton's white citizens expressed immediate disapproval. A petition circulated and, according to one newspaper account, "not a man to whom it was presented hesitated to attach his signature." The town's white leaders gathered to devise a plan for capturing the lawless perpetrators. At the meeting, former U.S. congressman Henry Persons commended Talbotton's response and said the murders had "cast a blot upon the fair page of the county's history." In their resolution, organizers acknowledged the "alarm" caused by rumors but concluded that "'Before Day Clubs' do not exist in Georgia to the extent that some fear and believe." Moreover, townspeople "earnestly" wanted to "promote the welfare of the community and encourage a spirit of fairness and justice." One newspaper observed that the "sentiment in Talbot County was clearly shown by this meeting to be in favor of guaranteeing to Negroes protection." The author then qualified this remark by noting that this "protection" came "so long as negroes remain in their proper sphere, at all cost." Area blacks were "as a rule, obedient, respectful and kind. The treatment which they receive from the whites is all that they could ask for or expect and they are contented and happy."[85]

Talbotton's Before Day club rumor, unlike the one in Statesville, did not have a dead white body attached to it. Instead, two black lives had been taken, freeing whites to denounce the lawlessness of the murders. Yet in the midst of this shared moment of concern, whites seized the opportunity to reinforce the "place" of blacks in society. Their good society extended some legal support to blacks but certainly not equality.

Rumors of a Before Day club reached Thomasville in September 1904. A newspaper claimed that James Horne, a white storeowner, received an anonymous letter that declared him "marked for slaughter by a 'Before Day Club.'" Soon after, Horne's store caught fire. Neighbors quickly extinguished the blaze, and so the store suffered only minimal damage. Immediately, Thomasville's mayor, Seaborne A. Roddenberry, called a meeting along with R. W. Branch, the presiding elder of Thomasville's AME Church. "The meeting seemed to clear the atmosphere," a Thomasville journalist suggested, "and it is now thought, that no trouble will follow. The negroes seem to be anxious to avoid the trouble. They have submitted the books and by-laws of all lodges to the inspection of the whites."[86] With rumors still proliferating, two hundred black leaders met in Thomasville and composed a resolution. "[We] regard the Before Day Club bug-a-boo as a relic of mythology." With unambiguous language, they disclaimed any knowledge of the clubs and asserted that they had never existed.[87]

Despite the resolution, rumors persisted in the Wiregrass South causing instability within black and white communities alike. On September 3, 1904, Nicholas Ware Eppes, the white superintendent of public instruction of Leon County, traveled from Tallahassee's downtown to his plantation home in Bradfordville. Along the way, an assailant carrying a shotgun shot and killed Eppes at close range. Shortly after the murder, authorities arrested three black men, Isom Edwards, George Caldwell, and Nelson Larkin.[88] Cognizant that a lynching was possible, police transported the suspects to nearby Live Oak. While in transit, Edwards supposedly confessed to the murder and declared himself a member of a Before Day club. The club reportedly met at Tallahassee's Mount Zion Church and planned to murder more area whites.[89]

Within days, Jacksonville's *Times-Union* alarmed Tallahassee residents, alleging that five other clubs existed in Leon County. Providing background, the article claimed that the club originated in Richmond, Virginia, through the efforts of an unnamed black man, "who made an incendiary speech, advising members of his race to do a manner of mean things." The report acknowledged the anxiety of Tallahassee's white community and assured its readers that the town's "best negroes" had no "sympathy with such an organization."[90] Another article expressed the hope that Tallahassee's white residents would remain "willing to see the negroes have a fair trial."[91]

Blacks and whites in Tallahassee knew the Eppes name well, so the violent death likely came as a shock.[92] One newspaper described the "spirit of sadness" that overcame Tallahassee after the murder. "His many admirable traits of character and his genial manner won him friends everywhere. His home life was beautiful, where he was devotion itself. Here is where he will be most missed and the hearts of hundreds go out to his bereaved family." Another article called his death "a thing too bad for words to depict." "No one ever dreamed of any one harming a man so universally known and so perfectly innocent. . . . His death was a shock to everybody, most especially coming from the source it did." The "source" of the murder was the mysterious Before Day club, but the author reasoned that Tallahassee's blacks did not sympathize with the group. Rather, many followed the lead of the black teachers who worked for Eppes, who felt the "sharp sting" of the loss and condemned "the parties accessory to the unmanly crime and want to see them punished to the fullest extent of the law." The article then applauded the white people of Leon County for their "coolheadedness." "We say in all crimes let the law take precedence—let us respect our laws—let us be law-abiding citizens." Another news article reported that blacks in Tallahassee held a meeting "at which resolutions were passed condemning the murder of Mr. Eppes, and promising vigorous co-operation with the whites at any and all times in maintaining law and order and putting down crime." The author called this "a step in the right direction" that would "tend toward the restoration of confidence in the colored population of Leon County, who have hitherto been considered law abiding, as a whole."[93]

Letters to Eppes's family denounced the murderers and extolled the murdered. Susan Bradford Eppes, the deceased's wife, received letters from well-wishers expressing remorse and anger. Writing from Monticello, Florida, Josir Kimudy lamented, "God alone knows how my heart goes out to you and your dear children in this dreadful hour of grief and trial." He called the murder "dreadful" and branded the suspected perpetrators a "gang of black ruffians."[94] The bereaved sister of Nicholas called her brother "grand and gentle and kind" and could not "fathom" how he became "the victim of such a plot." Expressing her concern for Susan, the sister concluded, "I feel so afraid for you all seem surrounded by a set of demons, God grant they may all be caught and punished."[95] Susan's sister, Martha, wrote to the *Times-Union* asking them to publish an obituary for Nicholas Eppes, who had the "very best blood of the South . . . in his veins" and was "faithful and loyal as a friend—upright and honorable in every walk of life."[96] Sympathy also came from area blacks. Robert Williams of Thomasville wrote on behalf of "the colored people who knew and loved Mr. Eppes." Area blacks, Williams shared, "feel deeply and keenly the awful tragedy that has caused such a sore affliction to befall our community. . . . He leaves as universally regretted and sadly mourned."[97]

While various voices hurried to identify Tallahassee's "best negroes," all eyes turned to the accused "black beasts" who sat in a Jacksonville jail. In an interview with the *Times-Union*, the detainees gave their accounts. Edwards spoke first. His circuitous account ultimately indicted Caldwell as the lone murderer. On the night of the murder, Edwards recalled that he went to Larkin's store, bought three shells, and borrowed Larkin's shotgun "to kill some bats." Edwards then left the store, but Caldwell took the gun and proceeded to confront Eppes, intending to retrieve some money that he had lent to the superintendent. This meeting ended with Caldwell shooting Eppes. While Edwards relayed his story, Caldwell and Larkin repeatedly interrupted, naming Edwards as the lone murder. "Isom Edwards," Caldwell asserted, "had me arrested as being an accomplice in the murder because I was with him at Larkin's store that night." The reporter claimed that the three fought throughout the interview but agreed on one point. "The three negroes stated positively that they were not members of any 'before-day' club, and that they never heard of the existence of such a club."[98]

Before Day club rumors quieted as the trial drew near. A preliminary hearing in early September concluded that Edwards was the principal murderer and that Caldwell and Larkin were accessories. An article covering the verdict briefly mentioned Before Day clubs, saying only that they were inventions of popular imagination. Most people believed that the crime was the result of a robbery.[99] The trial in January 1905 delivered three guilty verdicts and three death sentences. Lawyers for the accused appealed first to the state supreme court and then, after not winning there, to the state pardon board. Governor Napoleon Broward and the other members of the board upheld Edwards's sentence but agreed to reconsider the other two. The state set November 3, 1905, as Edwards's execution date. Just prior to his death, Edwards made two startling confessions. First, he admitted to having killed Eppes by himself. Then, Edwards claimed to have murdered Anna Paine three months before killing Eppes. Paine was a black mother of seven who lived near Lake Hall. According to the report, Edwards went to Paine's house, the two began arguing, and he choked her to death. "Nobody knew that I committed the murder, though at that time some of the negroes did accuse me of killing her." Edwards laughed as he told the reporter that he was a pallbearer for the funeral. The reporter queried why he had laughed, and Edwards responded, "I was just thinking that old woman tried to holler when I choked her." The article concluded, "[Edwards is] without a doubt the most cold-blooded murderer that has ever occupied a cell to the Duval County jail. . . . Now that he is doomed to die on the gallows he apparently cares nothing and freely tells about the murder and the way he committed the crime."[100]

A gathering of approximately five thousand people watched Edwards step to the gallows, accompanied by a Catholic priest. Before the crowd, Edwards confessed to the murders of Paine and Eppes and restated that Caldwell and Larkin were completely innocent. According to the *Times-Union*, "His statement was lengthy and he spoke with a strong, clear voice, warning members of his race and the public in general to avoid evil companions and to meet him in heaven." The crowd remained orderly throughout the hanging. Recollecting the story of the murder, the news report mentioned earlier claims about the Before Day club. "This confession caused much excitement in Leon County," but the paper assured its readers that the club had never existed.[101]

The Eppes family disagreed. Days before Edwards's execution, Governor Broward met with the convicted, who supposedly confessed to the murders and assured Broward that Larkin and Caldwell were without fault.[102] Almost a year later, Broward and the pardon board reduced Larkin's and Caldwell's sentences to life in prison.[103] This infuriated Edward Eppes, Nicholas's son, who was convinced that Caldwell and Larkin were the murderers and that Edwards was their pawn. In a letter to Isaac White, the editor of *The World* in New York City, Eppes claimed that his father's death was a "political assassination" orchestrated by the superintendent's political opponents. "[Certain] white politicians," the son fumed, bribed the "negro leaders" of a "criminal organization" to murder his father. Florida politics "had fallen into the hands of some very corrupt officials," who had approved secret and illegal public land deals. Eppes alleged that his father was "strongly opposed to all such corrupt practices." A "ring" of crooked politicians subsequently contracted the murder and orchestrated the commutation of Caldwell's and Larkin's death sentences. The supposed murderers, Eppes announced, "will never confess while they have any hope of escaping the gallows, and the white men who instigated the crime are therefore doing all they can in secret to save them." While Eppes avoided reviving the Before Day club rumor, he did invoke the image of a black criminal organization that was still "wide spread over this section of country."[104] To Edward Eppes, the supposed enemies of his father practiced a deficient form of Democratic Party politics, one that patronized black murder clubs.[105] He shared with others a fear of these clubs, which inverted a white vision of the good society, created a panic, and ultimately shed light on the ambiguous boundaries around the black "place" in society.

"The Almighty Maketh the Wrath of Man to Serve Him"

In September 1906, a mob of over ten thousand whites spent four days and nights laying waste to black neighborhoods in Atlanta. In Live Oak, Florida, a newspaper editor found a silver lining in this dark cloud. He accepted, as many others did, that the actions of the "brutal" mob were morally incomprehensible, and must be punished. "But even as the Almighty maketh the wrath of man to serve him," the editor added, "so in this case has the bloody work of the Atlanta hoodlums brought about a fortunate sequel which perhaps might not have been reached in years if less drastic medicine had not been used." The author suspected that the riot had been the culmination of years of "vile negro outrages," which the violence had eliminated. Moreover, the "educated negroes," such as preachers and teachers, who had taken to criticizing whites, were now "terrified into common sense and a sane view of the race question." So for the editor, Atlanta now had an opportunity to rebuild, along with the rest of the South. Because of the riots, the white South along with "the best elements of the negro race" could wage a "universal war" on "the swarming hordes of vagrancy from whose ranks rape fiends come."[106]

Of course, successful blacks — the so-called better sort — bore the brunt of the violence in the riots. As white mobs ravaged black colleges and businesses, they sent a clear message that no black person was safe, that no black person was equal, and that black freedom had limits. The Live Oak editor and other white apologists seemingly discounted the real target of the riots. Instead, they emphasized the redemptive quality of violence, feeding a civil religious discourse that endorsed all measures that might keep blacks in their "place."[107] But blacks had their own civil religious discourse, one version of which Christianized resistance to white dominance. By the time of the riots, Benjamin Jefferson Davis was a lawyer in Atlanta, where he had met and befriended a black minister who, during the riots, transformed his church into a "fort." The riots did not pacify the minister; rather, the violence made him even more forceful in advocating black freedom. In 1932, when Davis took part in the legal defense of an Atlanta black man accused of inciting an "insurrection," the minister arranged for Davis's protection from the Klan. Davis refused the offer. "It's our cross and we'll bear it. We don't want you to endanger yourself in any way on our account." The minister retorted, "Davis, this is the cross of the whole Negro population of Atlanta. It ought to be the cross of every white man with any Christianity or justice in his soul. But we're going to be with you just the same."[108]

The sheer power of white voices in the post-Reconstruction era might lead us to overemphasize their centrality in the region's civil religious discourse. This would, however, marginalize the varying civil religious interactions between and within black and white circles. Here, the "place" of blacks was highly contested, and the South's moral and physical geography remained unsettled even though white authority was pervasive. Voices like those of Davis and his minister would persist, imagining a place for themselves built on a vision of the good society that emphasized freedom and equality.

CHAPTER THREE

Female Voices, Male Voices

Devotion and the "Noble Daughters of the South"

"WHAT A STRONG POWER for good or evil is a woman's influence," decreed a Pensacola editor. "In all ages there have been instances where women have by their force of will or fascination of manner incited men to crimes or to the highest and holiest ambition." The "vilest" women corrupt men through subtle gestures, a smile or a teardrop. "On the other hand the womanly woman with her noble ambitions, her pure views of life and her sunny nature can spur a man on to higher and better work and let him see in her eyes the first glimpse of heaven." Accordingly, the author encouraged men to choose their spouse wisely. "With more noble, upright and true women in the world, there would be fewer dissolute, unprincipled men."[1]

For white men, the "true woman" was essential for family stability and, by extension, social stability. But the foil for this "handmaiden of the Lord" was the "handmaiden of the devil." In the post-Reconstruction era, both images assumed new forms and had an impact on how people understood the prospects of the Wiregrass Gulf South.[2] To be sure, the "true woman" was unique neither to the Wiregrass South, nor to the nation. Piety, purity, submissiveness, and domesticity were all the "cardinal virtues" of the "cult of true womanhood," according to Barbara Welter. In antebellum America, Welter argues, religion and family life became the "property" of women, who were often depicted as being "domesticated," "emotional," "soft," and "accommodating."[3] The antebellum southern lady also radiated these virtues. But after the war and Reconstruction, with fewer men living in the region and more women becoming engaged in social life, the "true woman" underwent redefinition. Women themselves used this gendered mythology in public life in participating in social campaigns such as prohibition, missionary work, and the Lost Cause. Southern Jewish women also took up benevolent causes, finding common ground with the majority on the significance of civic engagement and religious practice.[4]

Catholic women had more difficulty fitting in to the majority's "true woman" category. As nativist sentiments grew in the early twentieth century, the white Protestant majority became distrustful of nuns. Gender conflicts also existed within the Catholic hierarchy. Men were distrustful and wary of women religious who showed too much authority. Similarly, southern Protestant men supported women's civic work but criticized any expressions of womanhood associated with "woman's rights." Throughout the Wiregrass Gulf South, gender carried civil religious weight that when examined closely, offers a means for understanding how people envisioned what society ought to be.[5]

Devotion and the "True Woman"

In the years following Reconstruction, southern white men idealized female religious devotion, using it both as a standard for moral righteousness and as a contrast to moral deficiency. So a Pensacola newspaper relayed the following joke in 1900:

"Did you ever get religion?" asked the revivalist.

"Well, I should say so — 138 pounds of it," replied the man.

"A hundred and thirty-eight pounds of religion!" cried the revivalist. "How did you get that?"

"The only way that a good many men ever get religion," was the reply, "I married it."[6]

In 1901, Henry Partridge, a Methodist minister in Tallahassee, confided in his diary that his mother's "piety, teaching and prayers" gave his up-bringing an incredible "spiritual nature." Because of this, he explained, he knew from an early age, before he even understood Christian theology, that he was destined for the pulpit.[7] Partridge also credited his sister, Sarah Ann, whose pleasant disposition as a young girl "predicted the sweet, pure, gentle, loving, earnest womanhood of her after life." She was a teacher, Partridge wrote, whose instruction developed the intellect, morality, and spirituality of students. Partridge knew that his sister had a challenging vocation, but "she passed through the fire of trial to come out like the gold . . . to be fashioned for the vessel for the Master's use. Pure Gold." Sarah Ann died in 1873, but she left behind "an object lesson of what religion is, and will do."[8]

Women outside of his family would also morally influence him. When attending Wofford College in Spartanburg, South Carolina, Partridge lived with a "noble" attorney and his "gentle" wife. The husband was a prominent member of his church and society and was "honored and beloved by all." His wife "was a queen in her home" and the epitome of "womanhood." Their daughters likewise were "well read and intelligent; cheerful in disposition; easy and refined in manners; with high ideals of womanly purity." He rejoiced that the faith-filled atmosphere of his home "thus continued around me. . . . My Heavenly Father has thus most graciously prepared me for a true and noble life."[9] Just as he had with his sister and mother, Partridge found "true religion" in the "pure" women of his adopted family.

Partridge's memory cast both the Christian homemaker and the Christian teacher in the role of guiding moral influences. The female Christian educator was a relatively recent development, a product of the realities of the New South. The Civil War depleted the South's male population, leading to declining marriage rates in the decades that followed. Additionally, some women who had become socially active in wartime remained so in the years after. Lingering from the Old South was a belief that women were divine agents of social stability. In a post-Reconstruction South, though, this notion had a wider reach; the "new woman" of the New South employed metaphors of Christian motherhood in social reform campaigns, education, and a host of other public activities.[10] And the ubiquitous "handmaiden of the devil" lurked too, assuming new forms along the way. For example, men often expressed a fear that contemporary culture would lure women into "impurity," a euphemism for sexual promiscuity. In 1904, Methodist revivalist Sam Jones spoke to a crowd of over one thousand in Lake City, Florida. A "fact," he began, is "something that you can't get over, you can't get through it, neither can you get around it. It stands right there in your pathway an unmoved obstacle." Jones then pointed to the "fact" that "purity and character . . . are the only two pillars that hold [a] woman up in this world." If one pillar broke, the entire structure would fall. Thus, he called upon the honor of men in the crowd to take all measures in preventing the "fall of a girl." A journalist covering the event reported that the crowd listened attentively and agreed wholeheartedly "with all the hard things he had said."[11]

Here, a minister measured social stability by the purity of women and charged men with safeguarding it. In other settings, demands that female purity be protected came coupled with fears of racial intermingling. This civil religious package was toxic for blacks. Perceived black affronts to white womanhood—whether by rape or merely by accidental contact—registered as a supreme threat to white supremacy. Whites responded with sanctified violence, mobilizing their killing energy to reassert the boundaries between the races.[12] Some blacks made a point of addressing this fear, identifying rape as a major piece in the "race problem" puzzle. In 1898, a newspaper in Chipley, Florida, applauded William H. Councill, a black educator from Alabama, who pointed to what he believed was a rise in rape cases in the South and urged black leaders to police their own ranks, warning that the lynchings would not stop otherwise. "Let us restore that sense of security which white women felt fifty years ago in the presence of our fathers," Councill announced. "Let us make white women of this land, and of all lands, feel that our black arms are ever ready, backed by hearts as pure as truth, as guileless as babes, to defend their honor; that we are willing to throw our black bodies between them and their assailants, and shed our blood to the last drop in protecting them and hunting down and executing these brutes."[13] Councill's tone was unmistakably accommodationist. He fashioned a solution to racial discord by appealing to a white nostalgia for an imagined era of slave loyalty. Moreover, gender purity and male chivalry served as the bridge Councill used to connect his exhortation with a white civil religious discourse that would unflinchingly lynch any black person suspected of sexual contact with a white woman.[14]

In addition to sparking violence, female purity could also be invoked as a means of encouraging proper male behavior. Speaking before a meeting of commercial travelers, Sam Jones empathized with the challenges inherent to their lifestyle but called on them to "live as pure men." To accomplish this, he advised, "Never say a word anywhere that you could not say in the presence of a parlor full of ladies. And never go to a place that you don't want your sister or wife to go to. And whatever you do let your love and vows to your wife be kept as sacred as the word of God is sacred."[15] Similarly, Mobile's Episcopal bishop Richard H. Wilmer spoke ruefully of the "unreligion [sic] of our men" but at the same time chastened anyone who automatically assumed that women were ideal Christians from birth onward. He surmised that a parent "looks trembling to the future of his boys" yet "confidently to the time when his daughters shall unfold the graces and refinements of the Christian womanhood." The bishop dismissed the notion that God had produced this spiritual disparity, insisting that men were "originally not less religious than the woman." Instead, Wilmer warned that God's judgment extended to all, despite their gender.[16]

Still, for Wilmer, while women were not inherently more religious than men, they were exemplars of Christian morality and models for men to follow.[17] Preachers sometimes reversed this formula, putting themselves or other men at the center of Christian morality. Methodist minister Simon Peter Richardson recalled visiting Albany in 1851, a town he called "a hard place in more respects than one." During one of his sermons, the wife of a wealthy merchant grew visibly upset. Calling her Sister H., Richardson explained that she was an infrequent churchgoer who objected to his condemnation of "card playing and dancing." After the service, Sister H. complained to her husband, who was "a man of good sense and, though not in the Church, knew what a good woman ought to be." The husband's supposed moral intelligence led him to reject his wife's complaints, which in turn caused her to retreat into self-reflection. At the next morning's service, she arrived wearing a conservative sunbonnet, and when the appropriate moment came, she "rose up and gave the church a scrap of her experience." Sister H. thanked the minister and her husband for the rebuke, confessed her sins, and became thereafter "faithful to God and the Church."[18]

Richardson's account transformed Sister H. from an obstreperous complainer into an ideal Christian woman. He did not measure her Christian authenticity by her gender but rather by her conversion. In his mind, moral righteousness arose from individual salvation, which was not determined by gender. Elsewhere, though, Richardson more forthrightly emphasized the distinctiveness of female piety. Recalling his 1851 visit to Tallahassee, Richardson called it a place of "peace and prosperity" and "religion and morality." He credited the "deeply pious" women of Tallahassee's Methodist Church with nurturing such an environment, which influenced *nearly* everyone. One wealthy merchant who belonged to the church was also a whiskey seller. Aware of this, Richardson refused communion to him. The merchant had been a generous contributor to the church, and one church official was outraged by what Richardson had done. But Richardson reassured the official that the denied communicant would recognize the error in his ways. And sure enough, within days, discarded barrels of whiskey appeared in front of the merchant's store. Richardson visited the store, the two exchanged cordial greetings, and the merchant affirmed that he had forsaken selling whiskey. He then fitted the minister with a new suit, and the two became lifelong friends. Richardson concluded that "his convictions were right and in line with his preacher, but, like thousands of Church members, his life was wrong."[19]

Again Richardson made conversion central to his Christian moral map, this time drawing this map using pious women and alcohol-free streets as his landmarks. The preacher was more prone to highlight his own ethical superiority than that of his female counterparts. Others more directly emphasized the relationship between a "true woman," family, and society.[20] When Thomasville's Mary Ann Hansell died, a local newspaper wrote glowingly of her motherhood. A noted citizen in Thomas County, much of the obituary concentrated on her as "an example of true womanhood." Her family, the author extolled, lived in a household "surrounded by a Christian spirit and the sacred teaching of the Holy

Word." This would be her finest legacy in the author's eyes, who pointed to her five children as each being "a monument of the purity of the life she has lived."[21]

Monumentalizing domestic virtue and "true womanhood" had social implications for the author, who measured Hansell's worth by the moral character of her progeny. This image of the homebound "pious" mother would serve, for other men, as a rebuke to their moral indiscretions. In his diary, Samuel Floyd of Apalachicola, Florida, frequently lamented what he believed was his own sinfulness, worrying that his mother would disapprove. In 1872, this single twenty-six-year-old lumber inspector reminisced that in his mother "truth and honesty were virtues that never shone so brightly." While listing nothing specific, he worried that his frequent moral shortcomings dishonored his mother's example. Calling himself a "model moderner," Floyd wondered if the "improvements made in this human progression" had corrupted him, enabling him to purchase success "at the expense of morality."[22] Floyd's tortured self-examinations pulled female purity into ruminations about the nature of progress in the Wiregrass Gulf South. For many of his time, railroads, ports, and modern agriculture were proof that political redemption had been divinely ordained. In Floyd's case, though, wealth had a moral downside, and the example of his mother helped him navigate that minefield.

Elsewhere in the Wiregrass South, men negotiated new boundaries for the socially engaged "true woman." Southern educational reformers, for example, hoped to harness the presumed pious energies of women, reasoning that society could benefit from their motherly example. But reformers also refrained from granting women too much independence.[23] In promotional literature for Georgia's Southern Female College, Charles C. Cox described a typical evening on campus. Students and teachers, he said, could be found attending prayer meetings, reciting Bible passages, singing hymns, and praying earnestly in private. All of this, Cox proclaimed, spoke to the college's goal of organizing "Christians for practical, systematic work." This was the vision of the college's founder and first president, Milton E. Bacon. According to Cox, Bacon was a "knight" with uncommon "ability, zeal, and chivalry." Critics disapproved of the school, but Bacon was a determined advocate of the "woman's cause" and believed that the "ideal woman" was "consecrated and cultured." Cox averred that Bacon was a true product of the Old South, as was the school. Nothing would have insulted the founder more than "woman's rights," a "heathen" notion that "denied to woman the existence of soul . . . [and] her mind." Nothing in Cox's estimation could be more detrimental to women seeking to become "penitent servants of the Christian faith."[24]

While education was an expression of progressive reform, it had limits. For Cox, woman's rights—with its ties to the North, liberal Protestantism, and female suffrage—counted as a violation of "true womanhood," an affront to Christian female devotion. Cox and his fellow laborers worried about female independence and just how much authority women should have. Temperance reform saw similar conflicts. The Woman's Christian Temperance Union (WCTU) formed in Ohio in 1872 and made little headway in the former Confederacy initially. By 1890, however, every former Confederate state had a chapter. Helping this along was Frances Willard, who as the WCTU's national president toured every southern state from 1881 to 1883. As she encouraged the formation of more chapters, the northern-born institution found a home in the South. Southern ministers in particular were more concerned with waging a war on whiskey and less concerned with the regional origination of the group. Moreover, these ministers also wanted women to have more authority both in the church and society.[25]

So while Charles Cox spoke cautiously of female independence, Sam Jones wanted to open new terrain.[26] In one sermon, the former alcoholic urged churches to lend more support to the WCTU. Saloons, the revivalist proclaimed, are "the greatest obstacles which lie in the way of our triumph of Christ and His Church in the world." Jones complained that not enough people understood the "evil" of alcohol. But women and the WCTU did. Moreover, he advocated the "emancipation" of women, convinced that they could preach "the risen Christ" as well as any man. Jones cited as evidence the "sainted" Mary T. Lathrap. A Michigan native, Lathrap was a principal voice in the WCTU's formation. In 1878, she became a licensed Methodist preacher and gave a rousing sermon at a WCTU meeting at Grand Rapids, which quickly circulated throughout the state. With more women like Lathrap, Jones was certain the movement would grow and good things would result. He calculated that women made up two-thirds of his church's membership and described their "loyalty," "devotion," and "faithfulness" as exemplary. "Oh, woman, heed God's call to you," Jones concluded. "Join our ranks, and in addition to your church work, work for Him along the lines of prohibition and woman's emancipation."[27]

Jones's faith was undeniably active, engaged in transforming society through the labors of anyone willing to help, be they men or women. Alcohol, he averred, could only splinter society and alienate it from a Christian ideal that he sought to realize. With the power to minister, he hoped that "devoted" women would help actualize his good society. Jones's advocacy of temperance found favor among some women in the Wiregrass South. Writing in 1925, Mattie Coyle of Moultrie, Georgia, remembered the 1880s as a "turbulent period." This "era of lawlessness," she recalled, "was not checked until the good citizens of the County, after a hard fight, banished saloons." She remembered citizens voting on the matter twice. Both times, however, the results favored the "wet" advocates. Then Sam Jones arrived in 1902. He unleashed a fierce attack on the saloons, which, she conjectured, prompted the formation of a "dry council," composed of ministers and lay persons who pushed hard for prohibition. "The banishment of saloons was a forward step in the moral, religious and educational progress in the County," Coyle concluded. "Churches and schools came into existence, and the morale of the County rapidly improved."[28]

This transformational narrative of order emerging from chaos found Jones as the instigator of positive change. A dry town was a morally sound town, which saw prosperity as its reward. But Jones and others pressed ceaselessly for more women to take part, helping to reenvision "true womanhood." "Some people say they don't believe in woman's work," Jones quipped. "There is an old preacher down in Georgia who preaches against woman's work, and that preacher has not had a conversion since the war."[29] The gender ideals of Jones appeared in the Wiregrass Gulf South by way of people like Alfred L. Woodward, a Methodist minister in Tallahassee. Woodward frequently demonized drink and blamed it for the ills of the family and society. "Bless every man and woman, every agency and instrumentality," he announced, "which has for its object the abolition of the infamous traffic in intoxicating drink. A traffic which is the blackest blot on the civilization of the age, the remaining relic of a barbarous past." Liquor, in Woodward's mind, invaded the most sacred realm of southern society, the family. The "drunkard's wife" lives a lonely and loveless life, worried always of becoming a widow and anxious that her children would end up fatherless. In contrast, the wife of a sober man lives a "happy family life."[30]

Juxtaposing the drunken and sober man, Woodward equated alcohol consumption with shame—a shame that threatened female "purity," the family, and social stability.[31] For Woodward, women were not merely victims; they were also allies. In 1909, he served on the temperance committee for the Florida Conference of the Methodist Episcopal Church, South. One resolution expressed appreciation and support for Florida's WCTU and Anti-Saloon League.[32] Like Sam Jones's, Woodward's "true woman" was socially engaged and devoted to a cause that the public good demanded.

In the changing world of the New South, Wiregrass Catholics were also questioning the role of women. Mother Austin Carroll had a distinguished career with the Sisters of Mercy in New Orleans and Mobile. After arriving in Mobile in 1869, Austin directed the order's focus toward serving the poor. She launched a prison ministry, food pantry, and home for women. Additionally, by the time of her death in 1909, the Sisters of Mercy had opened sixty-five schools in Florida, Alabama, Mississippi, and Belize. Austin was also a tireless writer, penning numerous articles and nearly forty books.[33] Both Pope Pius IX and Pope Leo XIII wrote Austin to commend her activism and scholarship.[34] She drew additional praise from non-Catholics. Following her 1909 death, a Mobile newspaper wrote a lengthy obituary celebrating her as a "most remarkable woman," who not only served humanity but also possessed "splendid gifts of intellect." A Pensacola newspaper celebrated her "wonderful era of usefulness," which would remain "a monument" to her "untiring industry and fine enterprise."[35]

Publicly, Bishop Edward Allen of Mobile supported Mother Austin. But privately, he harbored reservations and resentment. In 1900, Allen wrote Austin to address charges leveled against her by the order's assistant, Mother Loyola. Mother Austin had apparently accused Loyola of violating her vow of poverty. To this, Allen rebuked, "I asked for proofs of the charges made against her and, as none has been given I must look upon the charges as groundless."[36] Writing to a colleague about Austin, Allen confessed that he had arranged Austin's impending transfer. The bishop called Austin "a woman insane with love for power," whose own order complained ceaselessly about her leadership. Specifically, the nuns charged that Austin belittled those sisters who she believed were rivals, intent on forcing them out of the community. It was all part of a pattern, Allen alleged. "She is a woman of great resources and can twist and turn things so as to make white appear black and black white. . . . She has a tongue that spares no one. Neither priest nor Bishop, the living or the dead is safe from her uncharitable and vitriolic remarks. She is a woman of whims, at one time observing her rule carefully and at another neglecting it altogether."[37]

Allen saw in Mother Austin a prime example of what Catholic female piety was not. He was not alone. Austin spent much of her career in conflict with the male hierarchy. One rector, upset that the Irish-born Austin had been asserting too much authority among New Orleans's German priests, grumbled that "it is simply the duty of the sisters to obey, as this is the natural order of things." He advised Austin that if she wanted the priests' cooperation, she and her sisters ought to remain "docile and obedient children."[38] But in addition to praise from two popes, Austin also attracted praise from American Catholic men. Henry Austin Adams, editor of *Donahoe's Magazine*, spoke favorably of Mother Austin. For Adams, she was not vocal enough, and he admired this. The "new woman" was threatening to the editor, who respected Mother Austin and her order for leading with actions not words. Thus, Adams's support for Mother Austin was grounded in a broader symbolic contest over religion and womanhood. His articles directly or indirectly contrasted Catholic and Protestant forms of womanhood, favoring the former for its presumed silent activism.[39]

Adams's belief that Austin was a woman of action rather than words notwithstanding, Austin was a noted voice in the South's public square. Among her many writings was *A Catholic History of Alabama and the Floridas* (1908), wherein, interestingly enough, she praised and thanked Bishop Allen, who "always found leisure to encourage the writer, and aid her with many judicious Apostolic suggestions." She credited him for bringing "extraordinary progress" to the region's Catholic populations, noting the increase in the number of priests and in the number of churches, schools, hospitals, and charitable institutions. Austin also praised her sisters. As teachers in Catholic schools, they became "'*the great moral force of society, the foundation upon which is built up the true greatness of states.*'"[40]

Mother Austin, like her Protestant counterparts, made women a "moral force" for the betterment of society. Catholics were a religious minority in the region, but they had established their presence in the physical and moral landscape. Their physical structures emerged from the broader progressive leanings of the time, and their moral geography included places where women were able to morally influence schools and society. But despite certain shared values, Catholicism—particularly as it appeared behind the convent walls—sat outside the majority's vision of the good society.

In July 1916, Alice Ketchman took her simple vows as a Benedictine sister at the Sacred Heart Academy in Cullman, Alabama, just north of Birmingham. Thereafter assuming the name Sister Fidelis, she was obliged to remain in the convent until July 2, 1919. In May 1919, however, Fidelis's stepfather, Ralph McCraney of Athens, Georgia, wrote to Bishop Allen in Mobile demanding immediate dispensation for his stepdaughter. McCraney alleged that Fidelis had entered the convent at age seventeen without parental consent. Moreover, he claimed that her mother was terminally ill and required Fidelis to accompany her on a trip to New York. Religious reasons also prompted the demand. "We being Protestants cannot take things in a Catholic light." Being Catholic was tolerable, McCraney added, but he did not "intend for her to be a nun." He closed on a contentious note, threatening to forcibly remove his stepdaughter with or without official dispensation.[41]

Allen responded, "I would not feel justified in dispensing Sister Fidelis from her vows because her relatives are opposed to her being in the convent." The bishop then rebutted the suggestion she was a minor when she entered the convent as an adult. Concluding sternly, Allen warned, "I would not advise you to interfere one day before that time. I have never yet seen anyone that interfered with a vocation of a son or a daughter happy over the result. Indeed I have seen more than one bitterly bewail the day that they interfered with a son or a daughter's vocation." He concluded his letter by noting that "no one has a right to come between the soul and Almighty God."[42]

Sister Fidelis wrote on her own behalf to Bishop Allen. She confided that religious prejudice fueled her stepfather's demand, a bias shared by her entire Protestant family. Fidelis worried that her family would "cause a great disturbance" at the convent if she remained. Thus, she felt God had called her to leave, and she asked for dispensation, assuring the bishop that she was "firmly enough instructed in my Holy religion to never fall."[43] Allen wrote back, "I cannot understand how the views of anyone should come between you and Almighty God." As far as the bishop was concerned, Fidelis's commitment to the order demanded that she fulfill her vows, so he denied her dispensation. The "whim of your parents or relatives is not a just reason for dispensing you or anyone from your solemn obligations to Almighty God." The bishop then reminded Sister Fidelis that she was twenty-two and "free to decide" if she felt "called to religious life." She could depart in July, he assured, "without any stain on your career" or "opposition from your superiors."[44]

The superior of the academy, Mother Ottilia, wrote to inform Allen that Fidelis had received his letter. Ottilia confirmed that Fidelis's mother was ill. However, Ottilia suspected that the entire affair was "a scheme of her non-Catholic relatives" who were suspicious of the faith. The bewildered mother superior then claimed that Fidelis's mother had actually visited the convent at one point, helping Fidelis with her religious garb.[45] In a later letter, Ottilia wrote Allen and confirmed that Ralph McCraney had forcibly removed Fidelis from the convent. "Under the circumstances it may be best that she did go," she noted with regret. "It might have caused an endless talk and scandal in the daily paper."[46]

The Sister Fidelis affair reflected deep civil religious tensions that existed in the South and nation during the 1910s. For Allen, Sister Fidelis's term was nothing short of sacred, and the stepfather's meddling would result in divine disfavor. McCraney saw no validity in the Catholic vocation and held an image of "true womanhood" that was decidedly Protestant and, embedded within this worldview, decidedly anti-Catholic. Both worldviews occupied southern soil, even though in 1916, Florida elected Sidney J. Catts as governor, an inexperienced candidate whose controversial anti-Catholicism undoubtedly won him a surplus of votes. Many white Protestants in the region distrusted Catholics, believing that their "patriotic" loyalties rested with Rome and Rome alone. Catholics rebutted that suggestion, arguing that nativist propagandists had manufactured these ideas, which had no foundation in reality. Moreover, they insisted that expressions of anti-Catholicism betrayed the foundations of American society. Protestants held the balance of power in the South, so the perceived transgressions of Catholics evoked a vociferous defense of their social boundaries. But the Catholic minority was still shaping the civil religious discourse of the region, directing it often through the focusing lens of gender.[47]

The Devoted "New Woman"

Southern white men often imagined the "true woman" as one devoted to family, faith, and society. Women also took part in defining the "true woman." In some settings, women wrote themselves into the Wiregrass Gulf South's redemption narrative. They emphasized the civil religious work of women laboring alongside men to facilitate the South's supposed metaphorical rise from the ashes of Reconstruction.

After the Civil War, Tallahassee's Susan Bradford Eppes recalled, legions of "[heart]-sick and weary" soldiers returned home, and southern women prepared to help them rebuild. The "Old South was dead, her economic system was in ruins, her wealth had taken wings, her manpower was depleted." Aware of this, the selfless women of the South "resolutely put aside all semblance of woe" and "performed the heaviest and most disagreeable tasks with a smile and a song." [48] Eppes then recounted a standard redemption narrative, one that rued Reconstruction politics and expressed gratitude for home rule. But she would also repeatedly acknowledge the work of women, whose supposed energy, faith, and optimism strengthened the South on its return to glory.

Despite her nostalgia, Eppes represented a new breed of southern woman. In 1894, Josephine Henry described the "New Woman of the New South" as educated, urbane, and socially active.[49] As Anastasia Sims explains, these "new women" kept a "tenacious hold" on their Old South ideals while using "the power of indirect influence and moral authority" to further social reforms. Long before they could vote, Sims claims, women became politically involved, completing "the chores of public housekeeping."[50] In this new era, many southern white women made themselves active civic participants in the hope that they might transform the region. While southern white men heralded the "pious" example of the "Christian mother," southern white women frequently told their own stories of the past or projected their own ideals onto the region's future.[51]

By the end of the nineteenth century, participating in missionary activity became one way that southern women were able to venture outside the home.[52] In the North, foreign missions attracted women who craved religious independence and the opportunity to minister in foreign lands. In the South, middle- and upper-class women had similar longings.[53] In 1882, a Baptist publication in Atlanta printed a letter from an anonymous female missionary who announced that, with the gospel in hand, any woman could take "her God-appointed place in human society." Since "the Fall," she explained, women had become fervent advocates of faith, offering "the divine remedy for sin." She reasoned that women were therefore suited to Christianize the world and that they could carry out this mission abroad or by ministering to "the spiritually destitute" of the South. The author then called out to readers, seeking financial support for the evangelization of those who were "far removed from the sanctuaries of God, shut out from Christian associations and Christian sympathy, denied, with their children, the sweet influences of God's holy day."[54] For this female missionary, the good society was a Christian society. Her scope was both domestic and worldly, and her agents of reform were devoted women.

Domestic missions were part of the female missionary campaign, but foreign missions attracted a unique set of southern women, who often brought the mores of their homeland abroad. An 1885 pamphlet by the Women's Missionary Society (WMS) of Florida printed a letter sent to Mary A. Turnbull of Miccosukee from Laura Haygood, a missionary in Shanghai, China. Born in Watkinsville, Georgia, Haygood began teaching in Atlanta in 1872. She also assisted domestic missions. In 1884, an Atlanta preacher's sermon on foreign missions inspired Haygood to join the endeavor. Her first mission was to Shanghai, where, before her death in 1898, she founded the McTyeire Home and School.[55] In her letter, Haygood beseeched readers to keep "broader room in your hearts" for the "work," "hope," and "plans" of the WMS. Describing the conditions of her mission, Haygood observed that Chinese parents had begun allowing their children to attend "foreign schools." There was suspicion, she admitted, but missionaries effectively quieted all such "prejudices." Haygood reasoned that it was only a matter of time before the missionaries would have success. With children in their schools, they had access to mothers—which, in Haygood's view, was the key to Christianizing China.[56] Haygood transported not only herself to China but also the gender norms of the Wiregrass Gulf South. In her homeland, a civil religious discourse equated the health of society with the health of the family, and the health of the family depended on the Christian influence of the mother. Armed with this worldview, the missionary hoped to remake the world in the image of a southern vision of the good society.

Prohibition was also a venue in which women wielded an authority gained through the "true womanhood" image. In 1907, Pensacola's WCTU drafted an open letter to "Christian" men, asking them to vote for a county prohibition law. In it, they summarily demonized liquor, calling it the "curse of the world," which left the county "groaning under its burden of cost and crime." The letter was more forthright in detailing alcohol's supposed toll on the family. This "deadly enemy of our happiness" had caused untold "sleepless nights" and "crushed hopes." For the safety and happiness of the county's families, and for the sake of the society that these families supported, the women called on those possessing "true manhood" to vote for a dry county.[57] The letter's urgent tone also reflected the lingering racial fears pulsing through the region as a result of the Atlanta riots. "IT WAS WHITE MEN'S LIQUOR IN THE FRENZIED BRAINS OF DRUNKEN NEGROES THAT CAUSED THE ATLANTA RACE RIOTS," shouted a Pensacola newspaper as the prohibition vote neared.[58] Still, the wet vote won—but not, as one commentator said it, owing to lack of effort from "moral people."[59] An editor in Live Oak charged wet advocates with corralling the "negro vote" in their favor and blamed the Fifteenth Amendment for negating the political will of whites.[60]

The women of the WCTU in Escambia County envisioned a good society that stood in direct contrast with the world around them, and they called on the honor code of men to actualize what they believed was God's will for the region. Tallahassee's Luella Knott used similar imagery in a 1905 address to a WCTU convention. Tallahassee's path to prohibition, she claimed, had been built through the devoted prayers of Christian women. In one critical town meeting, wet and dry advocates faced off in a debate. Women in attendance prayed in silence, petitioning God to "confuse" wet speakers and make the dry advocates "silver-tongued orators." "God heard all of our prayers," she affirmed. The otherwise "brilliant" wet speaker bumbled through his speech, while his opponent spoke eloquently. "God did that for us," Knott theorized. But the prayerful work of women was not complete. When time for the vote arose, wet advocates scoured the city for black voters, which would seemingly assure their victory. "We prayed that God would let the negroes put 'no' where they should put 'yes,' and 'yes' where they should put 'no,' and sign them in the wrong places—and they did just what we asked God to make them do."[61]

For Knott and her colleagues, practicing female devotion meant praying for prohibition. Coded in these prayerful gestures were assumptions about Tallahassee and the South's place within God's plan. Her exceptional South was a dry South, located in her middle Florida hometown. It was a message repeated by many female Wiregrassers. According to a WCTU member in Albany, prohibition resulted from the "prayer and unswerving faith" of Christian men and women. Prohibition had been a rather unpopular topic, the author claimed, but this changed when "the Empire State of the South" voted to prohibit alcohol consumption on July 30, 1907. In Albany, "church bells rang out the glad news," and the WCTU gathered to pray in thanksgiving.[62]

Nowhere did the author mention the Atlanta riots, but this was very much part of the statewide push for prohibition.[63] Wet and dry became contrasting symbols of chaos and order, heathen and Christian, and black and white. And WCTU members enlisted these potent symbols into their cause, writing their own redemption narrative. Armed with a dry vision of the good society, they issued dire warnings about how the family and southern society would be destroyed if alcohol was not banned.

Repeated Christian allusions made prohibition a holy cause, backed by the devotion of true women, who were legally barred from voting but not from praying and advocating.

While Protestants numerically dominated the Wiregrass Gulf South, non-Protestant women were also involved in social reform. The National Council of Jewish Women (NCJW) formed in 1893, after the Jewish Woman's Congress at Chicago's World's Columbian Exposition. By 1896, a chapter had formed in Mobile. The organization's stated purpose was to forge "closer relations among Jewish Women" and encourage social reform and philanthropy. In 1912, Mrs. J. S. Simon, the president of the Council, commended the organization's efforts to help with schools and hospitals in Mobile. She also discussed the group's influence on Jewish family life. "The aim of each member of this Council should be to revere and to sustain our religion, and to do our utmost to transmit religious fervor to our families." Drawing attention specifically to religious observance, she announced that "the efforts of the committee to protest against Sabbath shopping we endorse, as we should respect as much as we can our Holy Sabbath, and show our faith in Judaism by a more frequent attendance at Divine Worship."[64] Simon envisioned members of the NCJW as being religiously devoted agents of social reform. This meant, in her mind, protecting the Sabbath and building schools and hospitals.[65] Adopting positions like these gave southern Jews a means of forging civil religious accords with the Protestant majority. Indeed, while the Protestant South spoke an exclusively Protestant civil religious language, they often left doors open for Jews.[66]

The "Glorious Women" of the Confederacy

In the Wiregrass Gulf South, female devotion was a multivocal civil religious value. A devoted woman was both socially active and socially reticent. She was also a social progressive and an Old South romantic. "The highest symbol of Southern virtue was the Confederate woman," affirms Charles Reagan Wilson. "Southern ministers," he elaborates, "viewed woman as virtuous because she was the symbol of home and family." Moreover, women represented "the old-time virtue" that ministers set forth in contrast to New South change. Consistent with Wilson's observation, white male Lost Causers in the Wiregrass South often made women the epitome of "southern virtue." Idealizing her supposed nationalistic and religious devotion during and after the war, these men spoke glowingly of Confederate "true womanhood."[67] Women also participated in the Lost Cause. Wiregrasser women organized memorial activities, sought to question the idea that slavery was the sole reason for the Civil War, and cast Abraham Lincoln as an illegitimate idiot, thereby voicing their own "true history" of the South.

When Thomasville's Amanda Seward died in 1897, a veteran of the town's Confederate infantry remembered her "pure devotion to the Southern cause." Years had passed since the war, but the "boys in gray" would never forget Seward's "bountiful hand," "sympathetic spirit," and uncommon "generosity." He claimed that she selflessly gave what she had, sending provisions and clothing to soldiers throughout the war. On cold winter nights, reminisced the veteran, the men benefiting from her charity "[called] down the blessings of Almighty God upon Mrs. Amanda Seward."[68] In this instance, "pure devotion" amounted to wartime service. Elsewhere, men lauded the postwar efforts of women to memorialize the Confederacy. In 1897, Albany's United Daughters of the Confederacy (UDC) hosted a Confederate memorial day celebration. A local newspaper promoted the event, describing the tireless effort of the women committed to perpetuating the "spirit of their order," which included venerating those "who did so much for them in the past." The author was certain that the celebration would "touch a responsive chord in the breasts of our veterans."[69]

Lost Cause visions of the good society grew out of concerted efforts to construct a sacred history for the South. Specifically, the Old South and Confederacy became portraits of social stability and wartime virtue respectively. In transporting listeners to another time and place and then returning them to the present, Lost Causers created a history to contrast with a New South marked by industrialization, urbanization, and emancipation. Women occupied a central position in this narrative, and men delighted in emphasizing this point. At a Confederate memorial day celebration in Monticello, Florida, Scott D. Clarke recognized that monuments could never fully capture the heroism of Confederate soldiers. But at least they testified to the present generation's admiration of their "fallen heroes." The women of the UDC, he continued, were "instrumental" in the construction of monuments, just as they were critical to the war effort. "By their spirits and their deeds the women of the Confederacy are equal sharers with its soldiers of a glory which one could not have achieved without the other." For their "devotion," "heroism," and "Christ-like ministrations," Clarke predicted, Confederate women would no doubt be admitted to heaven.[70]

The intermingling themes of female devotion, religion, and Confederate nationalism also appeared in Park Trammell's 1910 speech to the UDC in Lakeland, Florida. While not a Confederate veteran, Trammell still felt "naturally proud" to be paying tribute to the veterans and "doubly proud" that the UDC had invited him to speak. Trammell offered a lengthy tribute to the women of the Confederacy, commending their work during the war both on the home front and for the soldiers. The UDC preserved this spirit, in the speaker's estimation, as evidenced by the town's Confederate memorial. For him, this captured both the sorrow of war and the "devotion" of the "noble daughters of the South," past and present. Those gazing on the monument, Trammell concluded, would see that "the patriotic love and devotion of the women of the South of those days has been transplanted into the minds and hearts of the women of the present generation."[71]

Women also took part in the enterprise of valorizing the men and women of the Confederacy. In 1865, as the war concluded, a woman identified only as "Miss B." addressed a group of Thomasville soldiers as they passed through Columbus. "Soldiers of the Army of Tennessee," she proclaimed, "the ladies of Columbus, [are] fully aware of the severe reverses which have befallen you." She extolled their "matchless valor" in war, and empathized with their feelings of demoralization. But Miss B. also assured them that there was no reason for shame, as they were simply overpowered and not defeated. History, she maintained, would remember favorably the "virtues" of the Confederacy. "Thank God," she declared, "the spirit that animated the martyred dead who have fallen in this contest for freedom still lives within you." Because of this, Miss B.

concluded, southern women had nothing to fear when considering the future.[72]

In this setting and elsewhere, support became a key dimension of Confederate womanhood. Mobile's Kate Cummings cited Ella K. Trader, a nurse during the war, as an exceedingly "patriotic and whole-souled woman." Trader died during the war, but Cummings had been particularly impressed with the nurse's postwar plans of opening a home for Confederate orphans. The author concluded, "Her noble life . . . will ever remain as a memorial of what can be done by a true woman."[73] Similarly, when Pensacola's Emily C. Jones died, the local UDC remembered her service during the war, and commended her for marrying a Confederate when the war ended. In the years that followed, her admirable qualities only developed further, as she became a "fearless champion of the 'Lost Cause.'"[74] Ella Davis of Albany had no shortage of praise for southern women like Lou Smith of LaGrange, Georgia. According to Davis, Smith's entire "heart and soul" was "devoted to the cause of the South." When Smith first learned of Georgia's secession, she was on a train. She enlisted the services of two other women, who managed to purchase material at a stop and stitch together a Confederate flag during the journey. Crowds cheered with unparalleled enthusiasm, Smith wrote, as the train arrived in Atlanta with the flag draped across the engine. Smith's work did not end there. She served the Confederacy throughout the war and formed the Ladies Aid Society after. In the years that followed, these women decorated Confederate graves and raised money to build a monument.[75] Grave decoration had become a common ritual for female Lost Causers in the Wiregrass region. Annie White of Thomasville remembered that from her youth on, women had gathered annually to place flowers on graves, "thus keeping fresh their services to home and Country." Gravestones became sites where women could practice their devotion to the past. "Wherever a Soldier was buried, throughout our Southland, someone made an effort to have his grave decorated."[76]

Sewing flags, spreading flowers, and erecting monuments: each gesture ritualized female Confederate devotion. Most of this activity happened under the auspices of the UDC, an organization that curiously occupied a negotiated intersection between an imagined past and lived present. Many UDC members countered the modern impulses embodied in growing populations, sprouting railroads, developing cities, and flourishing industry with reminiscences of the Old South and Confederacy. Still, as Edward Ayers observes, the UDC "was not simple evidence of Southern distinctiveness" but rather "ironic evidence that the South marched in step with the rest of the country." The UDC was one of nearly five hundred social clubs in the North and South, each forming an identity around shared histories and geographies. Many of the groups—the UDC included—used the innovative organizational techniques of the progressive era to "educate" the public.[77]

While not necessarily educating the South in institutional settings, many UDC members made it their principal aim to perpetuate a "true history" of the Civil War. This history, of course, emphasized the supposed righteousness of the southern cause. In the Wiregrass South, the call to educate southerners about their history sounded through monuments, newspaper articles, speeches, and public gatherings. With the stated goal of instructing "the children of the Southland," women in Pensacola formed a chapter of the UDC in 1899. Organizers foresaw the UDC instilling "loyalty and devotion to our country and our flag" in future generations while also promoting "admiration, reverence, and love [for] the brave men . . . who laid down their lives in defense of the purest principles of patriotism in 1861–65."[78]

To excite interest in the group, Pensacola's Mrs. A. E. McDavid began writing a monthly newspaper column in 1907. In her first article, she exhorted the "daughters of our dear Southland" to awake: "Before you is a great and noble work. Think of what your fathers and mothers bore and accomplished during the four long, weary years in which war raged in our fair country. Think of the brave boys who went to the front, never to return; of the dear ones at home, of the Confederacy." The Confederate past, McDavid worried, would be lost without the UDC's "noble work." She asked the community to band together for the sake of educating future generations about their heritage, which she believed was an endless source of morality and virtue.[79]

McDavid rejected any suggestion that the UDC's work would rekindle sectional discord. Illustrating this point, she told the story of two former Confederates who met at a memorial unveiling. One gently decried the monument, along with all Confederate organizations, reasoning that they only perpetuated existing tensions between North and South. Moreover, future generations would never move forward because they would always be hampered by their mutual hatred inherited from those who preceded them. The other veteran rebutted this argument, claiming that memorials and Confederate organizations would motivate new generations to "search for the truth" about the war. With this knowledge, they would be better able to make positive contributions to society. McDavid championed this position, confident that the members of the UDC would remain "devoted" caretakers of the South's "noble" history even as they preferred peace to war.[80]

Nevertheless, despite assertions to the contrary, in educating young southerners about the Civil War, the UDC clearly demarcated the North from the South, casting the former as the eternal foe. In 1907, Saint Augustine's UDC sold a pamphlet with a printed speech by a woman identifying herself only as "the Historian." Speaking in the third person, this woman confessed her undying love for the South, admiration for Confederate veterans, and high esteem for the women of the Confederacy. On this final point, she urged attendees to "represent their mothers not less than their fathers" in their remembrances. Both had lived "sacred lives," whose story needed to be told for the sake of preserving the South's "principles and ideals." She did not doubt that memorials suitably captured the "undying deeds" of the past, but she believed more work was needed. In particular, people needed to know the region's "true history" and to understand that their ancestors had not "died in vain." She demanded that southern women "chisel the principles" of the Confederacy onto the "hearts and souls" of their children, making sure to avoid rekindling "the smoldering ashes of enmity and wrath." With this, "no haze of ignorance" would linger in the South, and people would know that the "undying principle" of the Confederacy was "state's rights." She worried about the ramifications of forgetting this. "Federal encroachment" had persisted. The South was again threatened with the North's "misrule and tyranny." But, she exclaimed, southerners could draw strength from the "courage," "fortitude," and "steadfastness" of their Confederate past. While "heavenward" monuments could "display the glory of our dead, they shall have crumbled and faded" over time. She concluded:

> The Star Spangled Banner waves over an united country, God grant that it may continue to do so; but to that end teach the children to love and reverence it as the upholder of constitutional freedom, not military despotism, as the emblem of the Right and the Liberty for which its great God-father meant it to stand; and never let them forget that the Stars and Bars and the Starry Cross of the Southern Confederacy are twice holy; as the symbols of Eternal Truth, springing phoenix-like from the ashes of her dead defenders; and as the pass of Glory covering sacred graves.[81]

This "true history" did the civil religious work of cultivating a southern past designed to idealize state's rights and oppose northern political policies. Women were critical to this enterprise and in order to be truly devoted to the Lost Cause, they needed to be socially engaged in "educating" the public. Although the writer was exceedingly nostalgic, she was a product of her era. She spoke to a large audience in a time when southern women had a more prominent role in public affairs. Thus, she became one sort of "ideal woman" of the Wiregrass South, operating within the UDC just as other women did in the WCTU, the WMS, and the NCJW.

The UDC's educational focus generated offshoot groups, such as the Children of the Confederacy (CC), formed in Alexandria, Virginia, in 1896. When members gathered, they sometimes recited the following prayer: "We have met together, our Heavenly Father, to study and to discover the truth of history. Keep out of our hearts all bitterness—knowing that bitterness engenders strife; keep out of our minds all narrowness, knowing that narrowness weakens character; keep out of our hearts all injustice, knowing that injustice is sinful."[82] As CC chapters appeared in the Wiregrass Gulf South, each determined to "discover the truth of history." In Albany, Mrs. P. J. Nix organized a CC chapter, intending to enlighten new generations to the "nobility" of their "illustrious forefathers and mothers." One commentator noted that children in Albany were eager to participate and preserve their "history" and "ideals."[83] In

Thomasville, CC meetings opened with a pledge of allegiance to the United States and the Confederacy, the latter of which went "I salute the confederate flag with affection, reverence, and undying remembrance." Explaining the pledge, a CC pamphlet claimed the purpose was to "perpetuate, in love and honor, the heroic deeds of those who enlisted in the confederate army." Moreover, the pledge served to remind children "to preserve pure ideals" and remember "the truths of history." Parenthetically, the author mentioned that a principal "truth" was that "the War Between the States was not a rebellion, nor was the underlying cause to sustain slavery."[84]

With the same force that members emphasized state's rights, the UDC's true history also dismissed slavery as a cause of the war.[85] The aforementioned "historian" did just this, urging southern women to relate to children the "truth" that slavery was not a "potent" issue leading to secession.[86] Similarly, when recalling the early 1850s, Susan Bradford Eppes, a leading member of Tallahassee's UDC, lambasted the author of *Uncle Tom's Cabin*. "Mrs. Stowe knew nothing whatever of the South or its people," Eppes charged, because she "had never been South." Instead, Stowe used her "vivid imagination." The book, Eppes continued, came "just when the time was ripe for such a fire-brand; the abolition of negro slavery was 'the burning question of the hour.' . . . Brotherly love was lost sight of; Christian charity died a natural death and these apostles of abolition proclaimed 'A Higher Law.'"[87]

For a Lost Cause devotee like Eppes, Stowe's book offered a false history of slavery and thereby represented a perversion of moral order. Educating the public, in her view, meant convincing everyone that slavery was neither evil nor the cause of the war. This history did the civil religious task of absolving the South of its past misdeeds and, at the same time, elevating its principles and people to sacred status. It also created a cast of villains, which included Abraham Lincoln. Intent on discrediting the "great emancipator," Eppes sent a manuscript to a New York newspaper in which she argued that the South played no part in Lincoln's assassination. Rather, northerners had plotted the murder, many of them having become convinced of the president's incompetence. Eppes then alleged that Lincoln was the product of "THREE GENERATIONS OF ILLEGITIMACY," "three generations of unbridled passions," and "three generations of corrupt living and selfish disregard for the feelings and rights of others." When he won the presidency, she continued, Lincoln was "almost totally unknown." Moreover, "he was 'A POLITICAL MIS- TAKE'" and was "deplored by his constituents." How did he win? Eppes claimed conniving politicians had recruited Lincoln because they be- lieved he would be like "putty" in their hands. Over time they grew disil- lusioned by Lincoln's moral and intellectual ineptitude. "In the midst of the most serious consideration of the problems of War, when each mem- ber of the Cabinet was trying to concentrate on the subject of the hour, Mr. Lincoln would interrupt with some dirty joke or smutty story—but what else could be expected?" As far as his "great intellectual ability" shown in speeches, Eppes theorized that he may not have written them, noting that "we do not know the true source of these speeches." In any event, she added, "if he really entertained the views he expressed, then his actions prove him a consummate hypocrite—a moral and spiritual DERELICT—tossed about on the sea of life by the wind that blew the strongest."[88]

Lincoln's biographer, David Herbert Donald, notes that rumors of the president's supposed illegitimacy probably began circulating during the Civil War. Accidental castration or mumps, the stories usually claimed, left Lincoln's father ("Abraham Enlow") impotent. Eppes repeated this rumor, which Donald calls "utterly groundless."[89] While Lincoln was a hero to many, Eppes had a decidedly negative image of the president. An advocate of the Lost Cause, she went to great lengths to discredit his reputation and the entire northern wartime effort. In her vision of the good society, the South had always been righteous, just, and blessed by God. Spreading this vision, in her mind, was the duty of all "true women."

Intriguing Points of Agreement

Assessing the world of 1900, Dr. Albert M. Smith speculated that four nations were poised to dominate in the next century: Germany, Russia, England, and the United States. Whichever would prevail, "the future of these four nations and of all the world" lay "in the wonderful in- fluence wrought by the power of true womanhood." The significance of women, he attested, could not be underestimated. During the Civil War, women throughout the South worked at home alone, and "womanhood rose to its throne and there is not a single record of a negro approaching a woman in an unworthy manner." Those seeking inspiration, Smith advised, ought to read the letters from Robert E. Lee to his wife. "The power wrought by this woman over her husband and his unfaltering faith in her are wonderful." But womanhood was in peril, Smith suggested. While the "true" woman was the epitome of faith and family, there was another woman wandering about who was "responsible for the introduction into the world of the three greatest humbugs of modern times, Christian Science, Spiritualism and Theosophy." Worse, these women were leaving their homes and families to enter the workforce. "Women talk of women's rights, why, to my mind woman's rights is the last, dismal, despairing wail of a fallen angel." Never in history had women departed from their "proper sphere," Smith claimed, and if this trend continued, "the nation falls."[90]

Smith's audience listened from the seats of Green Ridge Baptist Church—in Scranton, Pennsylvania. A physician in Beaver Springs, Smith was also a leader in Pennsylvania's Grand Army of the Republic. In his speech, Smith also cited Cardinal James Gibbons, Abraham Lincoln, and Russell Conwell—all of whom, in his mind, understood the value of "true womanhood." Similar to his counterparts in the South, Smith linked the fate of the nation, and God's future vision for it, to the "true woman." He additionally challenged men to protect this feminine ideal. However, his preferred cultural resources had little regard for the Mason-Dixon Line or the theological distinctions separating Catholicism from Protestantism.

In the civil religious arena, North and South competed for ground and deployed unfavorable assessments of each other. But sometimes the two found intriguing points of agreement. Many men in the Wiregrass Gulf South would have no doubt cheered Smith's opposition to woman's rights and his admiration of Robert E. Lee. The former was an irredeemable threat to social stability, and the latter was a civic saint. From this, we might imagine North and South meeting on a narrow strip of ideological territory where their civil religious discourses overlapped. Each developed gender norms in light of their vision of the good society. And while operating in separate geographic quarters, they came to similar conclusions.

Finding such points of agreement requires us to wander off the beaten path, to turn our eyes away from the "solid South" and look for the so-called outsiders. After all, some outsiders were not outsiders at all. In the era of nativism, in a region known for religious conservatism, Wiregrass Jews managed to thrive in business, politics, and society. All the while, they found civil religious common ground with the Protestant majority.

CHAPTER FOUR

Jewish Voices, Gentile Voices

"The Soul of America Is the Soul of the Bible"

SHORTLY AFTER THE CIVIL WAR, Samuel Farkas, a Hungarian
Jewish immigrant, arrived in Albany, Georgia. Armed with little more
than a strong work ethic, he launched a mule-trading business and,
within ten years, rose to become a distinguished businessman and property owner. His horse, "Albany Boy," was a frequent sight at the race-
track. And after a scuffle with a business rival, the town's judge fined
Farkas's attacker, charging him with "quarrelling and cursing." Farkas
was no stranger to physical conflict. When a lion clamped down on its
trainer's head at a circus in 1908, Farkas was in the audience. The crowd
panicked as the lion gnashed away on the body of its victim. The ring-
master begged anyone with a gun to shoot the lion. Farkas did not have
a gun. But he did carry a cane, which he jammed in the lion's eye to
free the trainer.[1]

Farkas was one of many successful Jews in Albany, a town that had
over twenty Jewish-owned stores when he arrived.[2] They lived the southern white progressive's life, enjoying everything the New South had to
offer. Religion no doubt distinguished these Jews, who did from time to

time see the ugly face of anti-Semitism. But in Albany and the Wiregrass region, Jews found common ground with their Protestant counterparts, which resulted in both groups developing overlapping civil religious discourses. While small in number, Jews were active and visible citizens who engaged in politics and business, joined fraternal organizations, and served in the military. To each other, Jewish leaders emphasized unity, and expressed a need for coreligionists to hold to their traditions. They also drew connections between Judaism and American patriotism.[3] As one Mobilian declared, "An American Jew cannot be a true Jew unless he is a true American and he is not a true American unless he is a true Jew."[4]

Southern white Protestants often expressed admiration for the religious and social commitment of Jews. At first glance, this may seem counterintuitive. Journalist Wilbur J. Cash speculated that the "popular mind" of the South was rigidly anti-Semitic, clinging to "the notion that it was the Jew who crucified Jesus." Further, the "universal refusal to be assimilated" led southerners to think of the Jew as the "eternal Alien."[5] Certainly, the seeds of anti-Semitism frequently sprang forth in the South.

Still, even during the nativist 1910s, a collection of Jewish white men in the Wiregrass Gulf South immersed themselves in public life, earning, unlike Catholics, the highest respect of their Protestant peers. Sidney J. Catts, who was elected governor of Florida in 1916, may have been profoundly anti-Catholic, but his prejudice did not extend to Jews, reflecting a common pattern in the Wiregrass region. While Jews and white Protestants differed in their religious practices, they shared a commitment to philanthropic work, civic involvement, military service, and Democratic Party politics. Race was another story. According to Eric L. Goldstein, as a historically persecuted group, Jews tended to empathize with blacks—but only in private. Publicly, Jews "generally shied away from high-profile political engagement with racial issues." Doing otherwise could have compromised their personal safety and financial security.[6] Wiregrass Jews reflected this trend. Race simply did not figure into their public civil religious pronouncements, which focused more forthrightly on the intertwining of public and religious life.

The "Reform Spirit" of Southern Jews

After Reconstruction, southern white Jewish men, surrounded by Protestants, continually cast themselves as positive influences in social life. Most came from the Reform tradition, whose members tended to see in America their new homeland. By the early twentieth century, American Reform Jews practiced their faith in part by engaging in philanthropic efforts.[7] While mirroring the Protestant social gospel movement, Reform Judaism found its textual precedent in the prophets Amos, Isaiah, and Micah. The Jewish "civil religion" that emerged from the Reform movement, Jonathan Sarna writes, was the product of Jews who "linked their own destiny to that of the United States so as to legitimate their place in America and to demonstrate their sense of belonging."[8]

American Reform Jews in both the North and South made religion, nationalism, and philanthropy central to their corporate identity. While not a Reform Jew, Charles Wessolowsky of Albany, Georgia, was a prominent public figure who coupled Jewish unity with American citizenship. After serving in the Confederate army, Wessolowsky established residence in Albany. There, he performed rabbinical duties for the area's approximately thirty Jewish families, initiated a Sabbath school, and launched a men's and women's Hebrew Benevolent Society. He was also a politician, serving as the county clerk of the Superior Court from 1871 to 1875 and as a state senator in 1875. Wessolowsky belonged to a host of fraternal organizations, including the Masons, where he held the office of grand high priest of Georgia from 1895 to 1897. His public and religious reputation gained him favorable notice from coreligionists. Rabbi Edward Browne, editor of the *Jewish South*, a magazine that began publishing in Atlanta in 1878, recruited Wessolowsky to become the publication's associate editor. In this capacity, Wessolowsky traveled to Jewish communities in Alabama, Mississippi, Missouri, Arkansas, Louisiana, Tennessee, and Texas promoting the periodical in the spring of 1878 and 1879. During his travels, he repeatedly delivered a speech entitled "The Jew as a Citizen and Politician," encouraging Jews to become active participants in the South's emerging political, economic, and social structure.[9]

In letters to Rabbi Browne, Wessolowsky described the people and communities that he met and assessed their commitment to Judaism.

In Greenville, Mississippi, he credited the members of the Young Men's Hebrew Benevolent Society for helping unemployed Jews and Gentiles find work. In Uniontown, he noted a Jewish woman who, in the "spirit of true charity," opened her house to orphans of all religious denominations. In Farmersville, Wessolowsky applauded the "noble mothers, in Israel," who formed the Ladies Benevolent Society. And in Little Rock, Arkansas, the Hebrew Children's Mite Society drew his attention when they raised and donated funds to support the New Orleans Orphans Home.[10]

Acts of public kindness, for Wessolowsky, registered as a service not only to the community but to Judaism as well. Conversely, he sharply criticized communities that fell short of this standard. Wessolowsky chafed at the "lukewarm" and "indifferent" attitude of a number of Jews in Monroe, Louisiana, whom he called "an obstacle in the path of those who are anxious and desirous of promoting and elevating our holy cause." They embodied, for Wessolowsky, the "modern tendency" of Jews to distance themselves from each other and their faith. In contrast, he commended Mobile's B'nai B'rith lodge for being a place where Jewish men feel "*at home* and amongst brothers." Wessolowsky had no shortage of praise for the B'nai B'rith, provided the lodges lived up to his expectations. In Brenham and Hempstead, Texas, Wessolowsky came across some immigrants from western Prussia. While they had a lodge, members expressed neither "unity" nor "brotherly love." Instead, he was horrified to see Jewish children attending Christian Sunday schools, where they received "the most useful instruction that Jesus is the 'Saviour of all mankind.'"[11]

In the South, B'nai B'rith lodges represented a Jewish effort to engage in the era's fraternal culture. Literally meaning "sons of the covenant," the B'nai B'rith formed in New York City in 1843. Armed with the motto "Benevolence, Brotherly Love, and Harmony," founders sought to "unify" Jews from different ethnic backgrounds.[12] The order came South just like other northern fraternities, benevolent societies, and educational organizations. The white Protestant majority deliberately refashioned this northern-born institution, just as it did the chautauqua, to meet the white South's expectations. For Wessolowsky, a former Confederate, the northern origin of the B'nai B'rith was inconsequential. He showed more concern for unifying the region's disparate Jews and transmitting the message that civic involvement was a Jewish duty.

Like Wessolowsky, other Jewish political leaders in the Wiregrass region encouraged coreligionists to remain both communally active and religiously unified. A Democrat and member of Mobile's Reform temple, Lazarus Schwarz was a visible public figure in Mobile during the early twentieth century.[13] In 1911, the city's Orthodox community celebrated the laying of its synagogue's cornerstone. Then a member of the city council, Schwarz spoke at the event. "[The] American progressive spirit," he opened, "has taken root in the orthodox congregation." Schwarz commended the "reform spirit" of the synagogue, quickly adding that he meant not "reform of religious ceremonies" but "reform" in "the improvement of your standard of American citizenship." Jews, the councilman continued, "have always and everywhere been noted for their refinement, their charities to all creeds, and their love for the flag of our country." Schwarz predicted that the Orthodox synagogue would be no exception. He was also certain that the members would remain faithful to the nation that "opened its arms" to Jews, giving them refuge, protection, liberty, and freedom. Schwarz concluded by encouraging his Orthodox brethren to "impress" on their children a sense of "respect and honor for our flag."[14]

Schwarz's vision of society uniquely drew on Jewish history and identity, which he believed fit seamlessly into America's social fabric. His civil religious discourse also overlapped with the majority. For starters, Schwarz spoke highly of the moral value of progress. Additionally, in emphasizing "American" patriotism and not simply "southern" patriotism, he followed the lead of his white Protestant counterparts in the 1910s. Southern pride was still strong. But as the ranks of former Confederates decreased each year, the bitter partisanship born from the Civil War and Reconstruction was less potent. The Spanish-American War and World War I further instilled a sense of national pride. During World War I, white southerners rallied in support of President Woodrow Wilson, a native Virginian and son of a Presbyterian minister.[15]

Echoing this civil religious rhetoric was Rabbi Alfred G. Moses of Mobile's Reform synagogue, who also spoke at the Orthodox gathering.[16] "Rejoice that you live in a free country," the rabbi proclaimed, "where religious tolerance prevails and all bigotry is banished." The "blessings of religious liberty and freedom," Moses continued, both permitted and encouraged Jews to become active religious practitioners. "Religion means nothing if it is not practiced." For Moses, however, practice implied social action and a commitment to help those in need. He insisted that this would earn the respect of Gentiles, who themselves saw service as a patriotic act. The rabbi concluded: "Unfurl the banners of Israel and America and stand steadfast under both of them."[17]

Emphasizing religious freedom, philanthropy, and patriotism, Rabbi Moses gave voice to his hope that Jews would carve a space for themselves in Mobile and the nation. Additionally, he stressed the interconnectedness of America and Judaism, a common theme in his public speaking. In 1905, President Theodore Roosevelt designated November 30 a national day of thanksgiving. On that day, Mobile's Jewish community gathered to celebrate the 250-year anniversary of Jews in America and to pay respect to the nation's promise of civic and religious liberty.[18] Rabbi Moses was a featured speaker. He spared no expense in extolling the glories of Judaism and America, devoting considerable attention to those who he believed exemplified how Jews ought to function in the nation. Specifically, he praised Major Adolph Proskauer, who, during the Civil War, "marched forth from his city with many brave Jewish comrades to join the Southern army." This brand of national devotion was, for Moses, something that all Jews needed to aspire to, since it would only improve their condition. For the rabbi, the destiny of America and Judaism were the same. "Israel has at last found the spiritual paradise," Moses proclaimed. He puzzled over those who would not see America as their new Zion and chided Jews who clung to "encrusted" traditions at the expense of the "sublime teachings" of "progressive humanity." In Moses's mind, Jews served their faith by serving America, which required entering public service, whether as soldiers or as aids to the "poor and unfortunate."[19]

Moses combined progress, religion, and nation to create a distinctive Jewish position within a southern and American civil religious discourse. He was both respectful of Dixie and unconcerned with sectional differences. At stake for the rabbi was the future of Judaism and America, an intertwined pair of institutions, both of which required from peo-

ple more service and commitment. In his 1905 history of Mobile's
Reform congregation, Moses elaborated on this theme. The essence of
Judaism, Moses declared, was "the glorification of God in acts of humanity, kindness, charity and intellectual growth."[20] Mobile's Sigmund
Schlesinger, Moses believed, embodied this essence. The rabbi claimed
that Schlesinger "was not religious . . . if religion is measured by the yard-
stick of creed and dogma." If, however, "true religion means high and
exalted conduct, self-sacrifice and charity, a spotless character and an
unflagging devotion to duty, then he was truly a godly man." Schlesinger
was "a real believer," in Moses's estimation, whose ethics and actions
served the needs of others.[21]

The civil religion of Moses was similar to that of Wessolowsky and
Schwarz. Each advocated the idea that Judaism was a "religion of action" not a "religion of creed," as one southern rabbi put it.[22] Their
ideal Jewish community was a place where members of synagogues cultivated philanthropic, nationalistic, and Jewish interests. Their words
always carried a prophetic edge and contained encoded criticisms of
those residing outside of this civil religious territory. Moses, schooled in
the Reform tradition, continually heralded those who he believed were
"active" and, by default, "true" Jews. Rabbi Moses would further develop
his critique of the habits of Orthodox Judaism while promoting what he
called "Jewish Science." In the early twentieth century, Jews in the South
and nation worried about Christian Science and New Thought depleting
their ranks. As he advocated Jewish Science as a response, Moses would
blame Orthodox Judaism for these defections.

Jewish Science

Born in New Hampshire in 1821, Mary Baker Eddy suffered from a
series of physical ailments before meeting Phineas P. Quimby in 1862.
A mesmerist, Quimby emphasized the healing powers of positive thinking. Following his 1866 death, Eddy built upon this message to invent
"Christian Science." Like her predecessor, Eddy taught that sickness and
pain were illusions, the result of mental and spiritual misalignments
with the "infinite Mind" of God. Positive thinking could correct this.
Christian Science emerged alongside similar religious movements, such

as New Thought and Theosophy. The latter two, however, differed from Christian Science by deemphasizing Christianity, which Eddy, a committed Calvinist, believed was essential.[23]

Christian Science grew rapidly in the North during Eddy's time. By the time she died in 1910, there were nearly one hundred thousand adherents, some of whom were Jews. According to Ellen M. Umansky, urban Jews were comforted by Christian Science's "promise of health, peace, and comfort." The number of Jews who practiced Christian Science during its boom years of 1906 to 1926 remains unclear. Estimates range from four thousand to forty thousand.[24] Nevertheless, Jewish leaders were wary. In 1911, the B'nai B'rith announced that Judaism was fundamentally incompatible with Christian Science. In 1919, Henry Frank's *Why Is Christian Science Luring the Jew Away from Judaism?* argued that Jews were simply disenchanted with their own faith and found Christian Science to be novel and useful. Rabbi Max Heller of New Orleans agreed. "Christian Science has caught us napping," he wrote. An obsession with "knowledge and conduct," Heller theorized, had stripped the "vitality and intensity" from Judaism. He encouraged Jews to revisit the core of their tradition to find the "spirituality" of Judaism.[25]

For these Jewish commentators, meaningless religious practices were to blame for the Jewish exodus to Christian Science. Rabbi Moses agreed. In two books published in 1916 and 1920, Moses explained the tenets of "Jewish Science." He emphasized the Jewish foundation of mental and spiritual health, as evidenced by the proverb "As a man thinketh in his heart, so is he."[26] So Jewish Science was nothing new, according to Moses. He claimed that *chachmah*, the Hebrew word for "science," translated to "divine wisdom or truth." Accordingly, "the entire phrase of Jewish Science is in keeping with the faith and practice of Judaism."[27]

Moses's response to Christian Science both absorbed the new religious movement's basic tenets and put a distinctive Jewish stamp on it. He also used this platform to criticize Orthodox synagogues. "Faith," Moses affirmed, "implies deed, not creed. True religion according to . . . our prophets is an immanent process and not a far-off mystic speculation." For the rabbi, "true religion" meant both individual spirituality and a commitment to "social betterment." Under the symbolic canopy of Jewish Science, Moses also included American patriotism, extolling the nation's promise of "life, liberty and the pursuit of happiness." Because of this foundation, any American could achieve wealth and happiness. Poverty, according to Moses, was a mental abnormality that the Jewish Scientist could correct through positive thought and focused charity. "The greatest good cannot be done by merely giving the poor material means for food, clothing and shelter. A man is helped by being trained to help himself. By self-discovery and self-realization, one may find the road to success and achievement."[28]

Moses's thoughts on wealth and charity were strikingly similar to those of Pittsburgh's Andrew Carnegie, who penned the "Gospel of Wealth" in 1889. For Carnegie, three sacred principles of American progress were private property, free competition, and free accumulation of wealth. But Carnegie's ideal wealthy person did not horde his or her resources, nor did he or she thoughtlessly give his or her wealth away. Instead, the wealthy individual became a "trustee for the poor," judiciously and wisely distributing resources to those in need.[29]

Whether he intended to or not, Moses wrote a Jewish gospel of wealth into his vision for Jewish Science. He emphasized the redemptive power of hard work, perseverance, and positive thinking. A born southerner, Moses cited Abraham Lincoln as a great example of America's promise. Lincoln was of humble origins, but he rose to the office of president. "By faith and spiritual power, inspired by the Bible, the great emancipator overcame all obstacles and made himself the saviour of the Union. His example may be multiplied in every age of American history." For Moses, the nation would grant "great achievement and prosperity" to anyone who sought it, just as it did to Lincoln. "America has grown and prospered in accordance with the biblical teaching of liberty under law. Our blessed land, the home of the free, is the creation of the spirit of individual freedom that moved over the face of the wild wilderness." Punctuating his patriotic proclamation, Moses concluded, "The soul of America is the soul of the Bible."[30]

Moses's curious mention of Lincoln highlights a difference between Moses and the Lost Causers of his time. The rabbi did not appeal to the white southern rhetoric that made Lincoln an evil despot or bumbling idiot.[31] Instead, he used the former president to personify his convictions regarding poverty, American opportunity, and the responsibilities of the "true" Jew. Moses may not have shared the partisan worldview of many white southerners of his time, but his voice was present in the years after the war. He drew on symbolic resources available in American, southern, and Jewish history and tradition to form a Jewish civil religious discourse. The force of this discourse permitted Jews in the Wiregrass Gulf South to make a home for themselves and to gain the respect of the majority. Still, his optimistic portrayal of American religious freedom covered over the fact that the specter of anti-Semitism lingered in the South, even in his own hometown.

Anti-Semitism and the "Friendly Relations" of Jews and Gentiles

Remembering his childhood in Mobile, Joseph Proskauer spoke glowingly of his family lineage, making special mention of his "legendary" uncle, Major Adolph Proskauer, who fought in the Civil War. "I was, so I believed, a good boy. I was a patriotic American, and my uncle had surely earned for my family a deserved reputation for loyalty to Alabama." To the younger Proskauer's dismay, however, when he was walking home from school one day, a gang of classmates "bloodied my nose on the astounding theory that I was a 'Christ Killer.'" This would be, for Proskauer, one of many "physical and metaphorical" bloody noses. He recalled vowing then to "destroy this ugly excrescence on the American way of life." Proskauer later relocated to the North, where his struggle continued.[32]

For Proskauer, anti-Semitism was an insult to the "American way of life," a perversion of his good society. His ongoing battle against the prejudice also suggests that anti-Semitism was not unique to the Wiregrass region. Indeed, sometimes, bigotry traveled the railway southward. In 1865, George F. Thompson, an inspector for the Freedmen's Bureau, determined that Jews were irredeemably detrimental to society. He explicitly criticized Jacksonville's Jewish merchants for not closing on a national day of thanksgiving. "It is remarkable how the Jew finds his way into every nook and corner of the country, large enough to squeeze a three cent piece into it." Thompson was of the firm opinion that "this class" of people were anything but a "desirable population for any country."[33]

"Southern anti-Semitism borrowed from the national culture," writes Leonard Rogoff. At the same time, however, Rogoff notes that the potency of this intolerance was relatively low in the South. In 1910, North Carolina's Rev. Arthur T. Abernethy wrote *The Jew a Negro*, which attempted to tag Jews as "the kinsman and descendant of the Negro."[34] But, according to Rogoff, the book received little attention in the South because Jews had become an established presence there.[35] In the Wiregrass Gulf South, Rabbi Moses and likeminded coreligionists chose to praise the virtues of America and depict anti-Semitism as the product of an insufficient understanding of Judaism and the Constitution. Jews could will this problem away, they advised, by demonstrating their patriotism and testifying to the glories of religious freedom. While many white Protestants grew rather accepting of the Jewish presence in Mobile and the Wiregrass Gulf South, this sentiment was not universal. But even then, Jews had Gentile defenders.

In addition to the "Christ Killer" accusation, Wiregrass Jews also heard the "Shylock" stereotype, particularly in moments of financial crisis.[36] In 1862, a Union blockade along the Florida Gulf Coast made food and supplies scarce in Thomasville. Frustrated, Colonel J. L. Steward opted to shift blame to Jewish merchants, who he charged with profiteering. His scathing oratories motivated Thomasville's elected officials to pass a resolution banning Jews from the city. The measure drew quick criticism from a Savannah newspaper, which described the resolution as being "at war with the spirit of the age—the letter of the constitution—and the principles of religion." Thomasville's law, the editorial thundered, had its equal only in "the barbarism of the Inquisition and the persecution of the Dark Ages."[37] Also in Savannah, Charles Wessolowsky, who was a private in the Confederate army, led a protest. He lamented that his "adopted country" had dishonored Jews who were sacrificing their lives for the Confederacy.[38] A peddler before the war, Wessolowsky came to Georgia from Prussia in 1858. He was certain that the anti-Semitism of his homeland did not exist in the Wiregrass region but was distressed by the resolution. Wessolowsky was not alone. In Thomasville, little became of the resolution. Most Jews remained, and in the following years they built an active community.[39]

For Jews and sympathetic Gentiles, the Thomasville resolution betrayed a sacred trust. Throughout the Wiregrass Gulf South, both groups found common ground in their shared values, which included a profound belief in the redeeming power of progress. Accordingly, Jews in the Wiregrass Gulf South developed a redemption narrative that looked similar to that of southern white Protestants. Reflecting on the years following Reconstruction, Rabbi Edmund Landau of Albany recalled that the approximately three hundred Jews of his region "generously contributed" to the rebuilding of the city. Jewish businesses, the rabbi explained, provided a "foundation" that allowed Albany to become a "progressive community," distinguished by a chautauqua, a hospital, and various recreational facilities.[40]

Post-Reconstruction progress was, for Landau, a direct result of the Jewish presence. Many Jews in the Wiregrass South had the means and ability to bring needed goods to the inland region. In the 1850s, Jewish peddlers transported materials from Savannah and other ports. "Few things brought the isolated rural family more excitement than the visitation of a pack peddler," remarks Thomas D. Clark. As the region developed after the war, many peddlers continued their trade as established merchants providing goods to the largely Gentile population.[41] Grateful non-Jews occasionally validated Rabbi Landau's perception. In Valdosta, Georgia, a newspaper discussing the region's post-Reconstruction era called Jews "servants of God without whom progress would be unreal." This was nothing new in Valdosta. During Reconstruction, a newspaper chastened anti-Semitic grumblings in town, calling attention to the religious minority's "kindness" and commitment to the region's poor, widows, and orphans.[42]

For their role in developing the economy and their various benevolent endeavors, Jews won a favorable place in the redemption narrative of Wiregrass Gentiles. When anti-Semitism reared itself, voices from the Protestant mainstream came to the defense of the religious minority. But the majority sometimes looked at Jews as potential converts. As Jonathan Sarna explains, "Christians coupled their love for Jews and support for Jewish rights with the hope that Jews would ultimately be incorporated into the Christian fold."[43] Some Protestants believed that to be American one had to be Christian. But pushing Jews toward Christianity required a gentle hand.

As a student at the University of North Carolina, Stephens Croom of Mobile warned that if the "march of civilization" were to continue forward, Christians needed to abandon their anti-Semitic ways. He denounced Jewish persecution as "unlawful," "unchristian," and "unmanly." Croom then encouraged Christians to reach out to Jews with love in an effort to make them "true" Christians and Americans. This way, America could then demonstrate to God, "not that we have persecuted the Jew, but that we have converted him."[44] Croom's "true" American society was Christian, and Jews fell outside this boundary. But so too did anti-Semitism, a sin that he believed would deny America its rightful place in God's plan.

Similarly, Rev. Simon Peter Richardson, an itinerant Methodist minister from Augusta, Georgia, admitted that he had once harbored "prejudices" against Jews. Calling them "mistaken" in religion, Richardson confessed that Jews "are certainly true to their convictions" and "carry with them the revelation of the true God wherever they go." The minister specifically complimented southern Jews for their "remarkable moral record" and commitment to education. He then recalled a Jewish rabbi with whom he formed an acquaintance. The rabbi was a "broad-minded" man whose comprehension of the Old Testament had impressed Richardson. Richardson was also impressed with the rabbi's careful reading of the New Testament and noted that he had even attended Richardson's Methodist services. He "could accept Christ as the manifestation of God, but not as God," Richardson explained. He concluded that "if Christians would treat the Jews more kindly, they might do them more good. They feel that all Gentiles are their enemies, and that all Christians hate them. My friendly relations with the priest [sic] brought many of his people occasionally to my church."[45]

In public settings, Wiregrass Gentile observers often chose simply to commend their Jewish neighbors for their religious and patriotic values. In 1910, the regional convention of the B'nai B'rith was held in Mobile. The *Jewish South* reported that visitors "found the proverbial 'welcome' and the hearty greetings, typical of Southern hospitality." Mayor Pat J. Lyons gave an opening address, praising "the Jewish race" for being "one of the greatest civilizing agencies of the world." Jews, he continued, were known for advocating peace and stable government. As a result, in a city like Mobile, Jews were never found in jails or poorhouses. "You take care of your own poor and distressed in addition to lending aid to others."[46]

For the Protestant mayor, Jews were an invaluable social asset. They ensured stability within their own ranks and established benevolent campaigns that benefited the entire community. Mobile's Erwin Craighead painted a similar picture of the Jewish English immigrant, Israel I. Jones. Jones organized Mobile's Jewish synagogue in 1840, and, according to Craighead, contributed to numerous "progressive" endeavors such as the building of street railroads. The author found Jones to be profoundly charitable, "gentle as a woman and generous to a fault." Jones owned a house that abutted the Protestant Orphan Asylum and every Christmas he hosted an elaborate feast for the inhabitants. "Many is the Christian prayer," wrote Craighead, "that ascended to heaven in thankfulness for the kindly beneficence of that true-hearted Jew." And when Jones died, Craighead remembered all of Mobile mourning the loss.[47]

For Protestant onlookers, Jewish acts of philanthropy registered as a social good that validated the Jewish contribution to social stability. In Tallahassee, Julius Diamond drew accolades from the Masons when he died in 1914.[48] In a glowing obituary, the author called Diamond "an honored, useful and greatly beloved citizen," who had both a "strong mind" and a "[good] conscience." He was a "deep thinker," the author explained, who generously shared his "storehouse" of knowledge with anyone who asked. Additionally, his intellect and ethics made him a leader in "the cause of civic progress." Tallahassee was a better place because of Diamond, the obituary concluded, and the people of the city would remember him fondly.[49]

Methodist minister Alfred L. Woodward of Tallahassee bestowed similar praises on Diamond. Woodward met Diamond after the Civil War and found him to be "plain," "unassuming," and "rigidly upright." A devoted Jew, Diamond "was no sectarian," according to the minister. While "loyal to the faith of his Fathers . . . he 'loved his fellowmen' and his great heart included in its sympathies both Jew and Gentile." Woodward then highlighted his friend's political career, recalling Diamond's tenure as the chair of the board of Leon County commissioners. "[Diamond's] just and impartial rulings were recognized by all." In business, the minister described Diamond as thoroughly committed to his trade but "never too busy to pause in his work upon my entrance, adjust his pen behind his ear, and listen kindly and patiently to what I had to say." Woodward summarized: "Like Enoch of old in life [Diamond] walked with God, and now 'he was no more, because God took him away,' and God is keeping him against that day; for Jew and Gentile alike have this common faith in the resurrection of the just."[50]

For this non-Jewish observer, Julius Diamond was an exemplary citizen who shared a "common faith" with the majority. Sidney Diamond would follow in his father's footsteps. In 1915, Diamond ran for the county judge of Leon County. A Tallahassee newspaper quickly endorsed the young lawyer, calling him "intelligent," "brainy," "industrious," and "thoroughly competent for the position." If elected, the author reasoned, Diamond "would discharge the duties of the office without fear, favor, or affection" and run "a clean, just and equitable administration." The article then evoked the memory of his father, recalling the elder's exemplary service and "sterling" reputation as a businessperson.[51]

Diamond would continue serving the public and earning the respect of Protestant colleagues. During World War I, he applied for a position with the judge advocate general's department and solicited letters of recommendation from Florida's highest officials. Governor Sidney Catts described Diamond as "capable," "honest," and "exceedingly anxious to get into the service of the United States Government during this War." The governor expressed confidence that Diamond would serve "with great credit, honor and distinction," and could "be trusted with any and all secrets."[52] J. B. Christian, Florida's adjutant general, wrote that the "splendid lawyer" was "eminently fitted" for the position: "Mr. Diamond is personally well known to me as a gentleman of excellent habits, as to sobriety and moral character, standing high in his community as a good American Citizen, as well as a lawyer of the highest legal attainments, always progressive and identified with every movement looking forward to the best interests of State and Nation."[53] From the "highest to the most humble," exclaimed Florida secretary of state H. Clay Crawford, everyone knew Diamond as "a man that can be trusted with the most vital matters." Crawford then acclaimed the "patriotism," "ability," and "pleas-

ing personality" of Diamond, calling him a "valuable man."[54] Florida attorney general Van C. Swearingen likewise applauded Diamond's education and legal acumen: "[Knowing] him as I do I am sure his high sense
of honor and his ability, as well as his unbounded patriotism would make
him of inestimable value to any department of the service."[55]

All of this praise came in the wake of the 1913 trial and 1915 lynching of the National Pencil Factory superintendent Leo Frank in Atlanta.
Police charged Frank with the rape and murder of one of his employees,
thirteen-year-old Mary Phagan. Tom Watson's *Jeffersonian* stoked the fires
of anti-Semitism and cast Frank as a "lascivious pervert." At the trial, the
prosecution's evidence was circumstantial and flimsy. Nevertheless, the
jury took less than four hours to convict Frank, bringing cheers from the
crowd of over three thousand gathered outside the courthouse. After
two years of appeals, the case came before the Supreme Court. The
judges upheld the decision. Governor John M. Slaton became Frank's
final hope. Slaton received a petition on Frank's behalf that over one
million people—ten thousand of whom were Georgians—had signed
and commuted Frank's sentence to life imprisonment. The governor
fled Georgia fearing mob retaliation. Meanwhile, twenty-five men calling themselves the "Knights of Mary Phagan" broke into the prison
farm that housed Frank and proceeded to hang him from a tree near
Phagan's birthplace in Marietta.[56]

At the same time that Sidney Catts praised the Jewish Sidney Diamond,
he also befriended Leo Frank's principal agitator, Tom Watson. Catts
called Watson "the great Apostle of Americanism," and the Georgian
likewise labeled Catts a "friend and champion" of the white South. On
matters of religious prejudice, the two found common ground in anti-
Catholicism. But not anti-Semitism. When rumors of his anti-Semitism
circulated during the governor's tenure, Catts moved quickly to reject
the accusation.[57]

Catts's civil religious discourse fashioned a place for Jews, one that
Watson and his like were unwilling to acknowledge. The social location
of Jews in the Wiregrass Gulf South was the result of decades of negotiated exchange between the majority and minority. Jews and white southern Protestants developed a cordial relationship that was grounded in
mutual goals related to business, charity, religious devotion, and material

progress. This relationship unfolded through daily events, discussions, and transactions and represented a decided departure from the high-profile perspectives of Tom Watson and his sort, who through media and lynch mobs reinforced a civil religious discourse that was immanently hostile toward Jews and all perceived "outsiders."

The "True Jewish Spirit" of Leon Schwarz

"A Karl Marx for Hill Billies," Arkansas's Jeff Davis appealed to his state's disaffected population, who rewarded him with the governorship in 1900 and sent him to the U.S. Senate in 1907.[58] Along the way, Davis, a devout Baptist, befriended Charles Jacobson, a Reform Jew, and the two shared a law office in Little Rock. A result of this alliance, Jacobson was catapulted into public life, and in 1910, he won a state senate seat. Much like Davis, Jacobson's progressive politics embraced white supremacy and eschewed northern business. He vacated his position in 1914, perhaps a result of the post-Frank wave of anti-Semitism that led other Jewish politicians in the South to likewise give up their posts. But Jacobson stayed in Arkansas and practiced law for the remaining years of his life. "Despite his open and fervent commitment to Judaism, there was little, if any, of the outsider about him," explains Raymond Arsenault. Instead, in nearly every way except religion, Jacobson "was a classic New South gentleman."[59]

At nearly the same time as Jacobson, Mobile's Leon Schwarz also stood out as a "New South gentleman." Unlike Jacobson, though, Schwarz stayed visible in public life throughout his life. Schwarz was a soldier, fraternal "joiner," businessperson, politician, and member of Mobile's Reform synagogue. Raised in Perry County, Alabama, he was the son of a German immigrant, Ruben M. Schwarz. The elder Schwarz was a planter before the war, Confederate soldier during it, and successful merchant afterward. After his passing in 1909, the Knights of Pythias called Schwarz "one of our best known and most beloved members." They commended his "long and noble career," "splendid citizenship," "loyalty to friends," "patriotism," and "many kind and charitable acts." While committed to Judaism, Schwarz's "love of humanity and charity . . . knew no creed."[60] Military service, religious devotion, fraternal devotion, and charity all became Schwarz's marks of distinction, his noble legacy. The non-Jewish admirers of Schwarz's son, Leon, would say the same of him.[61]

Like his father, Leon Schwarz was a soldier. He served with the Alabama National Guard and fought in both the Spanish-American War and the Great War. While at the University of Alabama, Schwarz roomed with William Brandon, who later became Alabama's governor. As students, they published the *Citizen Soldier*, a monthly periodical devoted to the "welfare of the volunteer soldier" and the "military preparedness on the part of the citizen and the nation."[62] Schwarz's military activities won him notice as a young man. In 1892, Corporal Schwarz took an individual gold medal in a drill contest. The crowd applauded the choice, and the presiding officer commended the exemplary "preparedness" of this "best drilled soldier."[63] When the aged Captain Schwarz volunteered for active duty in 1918, the governor of Alabama, Charles Henderson, wrote a letter of recommendation commending his lengthy career and "unquestioned . . . loyalty to his country." General Hubbard similarly called Schwarz a "loyal, faithful and efficient" leader who "preached 'preparedness' at all times." Mobile's mayor, Pat J. Lyons, characterized Schwarz as "active and energetic in practically all matters pertaining to civic and public welfare." The mayor specifically lauded Schwarz's reputation of being "an advocate of the doctrine of national defense and preparedness."[64]

As a soldier, Schwarz earned praise for his military preparedness and patriotism. In public settings, Schwarz's military devotion spilled over into his reverence for the nation's Civil War veterans. But his Lost Cause advocacy had limits.[65] In 1907, letter writers inundated a Montgomery newspaper voicing concerns regarding "Confederate Memorial Day." Hoping to offer a suitable compromise, Schwarz proposed that the government designate one day as "Civil War Memorial Day." Schwarz envisioned citizens on this day decorating the graves of Confederate *and* Union soldiers, "for they died fighting for what each thought was the right." He reasoned that people needed to celebrate "American valor" while remembering "that our terrible internecine war is now but a sad memory and that the American people will never again be rent asunder by civil strife."[66]

Despite Schwarz's suggestion, Alabama designated the fourth Monday of every April "Confederate Memorial Day."[67] And even though he opposed the sectional implications of the holiday, he participated in its rituals. On the holiday in 1920, after returning from the war in Europe, Schwarz proceeded to the cemetery to honor Civil War veterans and those "buried under the poppy-studded sod of France." He explained that the Confederate soldier's "example in patriotism" had informed the heroism of Mobile's soldiers of the Great War.[68] Schwarz acted as both a nonpartisan and a traditional southerner, walking the line between venerating the past and living in the present. Violence in service to country had sacred status for Schwarz. But he was cautious in his reverence for the Confederacy and avoided mention of that era's enemy. Instead, Schwarz referenced the past to venerate the present, when North and South unified in opposition to a new enemy.

Schwarz's political persuasions also aligned with the majority's civil religious leanings. In 1906, he met William Jennings Bryan and asked, "Mr. Bryan, I am an Alabama Democrat—is that a good brand?" Bryan replied: "There is no better in the country."[69] Schwarz was a committed southern Democrat who supported the political career of his college friend, William W. Brandon, from the start. In 1906, Brandon ran for and won the office of state auditor. Writing Schwarz, Brandon offered his gratitude and commented that friendships like theirs "are more lasting and more beautiful than any perhaps, unless it be the strong tie that binds man to woman." Brandon continued: "I attribute my success as much to your efforts as to any other one man in Alabama, and I want you to know that next to my own family, there is no person in all Alabama who is closer to me or has a warmer place in my affection, than yourself."[70]

As a result of his friendship with Schwarz, Brandon contended that he better appreciated America's Jewish population. In 1907, Schwarz sent Brandon a book about Jews in America. Brandon replied by noting that "you know that I have been deeply interested in the study of the Jew, and this work gives me additional information as to their greatness and value as citizens." Brandon then criticized all "prejudices" against Jews as "baseless, groundless and unworthy of true American principle." He wished that everyone would recognize Jews as trusted friends, whose fidelity remains strong in both "the hours of prosperity" and "the hours of adversity." America's Gentiles, Brandon resolved, would do well to "study and emulate" the example set by Jews.[71]

Schwarz's alliance with Brandon propelled him into public life. In 1924, a "liquor upheaval" in Mobile resulted in the county sheriff resigning.[72] Brandon, Alabama's governor at the time, sent Schwarz a letter explaining that scores of Mobilians had written to suggest Schwarz as a replacement, praising him as "a business man who had not been handicapped by political entanglements or affiliations." The governor concurred. "Knowing, as I do, his boyhood habits, his ideals of constitutional government and enforcement of law, his love of his country and flag as demonstrated in two wars, his business ability, and his loyalty to his state, I am today, upon my own responsibility, appointing you, my old-time friend and companion, sheriff of Mobile County." Brandon assured Schwarz that this was not favoritism. "I would not appoint any man sheriff of this great and growing county whom I did not believe would rigidly enforce the law and bring to speedy justice all violators, great or small, rich or poor." He was confident that Schwarz would restore Mobile's "common bond" and make its "future prosperity an assured fact." Brandon concluded: "In the divine discharge of your important task, I ask the Divine Ruler to guide and lead you, and to crown your administration with achievements that will vindicate my judgments in thus placing in the hands of my friend this important office."[73]

This providential punctuation mark on Schwarz's appointment came amid a flurry of concurring civil religious values. The Gentile governor's perception of God was filtered through a southern Protestant lens, one that in other settings excluded Jews as "outsiders," threats to social purity. Brandon's "Divine Ruler," however, was not simply tolerant of Jews but also saw them as fundamental to the good society. Thus, anti-Semitism represented for Brandon a social sin, a corruption of the public good. Not surprisingly, Schwarz agreed. At a 1905 Thanksgiving Day celebration in Mobile, Schwarz encouraged Jews to thank God "for manifold blessings bestowed upon the people of our country." Elsewhere in the world, particularly Russia, Jews were not so fortunate. He prayed for God's intervention in such places where coreligionists suffered. Schwarz then spoke the gospel of American exceptionalism, lauding the unique

rights afforded to Jews, including "religious liberty and free speech."[74]
The disorder of anti-Semitism, for Schwarz, was not a part of America's
founding documents. Quite the opposite, in his homeland, the Jewish
southerner saw a shining example of how the world should treat people
of his faith. The history of persecution could come to an end, in his view,
if all nations would follow America's lead.

The social forces shaping Schwarz's vision of the good society flowed
inward from Jewish tradition, military service, civic participation, and
American history. In public pronouncements, he connected all of these
with religious liberty. Along with other Jewish leaders in Mobile, Schwarz
spoke at a 1911 groundbreaking for an Orthodox synagogue. The
Reform tradition, Schwarz explained, had "undergone changes which,
in the opinion of wise leaders of modern times, were deemed necessary
in the onward sweep of evolution." Those of "the old school" in the
audience, he observed, "worship their Maker and Creator in a form or
manner entirely different in name and plan." No matter the differences,
Schwarz encouraged them to remain committed to their faith, because
in America they could. He then imagined America standing with two
hands outstretched, one holding "the Tablets of Law which God gave
to your law-giver, Moses, on Sinai's Mount" and the other holding "the
greatest document ever penned by man, the American Declaration of
Independence." America was a nation where "God-fearing, law-abiding,
law-supporting, home-loving, and country-loving fathers, mothers and
children" could worship as they pleased.[75]

Internal divisions existed among the Jews of the American South.
Schwarz acknowledged these differences and showed respect for the
"old school" but invited them into his civil religious world. Practicing
this national faith implied, for him, both religious devotion and social involvement. And for the Jewish Mobilian, fraternal orders offered a setting in which to practice it.[76] In 1910, Schwarz outlined
ten reasons why he was "the most ardent Pythian who never held an
office."

1. Because I am a believer in a Supreme Being—and my membership in
a fraternal order is . . . evidence of such a belief.

2. Because I believe that the Supreme Being is Father to all mankind, thereby making every man my brother, "The Fatherhood of God and Brotherhood of man" is fraternal order doctrine.

3. Because I love and am devoted to my family—and I believe that those in my family are better protected if I hold membership in one or more fraternal orders.

4. Because I love my country—and my patriotism is strengthened by my membership in fraternal orders because they teach love of country, devotion to good government and antagonism to anarchy and revolution.

5. Because I believe that man should be charitable and benevolent—and both by precept and example are those virtues taught and urged upon those in the ranks of fraternal orders.

6. Because I believe in friendship and in forming friendships with my fellow men. There is no better medium for the promotion and cultivation of friendship and comradeship between man and man than in the lodge rooms of fraternal orders.

7. Because I believe in intellectual advancement and regard fraternal work and the association with those engaged in fraternal work as promoters of culture and intelligence.

8. Because I am a believer in temperance. This general application means that man should be temperate in drink as well as in all other things. The fraternal orders teach and promote this doctrine.

9. Because I believe in purity and chastity in our daily lives, having special regard for the maintenance of those holy principles in my own as well as in the families of my brethren. Membership in fraternal orders teaches, fosters and insists on the observance of such holy law.

10. To sum it all up—Because I believe that membership in a fraternal order and adherence in part or in whole to its teachings and principles and purposes makes a man a better citizen, better father, better husband, better son, better brother, a Better Man.[77]

A self-proclaimed "joiner," Schwarz saw a positive link between fraternal organizations and faith, nation, manhood, family, and morality. He
was also a member of the B'nai B'rith. At a 1907 regional B'nai B'rith
conference in Memphis, Schwarz served as a member of the committee
on intellectual culture. In a written statement, the committee reminded
readers that the B'nai B'rith aspired "to elevate the mental and moral
character of our people whether in or out of the Order." Accordingly,
they recommended that lodges conduct "English night schools" in locales where Jewish immigrants resided. The committee hoped that the
schools would Americanize newcomers, teaching them English so that
they could "earn a livelihood in this blessed land."[78] The schools aimed
not only to teach practical skills but to expose immigrants to a Jewish
civil religious discourse. Schwarz and his coauthors idealized American
freedom and the possibilities it offered and asserted a premise that any
Jew could achieve success through hard work.

For Schwarz, the B'nai B'rith served as a platform for transmitting his
optimism, his belief that America and Judaism were forever united—and
that this partnership made the nation exceptional. In 1907, Schwarz en-
treated his home lodge to host a "B'nai B'rith Day," with the purpose of
bringing "forcibly to the attention of our co-religionists the principles
and purposes of our benevolent order."[79] Mobile's B'nai B'rith conceded
and held the event that December. It began with a reading of the order's
constitution:

> The Independent Order of B'nai B'rith has taken upon itself the mission
> of uniting Israelites in the work of promoting their highest interests and
> those of humanity; of developing and elevating the mental and moral char-
> acter of the people of our faith; of inculcating the purest principles of phi-
> lanthropy, honor and patriotism; of supporting science and art; alleviating
> the wants of the poor and needy; visiting and attending the sick; coming to
> the rescue of victims of persecution; providing for, protecting and assisting
> the widow and orphan on the broadest principles of humanity.

The themes here—unity, patriotism, and benevolence—inundated
the following speeches. Schwarz heralded the B'nai B'rith's "platform"
as being "strong enough and broad enough for every Israelite, be he
Orthodox, Reform or otherwise." Similarly, Rabbi Brill commended the

order as a place where all Jews could work toward "promoting their high-est interests and those of humanity." The order's stress on intellectual and moral development, he explained, had resulted in noteworthy ef-forts to lessen poverty and eliminate prejudice.[80]

Sigmund Hass lauded the founder of Mobile's B'nai B'rith, the "sainted" Rabbi Oscar Cohen, who used the order to unify "those most interested in progress." A. Leo Oberdorfer then described the "new pa-triotism" modeled by the B'nai B'rith, which was also apparent in the words and deeds of Clara Barton. Barton's work with the Red Cross, he maintained, helped "alleviate the horrors of war" and direct "efforts toward the realization of a universal peace." Like Barton, the B'nai B'rith was devoted to "higher ideals of duty and honesty." Oberdorfer implored American Jews to unify and set aside religious differences and national backgrounds. A loud Jewish voice in America, he speculated, would awaken the nation's ethical awareness and practices of "brotherly love."[81]

The millennial tone of Oberdorfer's speech unambiguously tied the destiny of Jews to the destiny of America, defining that destiny in terms of a patriotism that stressed universal peace. Schwarz shared a similar vision, which, in turn, cast anti-Semitism as harmful to both Jews and America. In 1907, Schwarz exchanged a series of letters with a theater owner in Mobile over a play with a "Jew Pawnbroker" character. The manager, who was also Jewish, initially resisted Schwarz's criticism but eventually conceded the point. Schwarz would summarize the affair in the *Jewish Ledger*: "We do not intend to be offensively and obnoxiously caricatured on the stage in Mobile, and such can be stopped by Jews in every theatre in the country if the Jews will only watch it and protest." Echoing Schwarz, the *Ledger* encouraged Jews to adamantly protest any "offensive characters and caricatures" in their hometowns. Jews had to make their voices known and recognize that most people would listen to a reasoned objection. The editor encouraged "respectable Jews" to stop patronizing the theaters that "present offensive caricatures, be they Jew, Dutch, Irish or Dago."[82] Schwarz kept up his forthright stance against stereotyping in 1913, months before Leo Frank's trial in Atlanta. Writing to board members in his B'nai B'rith district, Schwarz encouraged the condemnation of all "offensive caricaturing of the Jew in moving picture

shows, vaudeville and other theatres." He explained that theater manag-
ers in Mobile had complied with his demands. But, Schwarz added, it
took constant agitation, complaint, and protest to accomplish it.[83]

Schwarz also combated prejudice at the legal level. In a 1913 address
to the B'nai B'rith, he called the recent veto of a federal immigration
bill "a source of gratification to American citizens truly imbued with
the American ideal of liberty, equality and opportunity in this land."[84]
The bill's author was a congressman from Alabama who assured Schwarz
that it would not target Jewish immigrants. Schwarz acquiesced on this
point but opposed the bill "as a matter of principle." He insisted that
America should remain a "haven" for all "honest" immigrants, no matter
their faith. Prejudice in all forms, Schwarz believed, was simply unac-
ceptable; it was also curable through education. "I believe that the more
knowledge the non-Jew has of the history and traditions of the Jewish
race the less prejudice and the more respect he has for him." Schwarz
spoke at a time when the fires of anti-Semitism were about to explode
in Atlanta. But he remained certain that the "true" American was religiously tolerant.[85]

Opposing Jewish caricatures and prejudicial laws was, for Schwarz, a
civil religious act, a manifestation of a belief that anti-Semitism in any
form was profoundly un-American, as well as offensive to Jews. Another
way Schwarz performed his civil religion was through generous deeds.
In 1908, the *Jewish Ledger* exclaimed that the B'nai B'rith "stands for
Jewish charity and is the champion for Jewishness all over the world."
Within the organization, the article noted, Schwarz's "good work" had
been exceptional.[86] From 1912 to 1913, Schwarz served as president
of his B'nai B'rith district, an honor awarded to him in "recognition of
his earnest and fruitful service in benevolent and philanthropic work
among his co-religionists."[87] In his first address as president, Schwarz
stressed the eternal bond between Judaism and America, they together
being the source of "humanity's two most precious documents," the Ten
Commandments and the Declaration of Independence.[88]

Philanthropy was among Schwarz's main concerns as district president. In a letter to the district, Schwarz suggested that the order's efforts
to do good "assume a wide scope." More lodges needed to "stand ready
to enter any field of endeavor where it may serve to uplift mankind — be

that non-Jewish as well as Jewish."[89] He also shared this message publicly. Speaking at an orphan home in New Orleans, he announced, "This is our home, just as it is your home, because it is a Jewish home, and these are your children and our children, because they are Jewish children." He implored Jews to become agents of "personal service," explaining, "there is none so exalted in station, social or financial position, to whom the call [to personal service] does not extend." While the faithful could "supply beautiful temples and synagogues," this was not enough for Schwarz. Serving society was an act of citizenship. "In citizenship it is not sufficient that you furnish good laws for your citizens, but through your personal service and example furnish good citizens for your laws."[90]

As the district president, Schwarz would have a wider screen on which to project his civil religious value system, which placed a premium on civic and religious service. In addition to philanthropy, Schwarz also advocated military service. He encouraged Mobile's lodge to support a new Jewish organization called the Patriotic League of America. Formed in New York, the group appealed to Schwarz because it promoted among Jews "patriotism and love for our common Country." He explained that for him, patriotism implied action and not mere words. Thus, the "Jewish patriot" would readily engage in military service. But Schwarz added that a patriot could also work as a private citizen, supporting the religious faith and welfare of Jewish and Gentile soldiers.[91]

Schwarz also implored members of the B'nai B'rith to serve their own by unifying the Jewish ranks throughout the southland. On assuming the district presidency, Schwarz wrote to Albert Herskowitz, editor of the newly founded *Oklahoma Jewish Review*. Schwarz expressed a hope that the publication would encourage the formation of more lodges in Oklahoma. Every "community where there exists a thriving B'nai B'rith lodge there is too at the same time a community there filled with the true Jewish spirit—supporting its congregation or congregations and everything else of a worthy Jewish nature as well—and in contrast, where a B'nai B'rith lodge does not thrive the Jewish spirit is likewise apathetic or decadent."[92] Schwarz's strident focus on unity knew no bounds, and he frequently reached out to the Orthodox community. To an Orthodox rabbi in Mobile, Schwarz proclaimed, "Our official position and titles differ but we are engaged in a common cause." This "cause," he continued, was "JUDAISM," and if the rabbi would support the B'nai B'rith, he would be helping the faith in all its diversity.[93]

Within the small southern Jewish circle were even smaller subsections. Schwarz represented one Reform Jewish voice, but there were others. In his mind, these distinctions were of little concern. He operated through a sincere belief that America's fate was the Jew's fate, and that America would only become greater if Jews were committed to their faith. Schwarz's recruitment tactics proved effective. The *Jewish Ledger* reported that the order experienced its highest single-year membership gain the year Schwarz finished his term. Approximately seven hundred joined, bringing the total to fifty-five hundred. The article credited Schwarz, explaining that he traveled "hither and thither . . . to solicit applications for membership."[94] His tenure would be remembered for years after. In 1920, the *Jewish Monitor* criticized recent presidents for allowing the numbers to dwindle and doing "absolutely nothing for the hundreds of Jewish men in the many army camps." The article proclaimed: "How the administration of Leon Schwarz looms up! Comparisons are odious—and they would be in the cases we have in mind. But we can't help recalling the glories of the Schwarz administration—glories which become the more illustrious as time goes by. We recall the sacrifice, the indomitable energy, the deep devotion of Leon Schwarz, to the cause—an attitude of mind which made the Order the greatest Jewish propaganda institution in the Southwest."[95]

"True Americans"

The 1905 Russian revolution resulted in a mass persecution of the country's Jews. In response, both Jews and Gentiles in the Wiregrass region shared their outrage and forwarded donations to the victims. Among the givers was a Methodist church in Montgomery, whose members Leon Schwarz thanked for their generosity as well as their "expressions of condemnation of the atrocities perpetuated on the Russian Jews."[96] Commenting on the outpouring of support, a newsperson in Tallahassee stated that he was not surprised. It was simply a showing of "brotherly love," which "is broader than mere sectarianism." Any "true American," the author asserted, would sympathize and support the distressed Russian Jew.[97]

Such expressions of solidarity fit within a broader pattern of civil religious exchange between Jews and Gentiles in the Wiregrass Gulf South. Jewish peddlers became established merchants in the New South. The trains that symbolized progress and prosperity to the majority also did to Jews. As their stock rose in the Wiregrass region, Jews made their presence known through fraternal orders, business, and politics. But Jewish leaders remained concerned with unity and sought to make sure the small communities of Jews stayed vibrant. Schwarz represented a Jewish citizen who found common ground with the majority by valuing civic and religious service. He was the son of a Confederate, a soldier, a Democrat, a "joiner," a businessperson, and a philanthropist. All of these activities fit within the majority's civil religious patterns, even though for Schwarz, they were filtered through a Jewish lens. Protestant admirers recognized the difference, but they were also comfortable including Jews within the ranks of "true Americans."

Tom Watson's vitriol and Leo Frank's lynch mob were powerful reminders of the reality of anti-Semitism in the American South. But for Schwarz and others, this was an anomaly and, more importantly, a threat to the American way of life. Judaism and America shared a common history and destiny, they argued, and to violate this bond was a supreme social sin. But at the same time that Jews were making inroads into the Wiregrass Gulf South, the majority's territory of religious liberty did not admit Catholics, casting them as the archetypal "untrue American."

CHAPTER FIVE

Catholic Voices, Nativist Voices

True and Untrue Americans

IN 1908, FATHER PATRICK BRESNAHAN settled at his missionary headquarters in Tallahassee. He would compliment the city for its relative lack of anti-Catholicism, crediting this to the "educated and cultured" population. "The bigotry that did show up," he noted, "was imported in vomitings of 'cheap' politicians seeking power or money." Bresnahan traveled throughout the state over the years, ministering to sparse Catholic populations in rural places. He knew why some areas grew, while others did not. "To me it is not strange to see that the communities that have flourished the most are those that formerly showed very little bigotry and no narrow mindedness." For the priest, a community's prosperity and stability could be measured by its tolerance of Catholics. He reasoned that anti-Catholicism was the product of ignorance, and ignorant people would never prosper. Tallahassee would remain, for Bresnahan, a model southern community. In the midst of a heated gubernatorial campaign in 1916, a representative of Sidney Catts spoke in Tallahassee. Bresnahan challenged the speaker's claim that America's bishops were demanding that Catholics vote against Woodrow Wilson. Bresnahan cowed the speaker, and he was certain the audience appreciated that fact. "I knew the Tallahasseeans—truly Southern, chivalrous, hospitable and fair minded."[1]

To be truly southern in Bresnahan's view was to be intelligent, cultured, and unbigoted. But alas, Sidney Catts would win that election, as scores of Floridians entered the polls certain that Catholics were anything but "true" Americans. Civil religion, observes R. Laurence Moore, can become "an arena of contested meanings where Americans make assertions about what makes them different from other Americans."[2] During the 1910s, Catholics and nativist Protestants in the Wiregrass Gulf South faced off in such an "arena of contested meanings," where each side argued that they knew who was and was not a worthy citizen.

The word "true" demarcated both Catholic and Protestant civil religious territories. A "true" American was either a southern white Protestant or someone who believed religious tolerance should be extended to Catholics. Of course, "true" marked boundaries elsewhere on the Wiregrass South's moral map. Many southern whites claimed that "true progress" came when redeemer Democrats secured home rule from "carpetbagger" northerners. "True womanhood" often implied a special devotion to religion and family. Lost Causers wanted to relay a "true history" of the Confederate past, one that made heroes of wartime leaders and challenged the idea that slavery was the primary cause of the conflict. For Reform Jews in the South, "true religion" both unified the faithful and prompted them participate in society through charity, military service, or political activism. Southern Catholics also spoke of "true citizenship" in this manner. Yet in the Wiregrass South, scores of non-Catholics refused to validate the idea of Catholic patriotism. While Catholics were small in number, during the 1910s, they became central to a civil religious discourse that created competing images of the "true American."

"An Arena of Contested Meanings"

America's nativists, writes Dan T. Knobel, "believed that they knew best who was *really* 'American.'" Their movement was powerful enough to mobilize mass portions of the electorate, and to do this, they created a "perception of world," complete with a symbolic system that separated insiders from outsiders. During the 1910s, Catholics sat firmly on the outside of this world. Nativists perpetuated a fear that Catholics were loyal to Rome and Rome alone. And if left unchecked, they would unravel the nation's social fabric.[3]

The rise of anti-Catholicism in the Wiregrass Gulf South coincided with nativist fears over immigration and the paranoid idea that if Catholicism were tolerated, papal rule would be imminent. It was a relatively new sentiment, one that reflected a national trend. But the story had an ironic twist. After Reconstruction, a number of southern white progressives conjectured that European immigrants could contribute to the region's financial growth. They also sold immigration as a solution to the "race problem." In 1904 and 1905, southern railroad executives hosted an Italian ambassador on a tour of Italian communities in the South. They hoped the ambassador would encourage more Italians to populate these locations.[4] In 1906, a Mississippi newspaper commended Louisiana for introducing foreign labor. The paper stated that European immigration not only had economic advantages but also had alleviated racial tension. "The influx of Italians between 1890 and 1900," the paper announced, "had made Louisiana a white state."[5]

Despite the optimism of progressives, much of the white South resisted the immigration movement. For starters, most planters reasoned that black laborers would willingly perform duties that white immigrants would not.[6] Additionally, groups like the American Protective Association, which had channeled the Know-Nothing spirit, gained influence in the region. As their voices grew louder, white southerners began questioning the wisdom of immigrant labor. One Memphis newspaper proclaimed that the "race question" had to be "solved on the old line of Anglo-Saxon and African. We do not want the ignorance and vice of Europe to complicate it."[7] In 1913, a New Orleans newspaper urged that "safety first for our native stock should be the watchword of the South in dealing with immigration. Material progress had better slacken than be furthered at the sacrifice of the higher good."[8] And in 1915, Methodist minister Alfred L. Woodward in Tallahassee implored legislators to confront the "urgent" and "pressing" matter of "white immigration." Although they may have been contributing to the region's prosperity, Woodward worried that outsiders like

Germans—with their "breweries and beer"—would morally degrade the state.[9]

There were limits to what white southerners were willing to accept for the sake of material progress. In this case, maintaining the "higher good" meant preventing immigrants from entering the South. But this was a difficult task in Florida, which engaged in a longstanding effort to attract foreign labor. In 1877, the state's Bureau of Immigration distributed pamphlets in Europe entitled "The Florida Settler" and "Florida Immigrant." When the native population began voicing opposition to the effort, the governmental push for foreign labor ended.[10] But immigrants still came to the state. From 1900 to 1920, Florida's foreign population grew while that of neighboring states did not.[11]

As more immigrants arrived in Florida, the state's Catholic presence swelled in urban centers and along the Atlantic and Gulf coasts.[12] Nativist legislators took note. In 1913, a pamphlet entitled "Knights of Columbus Oath, Extract 4th Degree" appeared in Florida's congressional records. While fake, the pamphlet spoke directly to nativist fears. The fictitious inductee pledged to "defend His doctrine and His Holiness's right and custom against all usurpers of the heretical or Protestant authority." He also promised to "wage relentless war" against Protestants, and "hang, burn, waste, boil, flay, strangle, and bury alive these infamous heretics, rip up the stomachs and wombs of their women, and crush their infants' heads against the walls in order to annihilate their execrable race." The invented inductee vowed to vote for Catholics only and to "place Catholic girls in Protestant families [so] that a weekly report may be made of the inner movements of the heretics."[13]

The nativist fear of Catholics was rooted in the premise that Catholics were an organized band of religious fanatics who planned to overthrow the nation's Protestant authorities. So pervasive was this fear that legislators created laws limiting Catholic rights. In 1913, Florida passed a law banning the instruction of whites by blacks and blacks by whites. The law had no overt markers of anti-Catholicism, but Catholic schools were the only places where interracial instruction happened. Not blind to its covert anti-Catholicism, Catholics immediately denounced the law as being profoundly un-American. In Saint Augustine, Bishop Michael J. Curley called the bill evidence of Florida's "wave of anti-Catholic hysteria." In the following years, Curley continued fighting the religious hysteria of his state. "Patriotism of the highest order," Curley proclaimed, "flows from the very essence of Catholicism."[14] Curley had supporters in Florida; however, if elections were any indication, the majority held the opposite view. Catholicism became a point of heated debate during Florida's 1916 election season. A candidate's position regarding the Catholic place in public life frequently determined his electoral success or failure.

Park Trammell and Florida's "True Patriotic People"

In April 1916, Governor Park Trammell received a petition claiming that white nuns teaching at the Saint Joseph's Convent in Saint Augustine were teaching black students.[15] He contacted the sheriff, confirmed the claim, and ordered the nuns' arrests.[16] In his public statement, Trammell was adamant that he had enforced "a good law." He dismissed the Catholic press, which charged him with prejudice. Trammell expressed a wish that all Floridians practice religion as they please. He was simply concerned with protecting the rule of white supremacy. "I do not think we should encourage anything which would tend to make the negro believe he is on social equality with the white people."[17]

A Jacksonville newspaper dismissed Trammell's justification for the arrests and speculated that anti-Catholicism motivated the governor. Moreover, the article applauded the "good sisters" for their work with blacks and averred that most people thought Trammell's actions were "deplorable."[18] Letters flooding Trammell's office, however, did not confirm the journalist's observations. Nor would they validate Trammell's contention that religious prejudice played no part in his decision, since they commended the governor as a "patriotic" protector of the white Protestant South. From Ft. Lauderdale, one supporter wrote approvingly of Trammell's handling of "the nigger teacher question." The author worried that "some of our courts will upset every thing when it comes to Catholics and the law."[19] H. Witaker of Muscogee applauded Trammell's "stand . . . on the side of the patriotic people . . . against Rome."[20] From Okeechobee, J. L. Crews called the law "one of the best" on the books. The author worried that if "something isn't done shortly that we the Protestant People" would have "some fight on our hands."[21] George Ensey, a postmaster and justice of the peace in Tropic Indian River, thanked Trammell for his "prompt, fearless action" against "the powerful Catholic Hierarchy." He charged that the "so-called 'Church'" had become "the most powerful political machine in the world."[22] J. B. George of Morristo warned: "Be on your guard as I think the Catholics are going to try to turn a trick on you. I have been told that the Catholics of South Florida are claiming that they are supporting you."[23]

Some letters gave more attention to the event's racial implications. R. C. Hodges, a former Confederate, proclaimed that Trammell's position "against Negro Equality" guaranteed that "all the old soldiers" would vote for him.[24] "I take sides with you commonly speaking," wrote Y. J. Holder. "I don't think white and black should class up with one another anyway. They think themselves on equality with white people. I hope you will get that law in force [so] that white teachers shall not teach in negro schools."[25] A. C. Pierce of DeLand wrote to assure Trammell "that as long as you stand as you do against the whites teaching negro schools you will have the People of the South for you."[26]

Some letter writers told Trammell that his actions in Saint Augustine would result in additional votes for his upcoming run for the U.S. Senate. When the June elections came, Okeechobee's chief of police William Collins wrote, "I will say that I am proud to know that I voted for [you]." Collins suspected "quite a number of people" in Okeechobee felt the same.[27] The principal of the Montverde Industrial School, H. P. Carpenter, pledged his vote. "Allow me to say that we are for you first, last, and all the time. All right thinking people approve of your action in the Saint Augustine affair."[28] Similarly, Dr. R. L. McMullen of Largo promised his vote, writing that he was "doubly endeared" to Trammell once he jailed the nuns.[29] D. A. Reid relayed that in Perry, support for the governor only grew after the affair.[30] R. L. Park, the editor of a newspaper in Crystal River, wrote that Catholics in his area had drafted a letter condemning the governor. "I refused to publish it," reported Park. "I assure you that I shall continue to do all in my power for you. I think you will carry this place almost solidly."[31]

Governor Park Trammell was a southern white Democrat living in a region where southern white Democrats dominated politics. For many sharing his political leanings, Catholicism and racial equality were both affronts to the common good. Not every Trammell supporter was a southern Democrat, however. C. A. Stanford of Minneola confessed that he was a Republican but nevertheless admired the governor's "stand."[32] Another northern Republican who had relocated to Ocala wrote emphatically that what Trammell had done was "THE PROPER THING TO HAVE DONE." The author suspected "nearly all right thinking people" of Florida would vote for Trammell because of it. He also conjectured that Catholics were secretly eyeing public schools, plotting to "'do' our school system 'dirty.'" Claiming to have voted against candidates who "[cater] to Romanism," the author proclaimed, "I believe the time has come when Americans must be put in office. Rome has had her day in office, and those that she now fills must be taken away from her as fast as Americans are found to take them, and hold them—for the good of America."[33] L. M. Drake of Daytona claimed he supported Trammell even though his wife and daughter were Catholics. He dismissed the "bitter" reactions of Trammell's opponents and regretted that the candidate would lose Catholic votes. Drake believed that "any fair-minded man" could see the governor was simply executing his "sworn duty." "Laws are made for all alike, regardless [of] politics or religion."[34]

Trammell gained a great deal of political momentum from the Saint Augustine affair. Publicly, he denied the assertion that religious prejudice motivated his actions. But supporters of all political persuasions and regional backgrounds praised what they believed was the governor's "noble" stand against Rome. Trammell's Democratic opponent for the Senate seat, Nathan P. Bryan, tried to use the governor's anti-Catholic image against him. In a pamphlet, Bryan alleged that Trammell belonged to a secret fraternal order, the Guardians of Liberty. The "chief purpose" of the Guardians, Bryan accused, was to keep "Catholics out of office," which violated the provision "that church and State should be kept separate." Trammell's political opponent saw in the Guardians an irredeemable flaw: "The Guardians of Liberty is Know Nothingism revived." For Bryan, anti-Catholicism was not an endearing political value, and he hoped that the state's Democratic voters felt the same. In addition to decrying Trammell, Bryan's pamphlet offered something of a defense for his having appointed Peter A. Dignan—a Catholic—as

Jacksonville's postmaster. Bryan's political opponents suggested that this appointment validated the candidate's secret ties with the Catholic Church. "I am not a Catholic," countered Bryan, "I did not recommend Mr. Dignan because he is one." Calling Dignan "my personal and political friend," Bryan maintained that he appointed Dignan because he was competent and trustworthy.[35]

In connecting Trammell with the Guardians of Liberty, Bryan gambled that Florida's voters would see both Trammell and the organization as being too extreme. The Guardians were an institutionalized product of the booming nativist print culture of the 1910s. The story of the Guardians begins in 1911, when Missouri's Wilbur Phelps began publishing the *Menace*, an anti-Catholic periodical. The publication reached 1.5 million subscriptions in four years. In Atlanta, Tom Watson's *Jeffersonian Magazine* became a southern version of the *Menace*. Watson published articles entitled "The Roman Catholic Hierarchy: The Deadliest Menace to Our Liberties and Our Civilization," "The Murder of Babes," "The Sinister Portent of Negro Priests," "How the Confessional Is Used by Priests to Ruin Women," and "One of the Priests Who Raped a Catholic Woman in a Catholic Church." In 1912, Lieutenant General Nelson A. Miles, ex-congressman Charles D. Haines, and Charles B. Skinner formed the Guardians of Liberty in Atlanta. With Tom Watson's support and a culture of anti-Catholicism brewing, the Guardians became a strong political force in the Wiregrass South.[36]

Trammell denied that he belonged to the Guardians, but he admired the organization nonetheless. "I am not a Guardian of Liberty," he announced, "but I know many of them who are good Democrats." Trammell continued, warning that Bryan's politics discriminated "against a large number of Protestants" and favored "a large number of Catholics."[37] On the matter of Catholicism, the white Democratic South was not an ideological monolith. Trammell's following was larger in number, thus eventuating in his victory. But the voice of Bryan relayed another value system. While less popular, his civil religious perspective relied on the idea that freedom of religion was constitutionally protected and a firm belief that Catholics could be "true Americans."

The Guardians occupied an ambiguous place in the Wiregrass Gulf South's moral landscape. Trammell guardedly supported the group but avoided association with them. It was both highly influential and highly controversial. And in the effort to discredit the organization, some Guardian opponents tried to prey on racial prejudices. Before the election, Bradford Byrd of the *Atlanta Journal* received a letter from Herbert Felkel, editor of Tallahassee's *Florida Recorder*. Not only were Trammell and Sidney Catts—a leading candidate for governor—Guardians, according to Felkel, but the Guardians had accepted black members into its ranks. Felkel requested that Byrd ask his cartoonist to draw an illustration showing blacks repeating the Guardian oath. "Have it in a negro lodge room," Felkel wrote, "with an alter [*sic*] and negroes and whites in the meeting in the background sitting together." Byrd sent an irate reply. "I must be candid and say that your proposed 'stunt' of cartooning a negro administering an oath to a white to be printed in a southern paper does not appeal to me personally." The implications were appalling to Byrd. "The placing of whites and blacks on the same level, by cartoon or story, creates in the negro the feeling of equality, and you know what that leads to. No white man, no matter what your personal feeling toward him may be, is low enough to be placed on the level with a negro." Byrd forwarded the letters to Trammell and assured him that the *Journal* would never assist the Tallahassee publication.[38]

Despite the scolding from Byrd, Felkel continued claiming that the Guardians had a substantial "negro membership." In one article, he wrote: "Oh! You Gardeens! Do you believe you can stand this, you men of the South, who fought with Lee, Jackson and Johnson? And how stand the sons of these men? Do you want a return to the troubles of Reconstruction days? If so, go to it. Organize the colored people into Courts of Guardians of Liberty; and the days of the 'Befo' Day Clubs' we sink into insignificance, and you'll have all the troubles you desire."[39] The statement pulled from all sides of the white South's symbolic universe, deploying images of good and evil via the heroes of the Confederacy and the horrors of Reconstruction. Additionally, Felkel evoked an image of supreme racial disorder in mentioning the Before Day clubs. By linking the Guardians with the Before Day clubs, Felkel implied that the organization's rise would trigger the downfall of Florida and the South.[40]

Many Trammell supporters saw the Guardians differently. Fred Taylor, the justice of the peace in DeLeon Springs, commended Trammel's stance against "nuns teaching negroes." Taylor speculated that voters "want clean, strong, bold, patriotic" Americans like Trammell. Then, using rather cryptic language, Taylor wrote: "I belong to a certain order, and I believe you also belong to the same at a certain lodge. . . . You received our endorsement unanimously." Taylor's letterhead read, "Are you a Patriot? Then subscribe to the *American Citizen*." Beside the letterhead Taylor had written in "and *The Menace*."[41] The *Citizen* was the official organ of the Guardians of Liberty, and thus it is likely that Taylor was a member. Trammell continued to claim that he did not belong to the organization, but for supporters like Taylor, the group represented all "patriotic" Americans.

Alas, the Guardians of Liberty was a political asset for Trammell; while for Bryan, the Knights of Columbus—a Catholic fraternal organization—became a political liability.[42] During the election, rumors surfaced that the Knights of Columbus had secretly supported Bryan's campaign. Letters coming to Trammell occasionally referred to the supposed link between Bryan and the Knights. From Tropic Indian River, one letter writer pledged that his family would provide "three easy votes" for Trammell. "We all glory in your spunk as regards this Catholic question." Bryan's chances were "dead," proclaimed the writer, "simply because he chose to affiliate himself with the Knights of Columbus."[43] After the election, more letters came in mentioning the Knights. Trammell won the Senate seat convincingly, receiving approximately twice as many votes as Bryan. In his concession speech, Bryan blamed his loss on his refusal to appeal "to passion or to prejudice."[44] Letters to Trammell confirmed Bryan's analysis. The "Catholic element," wrote W. S. Moore of Hawthorn, failed in its attempt to bring Trammell down.[45] In Lake City, Dr. Warren B. Rush claimed he recruited votes for Trammell and wondered why anyone would have voted for Bryan, "who stands for the whiskey ring and K. C." "Now I shall expect you to Stand against the Catholic," Rush stated.[46] T. J. Bunting of Milton called Trammell one of the nation's only "true patriotic" politicians. If more "patriots" like Trammell would win elections, Bunting noted, there would "not be so many [Catholics] in congress." Until that happened, the author advised Trammell to "watch the Catholic Senate and [Congress] and [do] not let them past [*sic*] any Bad Bills."[47] W. T. Brantley, pastor of the Apalachicola

Methodist Church, sent regrets that Franklin County did not vote for Trammell. "But, as you know, the Knights of Columbus and the Church of Rome are firmly entrenched here."[48] Frank E. Patten of Jacksonville wrote: "'Three Cheers for the Stars and Stripes' and another three to the manhood of the State of Florida." Florida's "true Americans" had made their statement. "The POPE of Rome must not rule America and I feel that this is only a beginning of what must come if we want to remain a free and independent people."[49] The clerk of courts for Escambia County announced regrets that the county could not offer more votes. "I presume you know something of what we had to contend with on account of Bryan playing to the Catholics."[50]

Trammell's enforcement of one law in Saint Augustine drew favor from white voters who believed that Catholicism and black equality were threats to the nation. Neither Bryan's attempt to use Trammell's religious prejudice to derail his campaign nor the newspaper's effort to undermine his candidacy by claiming that the Guardians favored racial equality was particularly effective. In the metaphorical river of civil religion of the 1910s, Catholicism became a particularly noticeable stream, and election campaigns came to revolve around it.

Sidney J. Catts and His "WHITE DEMOCRATIC VOTERS"

Senator Charles W. Jones of Pensacola was the first Democrat elected to the U.S. Senate from Florida during Reconstruction. After 1877, the Catholic politician's legislative efforts helped instigate the region's material developments. When Jones died in 1897, his devotees in Pensacola made the Catholic politician into a civic saint. They also obscured his inglorious end and apotheosized the "purity of his political reputation."[51] While Jones was "patriot" in 1897, by the 1910s, the image of a Catholic politician had become deeply threatening in west Florida. During the fall 1916 elections, the politically inexperienced Baptist minister Sidney J. Catts made an improbable run for governor. Catts came from DeFuniak Springs in west Florida, a region that produced, supported, and heralded Jones only a few years earlier.[52] But anti-Catholicism played no small part in Catts's campaign. Plank 4 on his platform read: "Nothing in Florida above the Nation's Flag. As Roman Catholicism puts her allegiance to the pope above the flag, Mr. Catts stands against the invasion of the state of Florida in her politics. As Roman Catholicism opposes our public school system, Mr. Catts opposes Roman Catholicism in the state of Florida in the realm of educational views. As Roman Catholicism believes in the celibacy of the priesthood and the confessional, Mr. Catts stands squarely against them, and is ready to fight from the state of Florida this great menace to the peace of home, the maintenance of our public schools, and the enjoyment of quiet religion at all hazards."[53] Catts banked his political future on an assumption that Florida's voters would respond positively to his stand against Rome. It proved to be a wise gamble.

During his campaign, Catts focused much of his attention on rural locales. Here, the candidate's anti-Catholicism sold particularly well. Of the total 24,650 Catholics living in Florida in 1916, 21,477 lived in eleven counties, most of which contained large urban centers like Jacksonville. Thus, Florida's rural population had limited contact with living Catholics and knew only what they read in the *Menace* or heard on the streets.[54] While Catts did not win counties with urban centers, he did manage to find support there. T. J. Morris of Jacksonville reported that he was "charmed" by Catts's "platform and your promise of allegiance to the American citizens of Florida." The concerned Morris wrote that "as day and night cannot abide together so papal rule and liberty can never exist together." The "gigantic political machine" of Catholicism, Morris asserted, opposed "fundamental American rights" such as "freedom of conscience, of speech and the press."[55] Another Jacksonville resident called Catts an "AMERICAN CITIZEN" whose platform was "bold and fearless." Terming Catholicism an "ungodly ecclesiastical body," the author lamented that more ministers were not more adamantly opposing "this politico-ecclesiastical machine." "If every minister of the Baptist, Methodist, Christian, Advent, Presbyterian and other Protestant churches would do their duty and enlighten the people of this state as well as other states we would soon break up the mighty political power of this so-called church."[56] Even though she could not vote, Mrs. Irvin Kelsey of Griffin assured Catts that "if I could and had ten thousand votes they would all be yours." Before coming to Florida and becoming a neighbor of the Seminole tribe, Kelsey reported, her family lived in a "Catholic neighborhood." For "a friend," she noted, "I prefer the Seminole. He is less treacherous despite the stories told of Indian treachery."[57] From Tampa, Herbert M. Brockell wrote to express support for Catts's "stand . . . in regards to Roman Catholicism."[58] In Dade City, O. N. Williams expressed his "great pleasure" with Catts's platform. The "Catholic loving papers" might criticize him, but Williams expected Catts to win. He worried, though, that the Knights of Columbus would "get" Catts, so he counseled the candidate to contact the *Menace*.[59]

Catts never needed to contact the *Menace*. From Aurora, Missouri, the publication's editor, B. M. Phelps, wrote Catts commending "the noble stand which you have taken against Romanism in Florida." Phelps explained that the *Menace* had been chronicling "the great work which was done by Patriots in the recent election in Iowa, Illinois, Ohio and New York" and thought the same could happen in Florida. The publication, Phelps assured, was "a great negative power in a campaign." He boasted that his articles had influenced local newspapers, which "begin running such ads as 'Mr. So and So' is a Roman Catholic, gives liberally to the church and attends mass." Such "trickery," he suspected, would propel Catts to victory.[60]

With the *Menace* and the Guardians on his side, Catts gained momentum. From Jacksonville, one avowed member of the Guardians of Liberty pledged his "moral support." The author hoped Catts would awaken "the people" to the "insidious efforts" of the "Roman hierarchy in attempting to control our government."[61] Another Guardian from Jacksonville anticipated that Catts would counteract the "counterfeit that calls itself the Catholic church." Catholics, warned the author, wanted "to get control of our country and destroy our institutions."[62] Catts also received a letter from "A POWERFUL SECRET SOCIETY OPPOSED TO PERVERSION OF AMERICAN RIGHTS." The "patriotic American issue" outlined in Catts's platform, announced the author, "attracted wide attention over all the State, and especially in Jacksonville." With a "growing sentiment against the invasion of American politics . . . crystallizing," the letter claimed, more people were prepared to "eradicate ecclesiasticism as a pest from American politics and government."[63]

With anti-Catholic feelings spreading by the day, talk of violence became more common in correspondence to Catts. Jacksonville's Richard

Hargrave advised Catts to gather more Guardian support. Hargrave worked for Van C. Swearingen, the former mayor of Jacksonville and organizer of Catts's campaign committee.[64] Hargrave reported that the Samaritan Knights and Masons in Jacksonville were reluctant to support Catts. There was, however, a "powerful secret order" that Hargrave estimated had become "the most promising of all the anti-papal organizations yet organized." He insisted that Catts might need the organization to combat the meddlesome Knights of Columbus. While the Guardians would "be ready for bloodshed if necessary," Hargrave was certain that the organization was morally superior to the "poor papists."[65] Catts secured the majority of his votes from rural counties. Yet, in Jacksonville, Richard Hargrave and others were strong supporters of the candidate, ready to go to war if necessary.

Catts did have detractors. From Tampa, one letter writer charged that Catts's platform "breeds hatred and is diametrically opposed to the tenants of the constitution of the U.S. and more important, the teachings of Christ."[66] A letter from Pennsylvania exclaimed "[I was] astonished that such a statement should come from a sane American citizen." Catholicism, the author assured, was essential in the forming of America. Moreover, it existed "a few hundred years before you were born, and will be here when everybody on this continent will have forgotten that Sidney J. Catts even lived, and the Catholic Church will be greater and grander than ever."[67] From Louisville, P. H. Callahan of the Knights of Columbus queried, "Would you kindly advise me just the conditions in the State of Florida, making it necessary to insert Plank No. 4 in your platform, which, according to the space allotted it, seems to be of greater importance, in your opinion, than any of the rest of your principles?" Catholic governors in Massachusetts and Illinois, wrote Callahan, brought "progress and development" to their states. Callahan called Catts's platform a fitting example of "religious prejudice" and proceeded to cite the liberal Protestant clergyman Washington Gladden: "[We] Catholics and Protestants are going to live together in this country and we might as well learn to do so in peace and harmony."[68]

In the minds of Callahan and others, Catts's anti-Catholic posture was an affront to America and Christianity. Tolerance of Catholicism was a feature of their vision of the good society, making Catts anything but a "true American." But Catts's supporters were always quick to come to his defense. Richard Hargrave wrote to Catts about Callahan's letter, theorizing that the Knight was acting on behalf of Rome, seeking to "strike a fatal blow at all America just while the war is at its height."[69] In a letter they sent to P. H. Callahan, Jacksonville's Guardians of Liberty admonished the Catholic, saying he had "absolutely NO JURISDICTION or part in the political affairs of Florida." The letter scolded Callahan for holding the "alien idea that a Pontiff has some jurisdiction in State affairs in Florida." But Callahan obviously did not want "the privileges" of "liberty and Justice" or "respect the liberties of fellow citizens to run on whatever constitutional platforms they please." Referring Callahan's plea to "come together," the letter writers explained that "we cannot go to you without prejudice to our liberties, which we will never surrender." The letter concluded by encouraging Callahan to declare his "complete independence of the Vatican at Rome":

> You should voluntarily cease to oppose freedom in all forms; to oppose free schools as these are the bulwark of enlightenment and help all religious faiths in proportion to degrees of light; to oppose the unrestricted reading of the Scriptures by the laity as this cannot jeopardize any faith; to oppose the Bible in the public schools; to seek to bastardize all children born without your sanction or marriages non-Catholic in performance; to practice the confessional in America, since it puts intelligence in the possession of a celibate order of friars non-compatible with the interests of free government; to maintain the cloister of American soil at all; to levy blackmail on the souls of human beings by pretending to ransom them from future perils for any consideration to the parish or priest payable; to maintain any longer the condition of celibacy as an order among priests.[70]

This diatribe left little doubt that for the Guardians, Catholics were neither genuine religious practitioners nor genuine American citizens. Opponents to the Guardians protested with similar normative language related to patriotism.

E. S. Morrison of Jacksonville asked, "do you expect to get the support of any real clean protestant if you do you are sadly mistaken, this B. S. you are hauling out won't make a vote for you and you bet here is one protestant that is going to work tooth and nail against you." Morrison then recalled that during the yellow fever epidemic, he "saw the protestant ministers flying." Yet, "the Catholic priests and sisters remained here worked with the sick it made no difference to them whether you were Catholic or protestant or black or white." Catholics, Morrison concluded, had always been great "patriots."[71] After receiving the letter, Richard Hargrave promptly wrote to Catts. The "brutal, vulgar and obscene" letter, he wrote, was inexcusable. The "term 'B. S.', used in the sense in which this brute employed it, constitutes a degree of obscenity which makes him liable to the incriminations of the Federal Postal laws for an improper use of the mails." He advised Catts to keep the letter "in case you might later wish to find and punish this rough-neck for his brutality."[72]

Hargrave pursued the matter further, theorizing that William Burbridge was the "vulgar" letter's author.[73] Writing as a representative of the "Florida State Committee of Civil and Religious Liberty," Hargrave informed Burbridge "that the highest consummation of Christianity and social culture is displayed in those men and women whose capacity for religious and sectarian toleration is most conspicuous." In contrast, he continued, the Catholic Church "is inimical to free speech, free press and free schools." Hargrave then turned to Rome, claiming that there was "widespread poverty and a high percentage of illiteracy" there. The scathing letter then described conditions in Spain and Central America, where "the 'Padre' is the alpha and omega of authority, illiteracy reigns supreme, and priestly benevolence reaches it's [*sic*] most sublime altitude in it's [*sic*] handling of the connubial relations." Hargrave suspected the Catholic hierarchy was eyeing America, intending "to strangle freedom of thought, conscience and education and usurp the powers of civil government."[74]

Hargrave's characterization of the oppressive Catholic sounded throughout Florida, and for those who listened, Catts became the antidote to "Roman rule." In the June primary election, after a great deal of confusion, the results showed Catts as the victor, he having garnered 33,893 votes and his opponent, William V. Knott, having earned 33,439 votes.[75] Knott brought the election before the Florida Supreme Court and with some political wrangling won the nomination. Infuriated, Catts

published an open letter. Catts suspected that Knott got the nomination by securing the backing of "the Supreme Court, the Big Moneyed
Interest, Roman Catholic Hierarchy, the Knights of Columbus, the Little
Court House Rings and the men who have been in office since they
were little Calves and they are now Crumpled Horned Steers." Catts
further charged that Knott would "qualify the Negroes" to gain more
votes. "I shall be elected," Catts announced, "as a 'WHITE DEMOCRAT'
by the 'WHITE DEMOCRATIC VOTERS.' Don't let anybody fool or
mislead you. I have an overwhelming majority of the WHITE DEMO-
CRATIC VOTERS supporting me and this support cannot be overcome
by any combination of Big Business, Political Crooks and the Roman
Hierarchy."[76]

To continue his campaign, Catts ran as a Prohibition Party candidate.[77] Catts and his supporters would continue linking Knott with the
Catholic Church. Knott adamantly denied the allegations while at the
same time expressing tempered respect for Catholics. Catts went on
to win the November election with 39,546 votes, compared to Knott's
30,343. In his victory statement, Catts downplayed his image as "a fanatic." Calling himself "broadminded," Catts pledged to "upbuild, not
tear down." "You have honored me by your vote, and whether you be
Catholic or Protestant, gambler or saint, rich or poor, you will receive
fair and considerate treatment at my hands."[78]

Catts's avoided anti-Catholic allusions in victory. But a Baptist newspaper theorized that his anti-Catholicism won over Florida's "common people."[79] Letters to the governor-elect confirmed this idea. A
supporter from Lisbon proudly dubbed Catts "the leader of American
Anti-Catholicism." The electoral victory was "God's will," and the author
hoped it would lead to "a national victory over catholicism." He then
suggested that Catts appoint people to educate the public about the
"abominable crafts" of Catholicism. Claiming to be a keen student of
Tom Watson's writings, the letter writer humbly offered his services for
this position, "regardless of salary." "I may have the great pleasure of being helpful in controlling Political Roman Catholicism."[80] In Orlando,
George R. Mauck complained about the "insults" of the anti-Catts press.
"I would like to see the same loyalty to Rulers in our great Country as is
shown the Kaiser of Germany; [when] a German says 'To Hell with the

Kaiser' he soon goes to that place himself, for he is shot down for the remark."[81]

Letters also commended Catts's prohibitionist rhetoric but frequently coupled this with favorable remarks about his anti-Catholicism. From Tyler, Alabama, J. A. Minter wrote, "I am glad that you won out over the forces of 'Rum and Romanism.'" He hoped Florida would set an example for Alabama, where "prohibition is certainly needed."[82] An avowed prohibitionist, LeGrand W. Jones of Texarkana "rejoiced when you put to flight the enemies of God, of Americanism and of good government."[83] G. W. Nance from Refugio, Texas, called himself "a strict Baptist prohibitionist" who never attended a dance or "knowingly darkened a saloon door" and firmly opposed "the hidden doings of the Romanists." Nance hoped the spirit of Catts's victory would imbue his hometown, where "the dance, the saloon, and Romanism" had become "popular evils."[84] J. P. Stephens of Tabor, North Carolina, expressed disappointment that Catts was "hissed at, and spat upon for doing good." He sent Catts a pamphlet entitled, "Behold I show you a Mystery—Christ and the Church." The pamphlet, Stephens summarized, predicted that between 1914 and 1921, "the old order (The Romanized system of governing the nations) [would go] to pieces." In its place would be "a righteous government" of "good laws (God's law)." "I have the feeling that God will use you prominently."[85]

Catts also heard from prominent members of his adopted party. Chicago's Virgil G. Hinshaw of the Prohibition National Committee expressed his pleasure with Catts's defeat over the "pro-Catholic, anti-prohibition people." Hinshaw expressed his earnest hope that Catts "be known as a party prohibitionist. It is not so much the party I desire to have aided as the prohibition cause." He suspected Catts's election meant that "some good men of the Democratic party" would join the prohibition effort and "bring about a moral regeneration of this nation."[86] The Prohibition Party's chairman in Drewry's Bluff, Virginia, predicted that Catts would be "our National standard bearer in 1920." The author protested that Catts had been "defrauded out of the [Democratic] nomination . . . by the machinations of a few sore headed politicians and the Catholic church." The letter speculated that Catts would create a "pure government" and do "great things."[87]

Clergymen from outside Florida also sent notes of congratulations. From the Evangelical Church in Laurel, Iowa, Pastor L. J. U. Smay was elated that Catts had won "upon the cleancut issues of PROHIBITION and AMERICANISM." Both issues, affirmed Smay, "are paramount to-day in American politics." He suspected members of the nation's "great patriotic societies" would carefully monitor the "progress of your legislative program in Florida." The "great battle" of Catts, the minister continued, "constitutes an epoch in the progress of true AMERICANISM and in the defense of our distinctively American institutions."[88] From the Swedish Baptist Church in Prentice, Wisconsin, Pastor Carl V. Anderson congratulated Catts for fighting "brilliantly against the machine element. . . . God grant that political Rome may feel itself in the sweat box during your administration as Governor of Florida and I hope the day may dawn soon when every state shall follow Florida's valuable example."[89]

The "great patriotic society" of this collection of voices made Catts a "valuable example" of political leadership. From North and South, supporters seemingly agreed on what they believed the good society *did not* include, namely alcohol and Catholicism. The *Menace* paid special attention to Catts's race, through which sympathetic northern readers received updates on the campaign. From Asbury Park, New Jersey, *Menace* subscriber Nelson Parker wrote, "You have won for our lord and savior Jesus Christ, I feel it my duty to let you know that my heart and soul is with you in the continuation of such work."[90] Also a subscriber, O. F. Garner of Chicago commended Catts's "hard work." When some "counted out" Catts, Garner claimed he never lost hope and that he always prayed for the candidate. "I was more rejoiced at your election than I was at our own state which put a Romanist out and a Protestant in as Governor." Garner hoped that as governor Catts would "continue the fight against Rome in politics and force open for inspection all Convents, Houses of Good Shepherd, nunneries, etc." Proudly declaring himself a prohibitionist, Garner proclaimed that he "would hail the day" that he could vote for him "for the highest office."[91]

Praise for Catts came from many corners of the nation. There were, though, vocal critics. When he was governor, Catts called for legislation to tax church property, test private school teachers, and give legal officials the authority to inspect convents.[92] The "inspection bill" eventually passed, but the state never enforced it. Bishop Curley in Saint Augustine was infuriated, calling it an "outrageous insult to women who rank with the best, purest and noblest on God's earth."[93] For Curley, the legislation was at odds with the nation's promise of religious liberty. For many nativist Protestants, however, the bill was an encouraging sign. Writing from Statesville, North Carolina, Thomas J. Conger commended Catts's "courage to stand for the Right." The bill, Conger hoped, would help "patriotic" Americans further reveal "the dark deeds of old Blind Rome."[94] From San Francisco, California, T. W. Morgan expressed his "pleasure and gratification" over Catts's law "establishing police protection for the inmates [of] parochial schools, convents and nunneries." Morgan hoped that other politicians would enact such laws that would protect the "guarantees" of "life, liberty, and the pursuit of happiness" that he suspected Catholics threatened.[95] A. D. Bulman of the "Patriotic Lecture Bureau" offered his services to help pass the bill. A circuit speaker, Bulman claimed to have evidence showing the "abominations" committed against "inmates of Roman Catholic institutions." He claimed to have had pictures of children, "debauched by both priests and nuns of the Catholic church" and "made sexual perverts by those same vampires." Enclosed in the letter was a flyer entitled "Romanism Exposed: The Man Who Put the TEST in ProTESTant." Outlining his three-day lecture series, the final evening was "for men only." During this meeting, the male audience would listen to what "celibate priests" taught "young brides," "married women," and "young boys and girls of tender age." This information was "so vile and filthy that it dare not be published in the English language because the publisher would be sent to prison for a long term."[96]

Catholics were relatively small in number in the Wiregrass South. But by 1916, Catholicism had become a prevailing concern in rural and urban locations throughout Florida and the nation. For admirers, Catts's victory represented a positive step in actualizing a good society free from the twin threats of "rum and Rome." Those who disagreed argued that Catts's anti-Catholicism was dangerous, ignorant, and decidedly "un-American." Dissenters lost the political battle, as anti-Catholicism inspired many to pull a lever for Catts and Trammell in 1916. By 1921, however, anti-Catholicism prompted one Methodist minister to pull a trigger.

The Coyle Affair

Following his victory in 1916, Catts traveled to Birmingham and visited his son and daughter-in-law. At the request of local officials, the governor-elect delivered a speech. Claiming that God "called" him to run, Catts explained that "the Catholics were about to take Florida and I told the people about it wherever I went."[97] The "True Americans," a secret influential anti-Catholic organization in Birmingham, joined others to express approval of Catts's speech. O. T. Dozier, a doctor in Birmingham, published pamphlets warning that "the Pope seeks to control American politics."[98]

In Birmingham, as in Florida, Catts found a receptive audience in the growing nativist population. He also drew a rebuke from Father James E. Coyle of Saint Paul's Parish. Commenting on Catts's speech, Coyle criticized the governor, claiming that his rhetoric belonged "in the malodorous gutter press of Georgia and Missouri."[99] Unafraid of entering the public debate, Coyle had long opposed the city's anti-Catholic forces. However, Bishop Edward Allen did not encourage Coyle's extra-ecclesial activity. In 1915, Coyle wrote a Saint Patrick's Day poem that sparked an anti-Catholic backlash. Calling the situation "unfortunate," Allen asked Coyle "to bring the discussion to a speedy close" and heed the instructions of Pope Benedict XV "to remain neutral and let the voice of Faith, Hope and Charity alone be heard about the clang of arms."[100] Coyle failed to follow the bishop's instructions. After Catts's speech, the Birmingham priest continued writing to newspapers. In a letter to Allen, Coyle claimed he could not remain silent. The "anti-Catholic atmosphere," he worried, was festering as the "True Americans" continued "stirring up trouble." The priest expected Birmingham would be "flooded with all sorts of nasty literature."[101] Coyle admitted to his "bad judgment" but insisted that he had to resist that "old quack Dozier" and his "glorified Baptist sheet."[102]

During Coyle's tenure, Birmingham's Catholic population grew rapidly, due in large part to the area's booming industrial culture. In 1908, Birmingham had only 38,000 residents. Two years later, "Greater Birmingham" grew to 132,000. Industry, in the form of iron and steel mills, transformed Birmingham into the "Pittsburgh of the South." As in other cities of the era, the limited supply of white labor prompted industrialists to seek foreign workers. The influx of Catholic immigrants, however, eventuated in a series of conflicts. In 1916, in nearby Pratt City, arsonists burned down a Catholic church and school. The following year, Birmingham's anti-Catholic factions plotted to burn down Saint Paul's, but federal authorities warned Coyle in advance. During the fall 1917 elections, the subversive True Americans led an effort to oust city commission president George Ward. The Episcopalian Ward drew criticism for not banning Sunday movies, for having a lukewarm position on prohibition, and for supporting Birmingham's Irish Catholic police chief, Martin Egan. During the election lead-up, the True Americans circulated literature warning that the Knights of Columbus were on the brink of overtaking the city and that Ward was their Trojan horse. Ward's opponent, Nathanial Barrett, won convincingly. On assuming his office, Barrett removed the Catholic police chief from his post.[103] As in Florida, politicians won or lost in Birmingham based on their relationship with Catholics.

Many successful politicians in the Wiregrass Gulf South during the 1910s appealed to the anti-Catholic prejudices of the electorate. For Catholics in the region, this tendency was a symptom of the region's disordered values. In his letters to Bishop Allen in Mobile, Father Coyle frequently referred to the problems of religious prejudice in Birmingham. Coyle mentioned a "bitter political campaign" in 1916 between two "fair and bigoted non-Catholics," a Baptist and a Methodist preacher, neither of whom offered hope for area Catholics.[104] His political observations were sometimes critical of fellow Catholics. "If we had any competent laymen with sufficient backbone to come and depend on the Church and point out the un-Americanism of the anti-Catholic campaign it might be a good thing." The city's "Catholic men," Coyle rumbled, "seem to have a streak of yellow and are afraid to offend their non-Catholic neighbors. It would of course be better still if some decent fair minded non-Catholics would come into the open but at least up here the decent element shrug their shoulders and say it's not our fight."[105] Coyle's ideal society necessarily included Catholics. Those who believed otherwise were, for the priest, "un-American."

By 1920, Birmingham's population had reached two hundred thousand. The city had twelve Catholic churches and the largest Catholic population in Alabama. That year Birmingham's Robert E. Lee Klan No. 1 drew a strong following through the recruitment efforts of James Esdale. The growth of the Klan paralleled the rise of religious violence in Birmingham. In nearby Sylacauga, a gang of twenty masked men severely beat Pearce H. DeBardeleben, a Catholic pharmacist. The attackers alleged that DeBardeleben was a philanderer and a threat to women in the town. Also, after the Klan held a parade in downtown Birmingham, members flogged a white man and woman, both Catholic, accusing them of separate acts of miscegenation.[106] On August 11, 1921, a heated confrontation between Edwin R. Stephenson, a Methodist minister, and Father Coyle ensued on the rectory porch of Saint Paul's Church. The point of dispute was Stephenson's eighteen-year-old daughter, Ruth. Coyle had just wed Ruth to Pedro Gussman — a forty-three-year-old Catholic Puerto Rican immigrant and widower of eleven years. The shouts grew louder and, suddenly, Stephenson pulled out a pistol and fired three shots. The forty-eight-year-old Coyle fell to the ground with one bullet lodged in his head. Coyle's sister, Marcella, heard the commotion from the rectory kitchen. She rushed outside only to find her brother mortally wounded. Coyle soon died in Saint Vincent's Hospital. Meanwhile, Stephenson stumbled to the courthouse, gun in hand, and confessed to T. J. Shirley, the chief of police.[107]

The murder of Father James Coyle quickly became a national sensation. Reporters from near and far flooded the city. Writing for the *Nation*, Charles Sweeney labeled Birmingham "the American hot bed of anti-Catholic fanaticism."[108] Anti-Catholicism was a key motive in the murder and played a central role in the ensuing court case, but race and gender were also factors. The olive-toned Gussman was not black, but the defense team feverishly tried to prove that he was. A fear of miscegenation along with the jury's staunch nativism spun a web of paranoia that all but assured Stephenson's acquittal.[109] The details of Coyle's trial reveal with utmost clarity the opposing value systems of Catholics and nativists.

Following the priest's death, Bishop Allen shared his indignation with the Catholics of Birmingham. Coyle "preached the word of God in season and out of season, visiting the sick, instructing the little ones, and helping the poor, the needy and the afflicted." Coyle's commitment to church life, the bishop continued, influenced his civic ventures. A "great patriot," Coyle "loved his native land" and "was devoted to the best interests of his adopted country." Referencing the Great War, Allen recalled that Coyle did all "that a leader of God's people could do . . . to advance the interest of our country during" it. The bishop reported having visited Birmingham twenty-five years prior. "[I] was highly pleased," Allen remembered, with the "cordial greeting" from Catholics and "our non-Catholic brethren," who were then "broad-minded," "generous," and "kindly." But by 1915, there was friction. "What brought about the change? What caused the distrust and suspicion in this community? Who is responsible for bringing in disreputable lectures . . . to misrepresent the doctrines of the Church, to assail her clergy, and malign her consecrated virgins, the noblest women in the land?" Allen answered that it was, "disreputable politicians and secret societies." For the angry bishop, the "true Americans are un-American, because they are false to American principles of charity, justice and equality for all." He suspected that "the great majority" of Birmingham's residents felt the same. However, Allen charged, "they allowed this miserable clique to misrepresent and dishonor them." The bishop closed by stating that "Father Coyle was a noble, self-sacrificing and devoted priest, a martyr to his duty."[110]

Letters to Allen repeated the "martyr" theme, expressing a hope that something good would come of Coyle's death. Philip Pullen of Saint Michael's church in Pensacola wrote: "We were all shocked and grieved at the news of Fr. Coyle's tragic death. He is a great loss to the diocese. Still his death may bring a blessing on us, since it was that of a martyr."[111] From Rhode Island, one letter writer expressed feeling an "awful shock" when hearing of the murder. "I can't keep the affair out of my mind," exclaimed the mourning Catholic, who "prayed often for poor Fr. Coyle." The letter writer went on, calling Coyle "a sterling good priest" and "a martyr like his ancestors." The author predicted that Coyle's "sacrifice" would rid Birmingham of its "religious bigotry."[112] From Pittsburgh, Mother Aloysia sent her "heartiest sympathy to you and the bereaved diocese." She prayed that "the zealous priest" would find "his eternal reward."[113] Mother Praxedes of Kentucky suspected that the "appalling tragedy" had likely impacted "the heart of the Bishop, whose spiritual son has been cut down by an assassin." Praxedes then wondered why this happened to "a man so good and useful, so widely known, respected and loyal." Coyle was a "martyr to duty," she wrote, and she condemned the South's "rampant [bigotry]. . . . The blood of martyrs must be productive of good; if Birmingham prove unworthy, some other part of the Diocese will be blessed."[114]

Bishop Allen was alone neither in his outrage, nor in his moral position. These letters strongly expressed the judgment that southern Catholics were wrongly subjected to religious prejudice. This brand of bigotry ran contrary to the American promise of religious freedom, a promise that they believed made the nation exceptional. Some expected vindication from the trial. They would be disappointed. On August 13, the county coroner J. D. Russum testified at a grand jury trial that Stephenson was guilty of first-degree murder. The evidence against Stephenson was overwhelming, but by the opening of the October 17, 1921, trial, many factors were playing in his favor. The foreman of the all-Protestant jury was the Klansman James Esdale. Arguing before Judge William E. Fort on behalf of Stephenson was a talented quartet of attorneys led by Hugo L. Black. Stephenson, who earned a living as a barber and by marrying couples at the courthouse, could not pay his legal team. A sympathetic band of supporters, likely the True Americans and the Klan, raised the necessary funds. Hugo Black was a successful politician in Birmingham, who had served as the police court judge and county prosecutor. He also was a supporter of prohibition and antigambling legislation. In 1923, Black joined the Klan along with seventeen hundred others. This alliance helped him win a U.S. Senate seat in 1926, a post he remained in until earning an appointment to the U.S. Supreme Court in 1937.[115]

Before the case opened, media attention focused on Stephenson's daughter, Ruth. Readers discovered that Ruth had a series of disputes with her parents over her religious affiliation. At the age of twelve, Ruth reportedly began asking Father Coyle about Catholicism. Thereafter, her interest in the faith developed. Her parents vehemently objected to the church. According to the daughter, Rev. Stephenson "wished the whole Catholic institution was in hell," and her mother "wished a bomb was under Saint Paul's." Ruth also alleged that her father belonged to fraternal organizations where members wore white robes. In April 1921, Ruth secretly began taking steps toward joining the Catholic faith. When her parents became aware of her activities, Ruth sought refuge with her Catholic godfather, Fred Bender, a Birmingham merchant. Rev. Stephenson and the police found Ruth at Bender's home. According to Ruth, when they got home her father beat her with a razor strap.[116]

The trial opened, and Joseph Tate, the prosecuting attorney, called five witnesses: Coyle's sister, three witnesses who were standing near the rectory, and the physician who examined Coyle's wounds. Tate wanted to prove that there was no physical encounter between Stephenson and Coyle before the shooting, and that Stephenson shot a seated Father Coyle. Black and his team then called witnesses for three days. Most testified positively to Stephenson's character and claimed that the minister never beat Ruth. Chief Shirley and his deputies claimed that Stephenson had a lump on his head and a broken belt. Black intended to use these testimonies to argue that a fight broke out before Stephenson had fired his pistol in self-defense. Then on October 19, Stephenson stepped to the witness stand dressed in his clerical garb. He described himself as a good citizen who held no religious prejudice. The minister then began recounting the details of the murder, alleging that he did not know that Ruth had married Gussman until Coyle arrogantly informed him on the rectory porch. Stephenson, then weeping, recalled having shouted at Coyle, "You have treated me as dirty as a dog . . . you have ruined my home, that man is a negro." Coyle then rose, according to Stephenson, and "told me I was a heretical son of a bitch, and knocked me to my knees against the post, and kicked me in the side, and caught me in the suspenders and jerked me to my feet . . . and I fired."[117]

When Tate questioned Stephenson, the prosecutor reminded the jury that the coroner found no physical evidence of a struggle. Such inconsistencies in Stephenson's testimony would prove inconsequential. Black's most effective defense strategy was Ruth's husband, Pedro Gussman,

who took the stand near the end of the trial. One news article reported
that when Gussman walked into the court, "lights were arranged . . .
so that the darkness of Gussman's complexion would be accentuated."
Gussman, who spoke with a thick accent, testified that he had been in
America for nearly twenty-four years and that his parents were of Spanish
descent. Black's initial questions accused Gussman of proposing to Ruth
when she was thirteen. Ruth had spread this rumor in her media inter-
views prior to the trial. In the courtroom, Gussman repeatedly denied
it. Black then showed the jury a newspaper photo of Gussman. The attorney wanted them "to see this picture taken before the witness had his
hair worked on." Black turned to Gussman and remarked, "You've had
the curls rubbed from you hair since you had that picture taken?"[118]

Black wanted the jury to believe that Gussman was, in fact, black — thus
appealing to both their religious and racial prejudices. Assistant solici-
tor John Morrow would try to rebut this claim in his closing arguments.
"The eyes of the entire country are turned upon this Birmingham jury,"
Morrow concluded. "They want to see whether a Southern jury will free
a murderer because of prejudice." In his final remarks, Black retorted,
"If the eyes of the world are upon the verdict of this jury, I would write
that verdict in words that cannot be misunderstood, that the homes of
the people of Birmingham cannot be touched. If that brings disgrace,
God hasten the disgrace." Continuing, Black insisted that Coyle's vocation did not make him "divine." Ruth could not have possibly converted,
Black said, without the undue influence of Coyle. "A child of a Methodist
does not suddenly depart from her religion unless someone has planted
in her mind the seeds of influence. . . . [No] man has the right to in-
vade the home of another in an attempt to induce any member of that
household to accept a new religion." Stephenson's behavior, the attorney concluded, was the result of "an uncontrollable impulse."[119]

Black appealed to the deepest fears of his white Protestant jury. Once
the attorney finished, the jury left for deliberations. Before the trial,
some Catholics were optimistic. Father Joseph Sheridan of Saint Anne's
in Albany wrote, "I do not think there is any danger of the dastardly
act being repeated." He believed that the verdict would be "the death
sentence of bigotry in Birmingham."[120] Others were less hopeful. Father
Kitrick of Ensley, Alabama, gave a dire prediction for Birmingham. "The

murder of Father Coyle and horrible subsequent comments show the intensity of hatred the non-Catholic citizenry in general have for a foreign born public man. The hatred was all the more intense because that public man was a priest and an Irish priest."[121] A member of Saint Catherine's in Pratt City observed that "the respectable elements" of Birmingham recognized the severity of the crime. The "viler class," however, were "outspoken in their approval of the murder."[122] Father Joseph Malone of Saint Catherine's wondered, "What will be the verdict? No one can tell." He had little confidence in the jury. "Stephenson will not get his just deserts," he predicted. "Some think there will be a quick verdict [and] claim there is no grounds for anything but an acquittal."[123]

After one vote and four hours, the jury delivered a verdict of not guilty. Stephenson wept and shook hands with Black, the jury, and the judge. "I am a broken-hearted man," Stephenson sobbed, "but I am going to try to live so that no man on the jury will ever be sorry for the verdict rendered." Judge Fort then proclaimed that "no one can properly criticize the honest verdict of twelve honest men." For many, the decision was anything but "honest." In the wake of the trial, Catholics and non-Catholics alike saw the decision as a fundamental injustice. Former Alabama governor Emmet O'Neal, a Presbyterian, called the acquittal a deplorable example of "religious intolerance and bigotry." The verdict "made an open season in Alabama for the killing of Catholics. . . . We have not advanced far from barbarism if murder is to be justified on account of the religious creed of the victim. Whatever may be our wealth and resources, they will be but dross in the balance if Alabama is a state where murder is justified and where religious hate and intolerance sway the admiration of the law." He advised the audience to "select judges of our criminal courts men who are able, courageous and learned lawyers, and not merely self-seeking politicians."[124] Expressing a similar opinion in a letter to Bishop Allen, John Gunn, the bishop of Natchez wrote, "I wish to offer you a word of sympathy on the infamous verdict which was given in Birmingham. It would seem that killing is no murder and no crime in that part of Alabama."[125] From New York, W. H. Zinn wrote Allen to warn that a priest in Anniston was making "imprudent remarks" that were drawing attention from the Klan. Allen replied: "If the reverend gentleman mentioned in your letter thinks it advisable to say a word of condemnation of the atrocious verdict in the Stephenson case, no one can reasonably blame him for this."[126] Critics saw only social disorder in the Coyle decision. Catholics, they suspected, would not find justice in a land where religious affiliation precluded the possibility of a fair trial. In Birmingham, the advocates of nativism believed otherwise. Their "true" American was both white and Protestant. For this Birmingham jury, there was insufficient support for the claim of Catholic patriotism.

Remoralizing the South

In 1941, writing for the *Catholic Weekly*, Helen McGough remembered the life, death, and legacy of Father Coyle. She had taken First Communion with Coyle, and while she knew many priests, she was particularly fond of him. So, like many others, McGough felt helpless and angry when Stephenson was "acquitted with honors." "But the death of Father Coyle was the climax of the anti-Catholic feeling in Alabama," she argued. "After the trial there followed such revulsion of feeling among the right-minded who before had been bogged down in blindness and indifference that slowly and almost unnoticeably the Ku Klux Klan and their ilk began to lose favor among the people." Anti-Catholicism still existed, McGough noted, but most Alabamans had come to accept Catholics. "Let us not forget the martyred priest," she requested, "who by his death was the instrument for bringing about in such large degree this happy state of affairs."[127]

McGough's story of tragedy and redemption was also a story of demoralization and remoralization.[128] Religious liberty was a shared value, she assumed, that the majority had lost sight of in the era of nativism. But alas, the murder served as a sacred exchange, Coyle's death secured the future safety of Catholics and the social righteousness of Alabama. Indeed, conditions did improve for Catholics in Alabama and the South after Coyle's murder. And perhaps the majority did become more tolerant. But the two former ideological foes were finding common ground elsewhere, namely on race. As the black freedom struggle unfolded, white Catholics and Protestants agreed on the necessity of segregation. So while Catholics had remoralized the South for themselves, blacks still had more work ahead.[129]

If historians can agree on little else, at least they
should rejoice in the realization that they have
many true stories to tell about the human past.

— MARK T. GILDERHUS

What If?

CAROLINE WALKER BYNUM has written, "My understanding of the
historian's task precludes wholeness. Historians, like fishes of the sea, re-
gurgitate fragments. Only supernatural power can reassemble fragments
so completely that no particle of them is lost, or miraculously empower
the part to *be* the whole."[1] This book has investigated "fragments" of
the post-Reconstruction South's civil religious discourse, concentrat-
ing on the ways people created, defined, and defended their visions
of the good society. It has examined the moral weight of daily discussions, private ponderings, physical places, and public pronouncements
in relation to subjects like progress, race, gender, and religion. Civil religions took shape through memories of the past, hopes for the future,
Judeo-Christian beliefs, and national-local loyalties. Operating either as
imagined foils or as active participants, minority groups played no small
role in the Wiregrass Gulf South's civil religious identity. All told, these
fragments of history show how visions of the good society existed in a
perpetual state of tension, as many voices strove to actualize an understanding for how society *ought* to function.

By limiting this book to a small subregion in the American South,
during a small slice of time, I hope to leave readers wondering "What if?"

What if we discarded the pesky yet persistent definitions of civil religion that assume that American society shares a set of values around which all agree? What if we accepted that concepts like freedom, equality, and justice as enshrined in America's sacred documents have dynamic definitions and applications? What if we accepted that civil religion is a valuable concept that refers to a particular vision of the good society, tied to a specific time and place and deployed for the purpose of legitimizing one set of values over another? And what if we applied this methodology not only to the entire New South era—a time when people of varying races, creeds, regions, and backgrounds engaged in redefining themselves and their social situation in the wake of the Civil War and Reconstruction—but also to America as a whole? I expect that the result would be a new wave of scholarship that would integrate new voices and new perspectives into new narratives.

I have endeavored to represent the minority voices that participated in the civil religious conversation, not for the sake of "diversity" but rather because these "outsiders" were influential in shaping debates about race, gender, religious liberty, and the like. There are, of course, other minorities I have not accounted for, such as freethinkers, an anomaly in both the Bible Belt and the historiography of southern religion.[2] In Kentucky, Charles Chilton Moore, the grandson of revivalist and reformer Barton W. Stone, left his pulpit in 1865 and announced that he was an atheist. In Lexington, he became a noted newsman who published the notorious *Blue Grass Blade*. In it, Moore criticized organized religion and made a number of outré claims. For example, Moore agreed with the biblical exegesis of Charles Carroll, whose *The Negro a Beast* argued that blacks were not human and were therefore subject to slavery for all of eternity. The choice for blacks, in Moore's mind, was clear: either remain an enslaved Christian or, "if you are an intelligent and honest Negro and claim the right to be a free man you must be an Infidel."[3]

Moore was by no means inviting blacks to join him and the freethinking community. He was not an advocate of racial equality. Indeed, he supported deportation as a solution for the "negro question."[4] Still, Moore was a controversial figure whose critiques of religion resulted in hostile exchanges with the Christian majority, who sometimes manipulated the law to silence the "infidel editor." When federal authorities tried to censor Moore, he blasted that "no citizen, no institution, no paper or periodical, in America can be, or ought to be, discriminated against because of its anti-religious or anti-Christian utterances, as the Constitutional guarantee of religious liberty includes the right to express a non-belief in god as it does to express a belief in god." For Moore, America was exceptional precisely because it allowed the freethinker to think freely. But the American South's ruling powers were not prepared to include atheists. Moore's irreverent comments about the virgin birth, slanderous remarks aimed at prominent ministers, and advocacy of birth control landed him in court on numerous occasions. In 1899, he received a two-year sentence for violating obscenity laws.[5]

Moore's journalistic career was an exercise in resisting Protestant visions of the good society. In doing so, he generated his own social ideal, one where unbelief was tolerated and censorship was not. Freethinking failed to gain a wide audience in the South, but Moore forced his voice into the New South's complex civil religious discourse.[6] Following generations would continue adding new layers to this discourse, reviving old themes to fight new battles. The Lost Cause rallying cry of "state's rights" sounded strong in the civil rights era, and so too would black calls for freedom.[7] But floating in this civil religious river were the voices of Catholics and Jews from the North and South.

In the civil rights era, alienated southern Catholics became a bit less alien. Alabama's anti-Catholic mood stayed strong in the decades after the Coyle affair. Public rituals, such as Reformation Day celebrations, became platforms on which southern Protestants confirmed their religious and national identity in contrast to Catholics. "Romanism and Communism are fundamentally totalitarian," thundered one speaker at a 1950 celebration in Mobile. A Catholic newspaper responded, excoriating the "foul nature" of the address and assuring readers that "sincere Protestants" in Mobile rejected such ramblings. A peculiar alliance during the civil rights era helped ease this tension. As the black freedom struggle reached a peak in the 1960s, many lay Catholics rose to defend segregation, finding common ground with their Protestant counterparts around the gospel of white supremacy. As Andrew Moore has explained, this accord allowed Catholics to became the South's "tolerable alien." Yes, there were Catholic activists. Mobile's priest-educator Albert S. Foley spoke openly in favor of desegregation. But the Protestant majority criticized the priest not for his religious affiliation but rather for his political liberalism.[8]

Hastening the Catholic clergy's entry into the civil rights struggle were the reforms of the Second Vatican Council, which called on the faithful to engage in social justice issues. A visible demonstration of this new activism came after the Bloody Sunday attacks in Selma, Alabama. A range of religious leaders traveled southward to protest, and among them were Catholic sisters. Meanwhile, the Sisters of Saint Joseph, who had an established presence in Selma, entered the fray in a more subtle manner, nursing those harmed in the conflict, visiting the imprisoned, and offering hospitality to the visiting protesters. They also had a long history of resisting the Jim Crow South through their labors in what Amy Koehlinger has named the "racial apostolate," a network of missionary activities that took sisters into black homes, neighborhoods, and schools. Such activities put the sisters on the radars of white supremacists. "The KKK is watching you," read a sign hung on the convent door in 1950. But the sisters persisted. Whether in the limelight or not, the fight for racial justice brought them out of the convent and into the contested public arena.[9]

Jews also traveled to Selma for the demonstration. Rabbis, students, and members of Jewish organizations all marched. Perhaps most notable among the Jewish participants was Abraham Heschel, who processed alongside Martin Luther King Jr. "I felt a sense of the Holy in what I was doing," Heschel confided in his diary, "as though my legs were praying."[10] There were also native southern Jews on hand, a fact that drew negative attention not only from white segregationists but also from coreligionists. Selma's Sol Tepper was a noted Jewish segregationist. For him, the sight of Jews marching registered as civic and religious disorder. Writing to one rabbi who participated in the march, Tepper fumed, "I am Jewish. I am proud of my Jewish heritage. I am not proud that you call yourself a Jew. In fact, I say you are not." According to Clive Webb, Tepper and other Jewish segregationists were not representative of the southern Jewish opinion on civil rights. Rather Webb points to Selma businessman Arthur Lewis and his wife, Muriel, as more typical. Although they had relocated from the North, the two had become part of the southern establishment. Secretly, though, they supported civil rights. Bloody Sunday drew them out of their shell, and the couple composed a letter to potential Jewish allies encouraging them to become involved. "We realize that we can no longer be afraid to speak out, but that does not mean that we are no longer a bit fearful, and we do not—nor should you—condemn our moderate friends for their silence. We know that this area is full of potential violence." Predictably, their public support of civil rights drew the scorn of the southern establishment. The stress likely precipitated Arthur Lewis's early death at the age of fifty-three. Still, he and his wife identified with the alienation felt by blacks and struggled to put their faith into action just as many other southern Jews of the era did.[11]

It cannot be overstated that in the South the most visible civil religious contest was waged between black and white Protestants. The 1954 *Brown v. Board of Education* decision motivated the white South to vehemently protest desegregation in schools and society. They argued that desegregation would destroy the very foundation of southern life, and ministers entering the fray cited texts like Acts 17:26 ("And [God] hath made of one blood all nations of men for to dwell on all the face of the earth, and hath determined the times before appointed, and the bounds of their habitation"). Capitalizing on the phrase "bounds of their habitation," preachers used the passage to insist that segregation was divinely sanctioned. At the same time, civil rights proponents referenced this very same passage, emphasizing the universal implications underlying "one blood of all nations."[12] In many respects, as Andrew Manis has framed it, this was a battle between "the South's two civil religions," one black and one white.[13] But the voices of Catholics and Jews add nuance to this history, showing how religious and social forces from outside the southern Christian world influenced the debate. Put bluntly, this was not *just* a story of black and white. It was instead a story of black, white, Protestant, Catholic, Jew, North, South, Republican, Democrat, and a host of others.

What if we put all of these voices together into one civil religious history of civil rights? And what if we applied a comparative, nonlinear, decentered approach to all of American history? Such a methodology offers numerous opportunities for contextualizing significant moments and movements in American history. Take manifest destiny, for example. As America debated the annexation of Texas in 1845, New York's *Democratic Review* called for an end to the quarreling. If the United States did not occupy this space, "other nations" would overtake it, thereby "thwarting our policy and hampering our power, limiting our greatness and checking the fulfillment of our manifest destiny to overspread the continent allotted by Providence for the free development of our yearly multiplying millions."[14] For this author and the legions who agreed, westward expansion was about fulfilling God's will for America. In the decades before and after this proclamation, movement into new territories represented a civil religious act of appropriating land, asserting authority, and sending a statement to the world. Part of this statement, for Presbyterian clergyman Lyman Beecher, was that America was *not* Catholic. "The moral destiny of our nation, and all our institutions and hopes, and the world's hopes, turn on the character of the West, and the competition now is for that preoccupancy in the education of the rising generation, in which Catholics and infidels have got the start of us. . . . If we gain the West, all is safe; if we lose it, all is lost."[15]

Beecher saw the western landscape through a Protestant lens and sought to coerce others to feel his fear. But this civil religious story had additional voices. Missionary priests charged Beecher and other purveyors of anti-Catholicism with betraying America's promise of religious freedom.[16] And for Native Americans, the Ghost Dance movement was a source of cultural pride, social unity, and hope in the midst of despair and displacement.[17] An interactive civil religious history of manifest destiny would account for all of these perspectives, showing how each position influenced the other.

While pockets of scholars have emphasized the need to democratize civil religion, the old model persists. American civil religion, according to George Marsden, celebrates soldiers who make "the supreme sacrifice" for their nation by fighting and dying in war. He calls Quakers, Mennonites, Amish, and Moravians the "major exceptions." These dissenters, Marsden explains, earn traitorous reputations from fellow Americans for "refusing to fight in a good cause."[18] Are these pacifists truly civil religious "exceptions"? Or do they have a *different*, albeit controversial, social ideal wherein nonviolence is an uncontestable "good cause"? And what about the exceptions? Major General Smedley D.

Butler, nicknamed the "fighting Quaker," was the most decorated Marine Corps officer of the early twentieth century, who as a civilian became a harsh critic of war.[19]

Americans have embraced war, rejected war, and in Butler's case, both. The task now is to consider each position and place them in conversation with each other. Rather than limiting America's past to one civil religious voice, we must begin inserting the voices of other groups—irrespective of their size or popularity. This will both breathe new life into old discussions and do justice to marginalized groups and ideologies in America's history. Minority groups have not simply resisted the status quo. They have also produced alternate visions of the good society using unique cultural resources. Acknowledging this will allow scholars to begin retelling the "many true stories" of America's civil religious history.

Population Data for the South and Wiregrass Region

Population in the South

YEAR	SOUTH	SOUTH ATLANTIC	FLORIDA	GEORGIA	ALABAMA
1870 TOTAL	12,288,020	5,853,610	187,748	1,184,109	996,922
(Black)	(4,420,811)	(2,216,705)	(91,689)	(545,142)	(475,510)
1880	16,516,568	7,597,197	269,493	1,542,180	1,262,505
	(5,953,903)	(2,941,202)	(126,690)	(725,133)	(600,103)
1890	20,028,059	8,857,922	391,422	1,837,353	1,513,401
	(6,760,577)	(3,262,690)	(166,180)	(858,815)	(678,489)
1900	24,523,527	10,443,480	528,542	2,216,331	1,828,697
	(7,922,969)	(3,729,017)	(230,730)	(1,034,813)	(827,307)
1910	29,389,330	12,194,895	752,619	2,609,121	2,138,093
	(8,749,427)	(4,112,488)	(308,669)	(1,176,987)	(908,282)
1920	33,125,803	13,990,272	968,470	2,895,832	2,348,174
	(8,912,231)	(4,325,120)	(329,487)	(1,206,365)	(900,652)

Source: "Historical Census Statistics on Population Totals By Race, 1790 to 1990, and By Hispanic Origin, 1970 to 1990, for the United States, Regions, Divisions, and States," U.S. Census Bureau, http://www.census.gov/population/www/documentation/twps0056.html (accessed Nov. 1, 2010).

Population in the Wiregrass Region

YEAR	LEON COUNTY (Tallahassee)	ESCAMBIA COUNTY (Pensacola)	MOBILE COUNTY (Mobile)	THOMAS COUNTY (Thomasville)	DOUGHERTY COUNTY (Albany)
1870 TOTAL	15,236	7,817	49,311	14,523	11,517
(Black)	(12,341)	(2,880)	(21,107)	(8,363)	(9,424)
1880	19,662	12,156	48,653	20,597	12,622
	(16,840)	(5,302)	(21,443)	(12,213)	(10,670)
1890	17,752	20,188	51,587	26,154	12,206
	(14,631)	(8,706)	(22,804)	(15,028)	(10,231)
1900	19,887	28,313	62,740	31,076	13,679
	(16,001)	(11,929)	(28,434)	(17,450)	(11,228)
1910	19,427	38,029	80,854	29,071	16,035
	(14,726)	(15,111)	(34,719)	(17,086)	(12,049)
1920	18,059	49,386	100,117	33,044	20,063
	(12,167)	(15,221)	(39,667)	(17,263)	(13,370)

Source: "County Population Census Counts 1900–90," U.S. Census Bureau,
http://www.census.gov/population/www/censusdata/cencounts/index.html
(accessed Nov. 1, 2010).

NOTES

ARCHIVE ABBREVIATIONS

ADAH   Alabama Department of Archives and History, Montgomery

CDA   Catholic Diocese Archives, Mobile, Ala.

FSA   Florida State Archives, Tallahassee

FSU   Florida State University Library, Tallahassee, Fla.

GSA   Georgia State Archives, Atlanta

THL   Thomasville Genealogical, History & Fine Arts Library, Thomasville, Ga.

THS   Thomas County Historical Society, Thomasville, Ga.

TMA   Thoronateeksa Museum Archives, Albany, Ga.

UF   Florida History Special Collections, P.K. Yonge Library, University of Florida, Gainesville

USA   University of South Alabama Archives, Mobile

UWF   University of West Florida Special Collections, Pensacola

INTRODUCTION

1. Charles Reagan Wilson, *Baptized in Blood*, 12–13, 98–99.

2. Harvey, "Religion in the American South," 394, 90.

3. Samuel S. Hill Jr., *Southern Churches in Crisis*, 73–88, 121–22.

4. Harvey, "Religion in the American South," 390.

5. Schweiger, *The Gospel Working Up*, 6.

6. Harvey wrote that "Wilson's anthropologically informed work will remain required reading for southern historians" ("Religion in the American South," 394). Wilson's recent work has given sufficient attention to the varied perspectives of southern life. In his general introduction to *The New Encyclopedia of Southern Culture*, Wilson explains that the volume "provides information and

perspective on the diversity of cultures in a geographic and imaginative place with a long history and distinctive character" (1:xv).

7. Gaines Foster suggests that the Lost Cause simply "eased the region's passage through a particularly difficult period of social change" (*Ghosts of the Confederacy*, 6). As the years passed after the Civil War, white southerners took up the culture of progressivism, and the nostalgic Lost Cause became less influential. Taking another approach, W. Scott Poole argues that "Confederate religion" (rather than "civil religion") cultivated a culture of conservatism in the South Carolina upcountry that led whites to "[practice] the values of the past in the present" (*Never Surrender*, 53). Poole modifies Wilson's Lost Cause thesis and limits his claims to one population and one region, thereby not overextending his sources.

8. Bellah, "Civil Religion in America," 168. French philosopher Jean-Jacques Rousseau first coined the phrase "civil religion" (*The Social Contract*, 115–25), a fact duly noted by Bellah. However, the work of another Frenchman, sociologist Emile Durkheim, provides the primary theoretical foundation for Bellah's work. Durkheim proposed that religion existed as a necessary element of social cohesion: "If religion gave birth to all that is essential in society," concluded the sociologist, "that is so because the idea of society is the soul of religion" (*The Elementary Forms of Religious Life*, 421).

9. See Mathisen, "Twenty Years after Bellah."

10. Cherry, introduction, 16.

11. Demerath and Williams, "Civil Religion in an Uncivil Society," 166.

12. Walker, "Liberators for Colonial Anahuac," 184, 199. Other studies employing the Demerath/Williams thesis include Woocher, *Sacred Survival*; Harrison, "School Ceremonies for Yitzhak Rabin"; Whillock, "Dream Believers"; Cristi, *From Civil Religion to Political Religion*.

13. See Semonche, *Keeping the Faith*; Meyer, *Myths in Stone*; Smith, *Daniel Webster*.

14. Chernus, review of *Myths America Lives By*, 541.

15. Bellah, "Comment," 147; Bellah et al., *Habits of the Heart*. Bellah's comments are a response to a literature review on civil religion by James Mathisen ("Twenty Years after Bellah"). In his rejoinder, Mathisen concedes that the "substance" of civil religion would remain an important topic.

16. Hammond et al., "American Civil Religion Revisited," 2, 5.

17. Williams, "Visions of the Good Society," 2. Williams did not intentionally follow Bellah and Hammond. However, he did "become frustrated with the task of 'finding' or 'identifying' civil religion as a distinct socio-cultural phenom-

enon." So he too jettisoned the phrase but kept the idea of civil religion in the background, examining "the moral formulations that shape political discourse and action" (e-mail from Williams to the author, Feb. 25, 2007).

18. Schofield, *Saving the City*; Etzioni, *The New Golden Rule*.

19. Bellah et al., *The Good Society*, 4.

20. Hammond et al., "American Civil Religion Revisited," 5; Williams, "Visions of the Good Society." See also Williams, "Constructing the Public Good"; Williams, "Religion as Political Resource."

21. Williams, "Visions of the Good Society," 30.

22. Wilson, *Baptized in Blood*, 79–83.

23. "Sorrow and Oppression," *Weekly Floridian* (Tallahassee, Fla.), May 22, 1877.

24. Parsons, "Durkheim's Contribution," 122; Bellah, *Beyond Belief*, 115.

25. "Florida as Great Cattle Growing State," *Pensacola (Fla.) Journal*, Jul. 14, 1907.

26. McGregory, *Wiregrass Country*; Crowley, *Primitive Baptists of the Wiregrass South*. As a historic region, the Wiregrass South starts north of Savannah and extends through southwest Georgia, northwest Florida, and southeast Alabama. I stick roughly to these boundaries, but I do not cover the entire region. Additionally, since the ports of Pensacola and Mobile arguably sit outside of the Wiregrass region, I included "Gulf" in the name.

27. Other books using this approach include Stowell, *Rebuilding Zion*; Schweiger, *The Gospel Working Up*; Moore, *The South's Tolerable Alien*; Coker, *Liquor*.

28. H. K. Brundydge, "The System Is All Wrong," *Weekly Tallahasseean* (Tallahassee, Fla.), Jul. 4, 1901.

29. Quoted in McPherson, *Battle Cry Freedom*, 761.

30. Diary entry, Mar. 6, 1864, reproduced in Eppes, *Through Some Eventful Years*, 261; Susan Bradford Eppes, "The Battle of Natural Bridge," speech, n.d., Susan Bradford Eppes Papers, FSU. See also Brown, "The Civil War," 244.

31. Grantham, *Southern Progressivism*, 60–64; Proctor, "Prelude to the New Florida."

32. For population data, see the appendix.

33. Woodward, *Origins of the New South*, 125–26; Grantham, *Southern Progressivism*, 47–51.

34. Rogers, *Thomas County*, 102, 98–127.

35. Blacks were lynched at a rate of 79.8 per 100,000 in Florida; 41.8 in Georgia; 43.7 in Louisiana; and 52.8 in Mississippi (Tolonay and Beck, *A Festival*

of Violence, 37–38; Ortiz, *Emancipation Betrayed*, 61–63). For a listing of lynchings in Florida, see Ginzburg, *100 Years of Lynching*, 256–57.

36. Litwack, *Trouble in Mind*, 290.

37. Grossman, *Land of Hope*; Cohen, *At Freedom's Edge*.

38. Cash, *The Mind of the South*, viii.

39. See Michael O'Brien, "A Private Passion."

40. Harvey, *Redeeming the South*, 17.

41. Stout, *Upon the Altar of the Nation*.

CHAPTER ONE. *Progressive Voices, Traditional Voices*

1. Crary, *Reminiscences of the Old South*, 97, 86, 124, 140.

2. Campbell, *Brother to a Dragonfly*, 22.

3. Crary, *Sixty Years a Brickmaker*, 68, 67.

4. Callahan, Lofton, and Seales, "Allegories of Progress."

5. Grantham, *Southern Progressivism*, xv; Gaston, *The New South Creed*. It should be noted that the origin and uniqueness of southern progressivism is a subject of historical debate. Grantham calls southern progressivism "an indigenous phenomenon" (25). But many historians since have emphasized the characteristics of progressivism shared by North and South, chief among them being Edward Ayers; see his *Promise of the New South*. For a comprehensive overview of the debate, see Samuel L. Webb, "Southern Politics."

6. Stowell, "Why 'Redemption'?"; Harvey, *Redeeming the South*.

7. Wilmer, *The Recent Past*, 30. Elected in 1861, Wilmer (1816–1900) was the second Episcopal bishop of Alabama and the only bishop consecrated in the Protestant Episcopal Church in the Confederate States. See Pennington, "Organization of the Protestant Episcopal Church."

8. Qtd. in Pruitt and Durham, *The Private Life*, 57–58.

9. Foner, *Reconstruction*, 587–601.

10. Ayers, *The Promise of the New South*, 8.

11. Shadgett, "Charles Jones Jenkins, Jr.," 220–44; Northern, *Men of Mark in Georgia*, 281–93.

12. Young Female College took its name from Elijah Remer Young, a Thomasville planter, and officially opened in February 1869 (Rogers, *Thomas County*, 220–21).

13. David S. Walker, "Commencement Address Delivered before the Graduating Class of Young Female College," Thomasville, Ga., June 25, 1872, Hopkins Collection, THL.

14. Cummings, *Gleanings from the Southland*, 10, 11. Cummings, who directed hospitals in Tennessee and Georgia, was one of the most famous Confederate nurses during the Civil War (Harwell, *Kate*; McPherson, *Battle Cry Freedom*, 478–80).

15. "Our Winter Climate Visitors' Pleasure," *St. Lucie County (Fla.) Tribune*, Dec. 23, 1910.

16. Brevard, *A History of Florida*, 124, 25. Brevard was an established member of Tallahassee's elite. One of her grandfathers, Richard Keith Call, was twice a territorial governor in Florida (1836–39, 1841–44) and was a wealthy planter in Leon County before the war. See Doherty, *Richard Keith Call*.

17. Wilmer, *The Recent Past*, 141, 43.

18. Brevard, *A History of Florida*, 203.

19. Wilmer, *The Recent Past*, 12–13.

20. Letter from William P. Homer, Thomasville, Ga., to H. S. L. Morse, Esq., Boston, Mass., May 30, 1876, in Joseph Tillman and C. P. Goodyear, eds., "Southern Georgia: A Pamphlet Published Under Auspices of the Savannah, Florida & Western Railway, Brunswick & Albany Rail Road, and Macon & Brunswick Rail Road," 1881, TMA.

21. Susan Bradford Eppes, "The Battle of Natural Bridge," speech, n.d., Susan Bradford Eppes Papers, FSU. "Vindication" was a common word in Lost Cause rhetoric. The history of white southerners often absolved the section from having done any wrong that would have led to the war (Wilson, *Baptized in Blood*, 161–82).

22. Susan Bradford Eppes, "What Does Florida Mean to the Tourist and What Does the Tourist Mean to Florida," n.d., Susan Bradford Eppes Papers, FSU.

23. John B. Jones, "Pensacola," draft copy of a speech, ca. 1920, Jones Family Papers, UWF; John B. Jones, "Historical and Descriptive Sketch of Pensacola, Florida," unpublished manuscript, Oct. 1924, Jones Family Papers, UWF.

24. Grantham, *Southern Progressivism*, 274. See also, Ayers, *The Promise of the New South*, 417–20; Link, *The Paradox of Southern Progressivism*, 124–59.

25. "Dedicating the New School Building," *Weekly Floridian* (Tallahassee, Fla.), Jan. 6, 1887.

26. Elma L. MaClay, "Public School Reminiscences: Pamphlet for the Dedication Exercises of the New Public School Building No. 1 in Pensacola, Florida," Jan. 3–4, 1887, Jones Family Papers, UWF.

27. Grantham, *Southern Progressivism*, 320–48.

28. Thomas P. Janes, "Handbook of the State of Georgia," 1876, Hopkins Collection, THL; Northern, *Men of Mark in Georgia*, 182–85.

29. Rogers, *Thomas County*, 385–87. Bryan was a lawyer in Thomasville who began his journalistic career in 1855 with his Whig-slanting *Southern Enterprise.* During the Civil War, the *Enterprise* ceased operations while Bryan served with Georgia's Fifty-seventh Infantry Regiment. In 1865, Bryan revived the newspaper, but by 1873, local competition combined with economic depression had forced him out of business.

30. Lucius C. Bryan, editorial, *South Georgia Agriculturist* (Thomasville, Ga.), Jan. 1878, 7–8, Hopkins Collection, THL.

31. Lucius C. Bryan, "The Thomasville Spring Fair," *South Georgia Agriculturalist* (Thomasville, Ga.), Apr. 1878, 151–52, Hopkins Collection, THL.

32. The phrase "redeemers of the soil" is the subtitle of an essay by Edwin Mims called "The South Realizing Itself."

33. "When Will Wonders Cease?" news clipping, ca. 1920, Hopkins Collection, THL.

34. Montgomery, "Radical Republicanism in Pennsylvania"; Wiggins, "The 'Pig Iron' Kelley Riot."

35. Kelley, *The Old South and the New*, 1–2, 19, 161–62.

36. Qtd. in Tindall and Shi, *America*, 846.

37. Proctor, "Prelude to the New Florida," 278.

38. Etemadi, "'A Love-Mad Man.'"

39. "The Election of Senator Jones," *Weekly Floridian* (Tallahassee, Fla.), Jan. 18, 1881.

40. "Florida and Senator Jones," *Weekly Floridian* (Tallahassee, Fla.), Jan. 25, 1881.

41. "An Address Delivered by Hon. Charles W. Jones," *Weekly Floridian* (Tallahassee, Fla.), Jan. 25, 1881.

42. "Ex-Senator Jones's Misfortune" *New York Times*, Nov. 24, 1887.

43. "Ex-Senator Charles W. Jones," *New York Times*, Oct. 16, 1887.

44. Etemadi, "'A Love-Mad Man.'"

45. John B. Jones, "Biographical Sketch of Charles W. Jones," manuscript, ca. Oct. 1897, Jones Family Papers, UWF.

46. Letter from William A. Blount, Pensacola, Fla., to John B. Jones, Pensacola, Fla., Nov. 30, 1897, Jones Family Papers, UWF.

47. "In the State He Loved," *Pensacola (Fla.) Daily Star*, ca. Oct. 1897, Jones Family Papers, UWF.

48. L. Hilton Green, editorial, *Pensacola (Fla.) Daily Times*, ca. Oct. 1897, Jones Family Papers, UWF.

49. "Charles W. Jones Dead," *New York Times*, Oct. 13, 1897.

50. See chapter 5.

51. Qtd. in Champion, *Giant Tracking*, 1–2.

52. Ibid.

53. Williamson, "W. D. Chipley."

54. Ibid., 334–35.

55. Rerick, *Memoirs of Florida*, 482. Rerick claimed that Elizabeth Chipley, William's wife, was in possession of the letter from Brown to Stephens.

56. "The Ashburn Murder Trial Suspended," *New York Times*, Jul. 23, 1868. For more on the Ashburn affair, see Jesse Earle Bowden, "The Colonel from Columbus."

57. Editorial, *Pensacola (Fla.) Commercial*, Nov. 10, 1883.

58. Woodward, *Origins of the New South*, 6–10.

59. Johnson, "The Florida Railroad"; Standiford, *Last Train to Paradise*.

60. Charles H. Bliss, "Pensacola's Social Features," *Bliss Quarterly*, Jan. 1897, 121, UF.

61. Morgan, "History of Albany," 18. See also McGuire, "The Railroads of Georgia," 98–127.

62. Ayers, *The Promise of the New South*, 9–13; Johnson, "The Florida Railroad"; Summers, "Railroads," 656–58.

63. Qtd. in Williamson, "W. D. Chipley," 339.

64. Ironically, Call had once unknowingly defended Chipley on the federal senate floor when Chipley had been accused of murdering Ashburn (Roberts, "Wilkinson Call, Soldier and Senator," 2:194).

65. Peter Stanley, "An Interesting Story of Col. W. D. Chipley," *Pensacola (Fla.) Journal*, Nov. 8, 1908.

66. Boylan, *Sunday School.*

67. Rieser, *The Chautauqua Movement.*

68. Ibid., 12, 142, 39–45; Griffith, "Chautauqua."

69. Qtd. in Griffith, "Chautauqua," 276.

70. Grady, "The New South," 13.

71. Rieser, *The Chautauqua Movement*, 143.

72. Gaston, *The New South Creed*, 86.

73. DeBolt, "The Florida Chautauqua"; Beemer, "The Florida Chautauqua as Text."

74. "The Florida Chautauqua," program for the first annual session, Feb. 10–Mar. 9, 1885, UWF.

75. John L. McKinnon, "History of Walton County," typescript, ca. 1911, 161, FSU.

76. "The Florida Chautauqua," program for the first annual session, Feb. 10–Mar. 9, 1885, UWF.

77. Link, *The Paradox of Southern Progressivism*, 54; Ownby, *Subduing Satan*, 122–45; Schweiger, *The Gospel Working Up*, 145–46.

78. "Sabbath Desecration," *Weekly Tallahasseean*, Aug. 8, 1901.

79. "Strong Sermon by Dr. Sibley," *Pensacola (Fla.) Journal*, Mar. 23, 1909.

80. A group of professors at the 1885 chautauqua discovered that the lake was actually a spring (DeBolt, "The Florida Chautauqua," 8).

81. W. F. Mallalieu, "Another Chautauqua," *Mount Dora (Fla.) Voice*, Apr. 23, 1886.

82. DeBolt, "The Florida Chautauqua," 360. Chipley was active in education, sitting on the board of trustees for the Florida State Agricultural College, Stetson University, and the Tallahassee Seminary (Champion, *Giant Tracking*, 2). Williamson mentions that he's active in education, but Champion lists the institutions, which are also named on his monument.

83. George B. Loud, "A Chautauqua in the Wilds of Western Florida," program for the twelfth annual session, Feb. 20–Mar. 18, 1896, 4–5, UWF.

84. Rerick, *Memoirs of Florida*, 482.

85. *Pensacola (Fla.) Advance-Gazette*, Oct. 1887; "Pensacola," *Weekly Floridian* (Tallahassee, Fla.), Oct. 13, 1887.

86. Williamson, "W. D. Chipley," 348–52.

87. *Daily Florida Citizen* (Jacksonville, Fla.), May 15, 1897; *Pensacola (Fla.) Daily News*, May 19, 1897.

88. *Pensacola (Fla.) Daily News*, June 8, 1897. Chipley had initially funded this newspaper and first announced his intention to run for senator in it (Bowden, "Editors and Other Hell Raisers," 14).

89. *Pensacola Daily News*, June 8, 1897.

90. "Old Campaigner on Politics and Politicians," *Pensacola (Fla.) Journal*, Feb. 10, 1907.

91. Roberts, "Wilkinson Call, Soldier and Senator," 2:186.

92. "Last Sad Rites over Remains of Hon. W. D. Chipley," *Pensacola (Fla.) Daily News*, Dec. 4, 1897.

93. Ibid. The faculty of Florida Agricultural College added, "We share in the grief of their surviving loved ones and extend to them our deepest sympathies, cheering them with the thought that faithful workers for the good of others lose not their reward in the life beyond."

94. Letter from A. Stoddard, New York, N.Y., Dec. 1, 1897, printed in the *Pensacola (Fla.) Daily News*, Dec. 4, 1897.

95. "The Florida Chautauqua," program for the fourteenth annual session, Feb. 17–Mar. 23, 1898, 5, UWF.

96. "Resolutions and Remarks of the Memorial Exercises in the Senate of Florida on the Death of Hon. W. D. Chipley and Hon. Chas. J. Perrenot," pamphlet, Apr. 13, 1899, FSU.

97. Ibid.

98. Ibid.

99. Contract between the W. D. Chipley Monument Committee, Pensacola, Fla., and the Muldoon Monument Company, Louisville, Ky., Jul. 12, 1899, Beggs and Lane Collection, Blount and Blount and Carter Papers, UWF.

100. Qtd. in Stowell, "Why 'Redemption'?" 141.

CHAPTER TWO. *Black Voices, White Voices*

1. Benjamin J. Davis, *Communist Councilman from Harlem*, 22, 26.

2. Cresswell, *In Place/Out of Place*.

3. "Jefferies Won't Fight?" *New York Times*, Oct. 25, 1909.

4. Qtd. in Ward, *Unforgivable Blackness*, 283.

5. "Attacks Johnson Marriage," *New York Times*, Dec. 12, 1912.

6. Qtd. in Ward, *Unforgivable Blackness*, 322.

7. "Jack Johnson Wedding Denounced in Congress," *New York Tribune*, Dec. 12, 1912. The article notes that Roddenberry's speech to Congress was met with continuous cheers from fellow southerners.

8. Bailey, *Race Orthodoxy in the South*, 92–93.

9. Haller, *Outcasts from Evolution*; Frederickson, *Racism*, 49–96.

10. Dunning, *Essays on the Civil War*, 74–80. See also Smith, *An Old Creed for the New South*.

11. Craighead, *From Mobile's Past*, 128–32.

12. Cummings, *Gleanings from the Southland*, 9, 259, 264.

13. Editorial, *Weekly Floridian* (Tallahassee, Fla.), May 15, 1877.

14. Eppes, *Through Some Eventful Years*, 301.

15. Eppes, *The Negro of the Old South*, 182–83. Eppes's condemnation of black religion was echoed through the white South. See Harvey, *Redeeming the South*, 107–35; Dorsey, *To Build Our Lives Together*, 69.

16. Eppes, *The Negro of the Old South*, ix, 175.

17. Crary, *Reminiscences of the Old South*, 61–62.

18. Litwack, *Trouble in Mind*, 211; Luker, *The Social Gospel*, 30–56.

19. "White Man's Whiskey, and the South's Great Race Problem," *Pensacola (Fla.) Journal*, Sept. 22, 1907.

20. Coker, *Liquor*, 124–73.

21. Ayers, *The Promise of the New South*, 310–38. On the promotion of the Wiregrass Gulf South, see Rogers, *Thomas County*, 146–53; Paisley, *From Cotton to Quail*; Hackney, *Populism and Progressivism in Alabama*; Ortiz, *Emancipation Betrayed*, 12–17.

22. Grady, "The New South," 11, 9.

23. William D. Chipley, "Pensacola (The Naples of America) and Its Surroundings Illustrated," pamphlet, 1877, UWF.

24. H. W. Hopkins, "Thomasville, Georgia: The Health Resort," 1891, Hopkins Collection, THL.

25. Tallahassee Board of County Commissioners and the Board of Trade, "Tallahassee Leon County Florida," n.d., UF.

26. Qtd. in Litwack, *Trouble in Mind*, 218.

27. G. B. Zimmerman Diary, Mar. 24, 1895, GSA.

28. Samuel Proctor, "Prelude to the New Florida."

29. Erastus G. Hill Diary, Jan. 19, n.d., Feb. 2–3, 1877, Florida Miscellaneous Manuscripts Collection, UF.

30. William George Bruce, "A Short Visit South Milwaukee-Wisconsin," ca. 1921, William George Bruce Papers (1881–1978), UWF. While school segregation was not always a legal norm in the North, it was part of the cultural code of the region. See Douglas, *Jim Crow Moves North*.

31. Interview with J. E. Callahan, "The Carpet-Bagger's Defense," Oct. 13, 1907, Florida Miscellaneous Manuscripts Collection, UF.

32. Pasquier, "'Though Their Skin Remains Brown,'" 369.

33. Bresnahan, *Seeing Florida with a Priest*, 77.

34. Qtd. in Davis and Phelps, *"Stamped with the Image of God"*, 97.

35. "An Important Movement for Colored Catholics," *Mobile (Ala.) Josephite*, Dec. 1909.

36. Letter from Edward Allen, Mobile, Ala., to Thomas B. Donovan, Montgomery, Ala., Jan. 1901, Bishop Edward Patrick Allen Collection, CDA.

37. Qtd. in Ochs, "The Ordeal of the Black Priest," 50.

38. Letter from Edward Allen, Mobile, Ala., to Thomas B. Donovan, Montgomery, Ala., Jul. 25, 1902, Bishop Edward Patrick Allen Collection, CDA.

39. McGreevy, *Catholicism and American Freedom*, 207–09.

40. Qtd. in Ochs "The Ordeal of the Black Priest," 64. On the mix of anti-Catholicism and racism evoked by Dorsey, see Woodward, *Tom Watson*, 421.

41. Qtd. in Raboteau, *A Fire in the Bones*, 126, 127–28. See also Bennett, *Religion and the Rise of Jim Crow*, 193–228.

42. "Communications: From Two Well Known Colored Citizens of Albany," *Albany (Ga.) Daily Herald*, May 13, 1899.

43. Oltman, *Sacred Mission, Worldly Ambition*, 15–33.

44. "Negro Leadership," *Waycross (Ga.) Gazette and Land Bulletin*, Jan. 27, 1900.

45. Bragaw, "Status of Negroes."

46. F. E. Washington, "Pensacola's Colored People," *Bliss Quarterly*, Jan. 1897, UFL.

47. Booker T. Washington, *The Negro in Business*, 230, 236.

48. Rogers, *Thomas County*, 188–89.

49. Qtd. in ibid., 188.

50. Qtd. in Love, *History*, 90, 98–99.

51. Qtd. in ibid., 100

52. Ayers, *The Promise of the New South*, 142–43.

53. James Melvin Washington, *Frustrated Fellowship*, 147–51.

54. "Race Prejudice," *New York Times*, Sept. 13, 1889.

55. Qtd. in Washington, *Frustrated Fellowship*, 150.

56. E. K. Love, "Emancipation Oration!" speech, Jan. 2, 1888, Daniel A. P. Murray Pamphlet Collection, Library of Congress, Washington, D.C.

57. Qtd. in Montgomery, *Under Their Own Vine and Fig Tree*, 248.

58. William Watson Davis, *The Civil War*, 586.

59. Ortiz, *Emancipation Betrayed*, 61–84.

60. Qtd. in ibid., 69.

61. Foner, *Reconstruction*, 77.

62. Marvin and Ingle, "Blood Sacrifice and the Nation," 767, 774. Their use of "totem crisis" is an adaptation of René Girard's concept of the "sacrificial crisis" (*Violence and the Sacred*, 36–67).

63. Mathews, "Lynching."

64. "The Strongholds of Democracy," *New York Times*, Dec. 4, 1876. The article is unclear as to what authority the correspondent had to collect the election results.

65. Williamson, *Florida Politics in the Gilded Age*, 36–37.

66. "Political Murders in Florida," *New York Times*, Jul. 29, 1877.

67. Rivers and Brown, *Laborers*, 24–28, 91, 103; Brown, *Florida's Black Public*

Officials, 128–29. Born a slave in Decatur County, Georgia, and sold to a family in northeast Florida, Stewart earned his education during the Civil War when he was an escaped slave living in Beaufort, South Carolina. In June 1865, after his ordination, Stewart relocated to Jacksonville and soon moved to middle Florida, where he ministered to black Floridians. He became a prominent Republican leader in Tallahassee during and after Reconstruction. In 1873, he served both in Florida's House of Representatives and on the Tallahassee City Council. This same year he became the postmaster, a position he held until 1886.

68. W. G. Stewart, "The Tallahassee District," *Weekly Floridian* (Tallahassee, Fla.), Nov. 20, 1877.

69. C. E. Dyke, editorial, *Weekly Floridian* (Tallahassee, Fla.), Nov. 20, 1877.

70. Stewart was also highly respected within Tallahassee's black community. After his passing in 1911, S. S. Herndon, the presiding elder of the AME Church, wrote a letter to Tallahassee's white newspaper subtly criticizing the paper for not printing an obituary. "The news of his death failed to reach many who would have been glad to pay a tribute of respect to this great, good and useful and exemplary husband, father, citizen and churchman." Herndon called Stewart a "progressive pastor" who "was of usual high moral character," noting that the "excellent characteristics he possessed and displayed are rare and seldom found in his age" ("Tribute to a Most Worthy Negro," *Tallahassee (Fla.) Weekly True Democrat*, June 16, 1911).

71. Long, *Florida Breezes*, xvii.

72. Ibid., 65.

73. E. K. Love, "A Sermon on Lynch Law and Raping," speech, Nov. 5, 1893, Daniel A. P. Murray Pamphlet Collection, Library of Congress, Washington, D.C.

74. "As to Lynchings," *Pensacola (Fla.) Daily News*, Feb. 6, 1897.

75. Raboteau, *Slave Religion*, 163–65; Chidester, *Christianity*, 403–5.

76. "Awful Work of Turner," *Richmond (Va.) Times Dispatch*, Aug. 28, 1904.

77. Litwack, *Trouble in Mind*, 71, 197–216; Ayers, *The Promise of the New South*, 426–32.

78. "Where Mr. Baker Misses It," *Pensacola (Fla.) Journal*, Apr. 23, 1908.

79. Dittmer, *Black Georgia in the Progressive Era*, 132–35; Moseley and Brogdon, "A Lynching in Statesboro."

80. *Savannah (Ga.) Morning News*, Aug. 15, 1904.

81. Dittmer, *Black Georgia in the Progressive Era*, 132–35; Moseley and Brogdon, "A Lynching in Statesboro."

82. *Savannah (Ga.) Tribune,* Nov. 5, 1904.

83. *Statesboro (Ga.) News,* Sept. 23 and Oct. 4, 1904.

84. "Negro Preachers Score Lawlessness," *Atlanta Constitution,* Sept. 20, 1904.

85. "Two Negroes Shot Apparently without Cause" and "No Before Day Club," *Talbotton (Ga.) New Era,* Sept. 22, 1904; "Mass Meeting Denounces Shooting of Negroes," *Talbotton (Ga.) New Era,* Sept. 29, 1904; "A Proclamation," *Talbotton (Ga.) New Era,* Sept. 29, 1904.

86. "Thomasville Man's Store Fired, Professedly by Before Day Club," *Florida Times-Union* (Jacksonville, Fla.), Sept. 16, 1904.

87. Qtd. in Rogers, *Transition to the Twentieth Century: Thomas County, Georgia, 1900–1920,* 152.

88. "N. W. Epps [*sic*] Brutally Assassinated near His Home in Leon County," *Florida Times-Union* (Jacksonville, Fla.), Sept. 5, 1904. See also Eppes, *Through Some Eventful Years,* xvi–xx. In this introduction, Joseph D. Cushman gives a brief recounting of the murder and the events surrounding it.

89. "Before Day Murder Club Has Organized in Leon County," *Florida Times-Union* (Jacksonville, Fla.), Sept. 6, 1904.

90. "Five Before Day Clubs Organized in Leon County," *Florida Times-Union* (Jacksonville, Fla.), Sept. 7, 1904.

91. "Eppes' Murderers Brought Here," *Florida Times-Union* (Jacksonville, Fla.), Sept. 8, 1904.

92. Eppes was a wealthy Confederate veteran and a prominent political figure in Tallahassee. His father, Francis, who came to north Florida from Virginia, was Thomas Jefferson's grandson, a successful planter, a principal lay figure in the Episcopal Diocese of Florida, and the mayor of Tallahassee. A biographical sketch is included in the Pine Hill Plantation Papers, FSU.

93. News clipping, n.d., Pine Hill Plantation Papers, FSU.

94. Letter from Josir Kimudy, Monticello, Fla., to Susan Bradford Eppes, Bradfordville, Fla., Sept. 7, 1904, Pine Hill Plantation Papers, FSU.

95. Letter from Martha Virginia Greetham, Orlando, Fla., to Susan Bradford Eppes, Bradfordville, Fla., Sept. 9, 1904, Pine Hill Plantation Papers, FSU.

96. Letter from Martha Bradford Houston, Ashville, N.C., to Susan Bradford Eppes, Bradfordville, Fla., Sept. 15, 1904, Pine Hill Plantation Papers, FSU. The letter is handwritten and is likely a copy of the one Houston sent to the *Florida Times-Union.* I could not determine whether the letter was published.

97. Letter from Robert Williams, Thomasville, Ga., to Susan Bradford Eppes, Bradfordville, Fla., Sept. 7, 1904, Pine Hill Plantation Papers, FSU.

98. "Edwards Insists That He Had Help," *Florida Times-Union* (Jacksonville, Fla.), Sept. 9, 1904.

99. "Coroner's Verdict in Eppes Murder Case," *Florida Times-Union*, Sept. 10, 1904.

100. "Self-Confessed Double Murderer Laughs as He Tells of Crimes," *Florida Times-Union* (Jacksonville, Fla.), Nov. 2, 1905.

101. "On to Death Goes Isham Edwards," *Florida Times-Union* (Jacksonville, Fla.), Nov. 3, 1905; "Confessed Crimes on the Gallows," *Florida Times-Union* (Jacksonville, Fla.), Nov. 4, 1905.

102. *Florida Times-Union* (Jacksonville, Fla.), Oct. 23, 1905.

103. "Death Sentence Was Commuted," *Florida Times-Union* (Jacksonville, Fla.), Aug. 4, 1906.

104. Letter from Edward Eppes, Tallahassee, Fla., to Isaac D. White, New York, N.Y., Nov. 23, 1905; letter from White to Eppes, Dec. 7, 1905; letter from Eppes to White, Dec. 10, 1905, Pine Hill Plantation Papers, FSU.

105. Letter from an anonymous author to the editor of the *Tallahassee (Fla.) Weekly True Democrat*, ca. May 1906, Pine Hill Plantation Papers, FSU. Eppes was probably not alone in keeping the rumors alive. An anonymous letter to a Tallahassee newspaper also expressed outrage over the pardon of Caldwell and Larkin. This account made no mention of conniving politicians but instead charged the duo with having been the prime actors in the murder. The author claimed Edwards was "the tool" of his more "charming accomplices," Caldwell and Larkin. At Larkin's store, which was full of stolen merchandise, the letter read, blacks "gambled and fought." Mothers of the neighborhood's "better class," claimed the author, "openly bewailed [Larkin's] evil influence over their young sons, saying Larkin was too smart and cunning to be caught himself and that he did not mind what trouble he got them into." The writer then recalled the events of the murder and claimed that Edward Eppes, investigating the crime scene, found the blood-soaked shirt of Caldwell. "[Respectable] colored men in the community said they would swear to it the clothes belonged to George Caldwell."

106. "Gain from the Atlanta Riot," *Live Oak (Fla.) Daily Democrat*, Sept. 27, 1906.

107. Dorsey, *To Build our Lives Together*, 147–66; Mixon, *The Atlanta Riot*.

108. Davis, *Communist Councilman from Harlem*, 70–71. The defendant was nineteen-year-old Angelo Herndon, a black communist, whose passion in the face of oppression impressed Davis enough that he joined the Communist Party.

CHAPTER THREE. *Female Voices, Male Voices*

1. "Woman's Tears and Smiles," *Pensacola (Fla.) Journal*, Mar. 19, 1905.

2. Braude, "Women's History." Braude discusses the contrasting images of women as "handmaidens of the Lord" and "handmaidens of the Devil" as a dialectic that persists in American religious history. "While the shift toward positive views of woman's nature is a major event in the story of American religion, it is crucial to remember that it remains by definition incomplete, that it is not a positive valuation of woman qua woman, but rather of an ideal that few women ever can attain" (100).

3. Welter, "The Cult of True Womanhood"; Welter, "The Feminization of American Religion," 138.

4. Scott, *The Southern Lady*.

5. Fessenden, "Gendering Religion"; Lyerly, "Women and Southern Religion." After summarizing Welter's influence on discussions of religion and gender, Fessenden pleads "for the kinds of subtle, pluralizing inquiries into religion that have opened up other areas of experience when gender becomes a focusing lens" (167). Similarly, Lyerly writes, "Focusing on women transforms our view of southern religion; focusing on women and religion transforms our view of southern history; and doing so suggests ways in which southern honor was contested by women early in the republic and later in the twentieth century" (247).

6. "How He Got Religion," *Pensacola (Fla.) Daily News*, Nov. 29, 1900

7. Henry Partridge Diary, 1873–88, Aug. 24, 1902, FSA.

8. Henry Partridge Diary, 1873–88, Apr. 19, 1873, FSA.

9. Ibid.

10. Wheeler, *New Women of the New South*.

11. Sam Jones, "A Synopsis of Rev. Sam Jones' Lecture Delivered at Lake City, Fla.," ca. 1904, Samuel Porter Jones Papers, Woodruff Library Special Collections, Emory University.

12. Hodes, *White Women, Black Men*, 198–202; Sommerville, *Rape and Race*, 223–59.

13. "Well Said," *Chipley (Fla.) Banner*, Sept. 11, 1897.

14. Councill was the president of Alabama A&M Institute in Huntsville between 1875 and 1909 and positioned himself as an accommodationist (Morris and Morris, *The Price They Paid*, 17–27).

15. Jones, *Sam Jones' Own Book*, 225–26.

16. Richard Hooker Wilmer, "Counsel to Men: A Sermon Preached at Christ Church, Mobile," pamphlet, 260, UWF.

17. Ownby, *Subduing Satan*, 103–21. "Central to white Southern culture was the notion that men were more sinful than women" (11).

18. Richardson, *The Lights and Shadows*, 122–23.

19. Ibid., 105–6.

20. See Ownby, *Subduing Satan*, 5; Friedman, *The Enclosed Garden*, 110–27.

21. *Thomasville (Ga.) Press*, Aug. 15, 1906, Hopkins Collection, THL. See also Rogers, *Transition to the Twentieth Century*, 124. Hansell's husband, Augustus, was a judge and politician in Thomas County.

22. Samuel A. Floyd Diary, Jan. 3, 11, 19, 1872, FSA.

23. Schweiger, *The Gospel Working Up*, 154, 155.

24. Charles C. Cox, "Souvenir of the Southern Female College," pamphlet, 1896, 23, 28, 32, 39–40, Geiger Family Papers, GSA. See also Southern Female College Records, Troup County, Ga., Archives. In 1895, Cox moved the college from LaGrange, Georgia, to College Park.

25. Bordin, *Woman and Temperance*, Coker, *Liquor*, 200–13.

26. Richard L. Wilson, "Sam Jones."

27. Sam Jones, "Why Should a Church Member Belong to the WCTU?," typescript, n.d., Samuel Porter Jones Papers, Woodruff Library Special Collections, Emory University. On Jones and his reform efforts, see Minnix, *Laughter in the Amen Corner*. On Lathrap, see Bordin, *Woman and Temperance*, xiii.

28. Mattie Oglesby Coyle, "History of Colquitt County, Georgia and Her Builders," 1925, pamphlet, Hopkins Collection, TLH.

29. Jones, *Sam Jones' Own Book*, 174.

30. A. L. Woodward, "Eloquent Prayer for Prohibition: Extract of a Prayer Offered in Trinity Methodist Church, Tallahassee," *Tallahassee (Fla.) Daily Democrat*, Apr. 12, 1915. This prayer came a day before Florida's vote for prohibition that passed 57–14 in the House of Representatives.

31. Coker, *Liquor*, 175–98.

32. *Journal and Yearbook*, 10.

33. Ewens, "Women in the Convent," 27–32; Muldrey, *Abounding in Mercy*.

34. "In Many Lands," *New York Times*, Mar. 26, 1904.

35. "A Tribute to Mother Austin Carroll," *Pensacola (Fla.) Journal*, Dec. 4, 1909; "Mother Austin Carroll Passed Away in Mobile," *Pensacola (Fla.) Journal*, Nov. 30, 1909

36. Letter from Edward Allen, Mobile, Ala., to M. Austin Carroll, n.p., Feb. 16, 1900, Bishop Edward Patrick Allen Collection, CDA.

37. Letter from Edward Allen, Mobile, Ala., to I. Heslin, n.p., Aug. 14, 1900. Bishop Edward Patrick Allen Collection, CDA.

38. Qtd. in Fialka, *Sisters*, 75.

39. Cummings, *New Women of the Old Faith*, 26–27.

40. Carroll, *A Catholic History*, 23, 368, 357 (her emphasis).

41. Letter from Ralph McCraney, Athens, Ga., to Edward Allen, Mobile, Ala., May 19, 1919, Bishop Edward Patrick Allen Collection, CDA.

42. Letter from Edward Allen, Mobile, Ala., to Mr. and Mrs. McCraney, n.p., June 2, 1919, Bishop Edward Patrick Allen Collection, CDA.

43. Letter from M. Fidelis, Florence, Ala., to Edward Allen, Mobile, Ala., May 31, 1919, Bishop Edward Patrick Allen Collection, CDA.

44. Letter from Edward Allen, Mobile, Ala., to M. Fidelis, Florence, Ala., June 2, 1919, Bishop Edward Patrick Allen Collection, CDA.

45. Letter from M. Ottilia, Cullman, Ala., to Edward Allen, Mobile, Ala., ca. May–June 1919, Bishop Edward Patrick Allen Collection, CDA.

46. Letter from M. Ottilia, Cullman, Ala., to Edward Allen, Mobile, Ala., June 7, 1919, Bishop Edward Patrick Allen Collection, CDA.

47. On anti-Catholicism during this period, see chapter 5.

48. Eppes, *Through Some Eventful Years*, 267, 370.

49. Henry, "The New Woman."

50. Sims, *The Power of Femininity*, 4.

51. Historians debate the level of authority gained or lost by southern white women after the war and Reconstruction. Those arguing that women gained authority tend to look at women's participation in temperance, suffrage, non-violence campaigns, education, mission work, and welfare reform. See Scott, *The Southern Lady*; Tetzlaff, *Cultivating a New South*; Wheeler, *New Women of the New South*; McDowell, *The Social Gospel in the South*; Sims, *The Power of Femininity*; Hewitt, *Southern Discomfort*. On the other side, the argument generally examines the backlash men unleashed when they returned from the war. See Whites, *The Civil War*; Lebsock, "Radical Reconstruction."

52. Schweiger, *The Gospel Working Up*, 163; Lyerly, "Women and Southern Religion," 252.

53. Hill, *The World Their Household*.

54. "An Earnest Appeal to the Baptist Women of the South," *Atlanta (Ga.) Christian Index*, Mar. 30, 1882.

55. Yrigoyen, "Haygood, Laura Askew."

56. Laura A. Haygood, "A Message from China to the Woman's Missionary Society of the Methodist Episcopal Church, South," pamphlet, Oct. 19, 1885, Yarbourgh Family Papers, 1880–1940, FSA.

57. Pensacola WCTU, "An Earnest Appeal," pamphlet, Oct. 1, 1907, Pensacola

Miscellaneous Items Concerning Prohibition, Florida Miscellaneous Manuscripts, UFL.

58. "White Man's Whiskey, and the South's Great Race Problem," *Pensacola (Fla.) Journal*, Sept. 22, 1907. See also Guthrie, *Keepers of the Spirits*, 14–18.

59. "The Prohibition Elections," *Tallahassee (Fla.) Weekly True Democrat*, Oct. 4, 1907.

60. Editorial, *Live Oak (Fla.) Daily Democrat*, Oct. 4, 1907.

61. *Tallahassee (Fla.) Weekly True Democrat*, May 12, 1905. Knott was the wife of then state treasurer William V. Knott.

62. "History of the Albany Womans Christian Temperance Union," 306, 307.

63. Dittmer, *Black Georgia in the Progressive Era*, 112.

64. "The Year Book, Mobile, Alabama, Section Council of Jewish Women, 1911–1912," pamphlet, Leon Schwarz Scrapbook, MMA.

65. See Rogow, *"Gone to Another Meeting."*

66. See chapter 4.

67. Charles Reagan Wilson, *Baptized in Blood*, 13.

68. "A Noble Woman," *Thomasville (Ga.) Times-Enterprise*, Sept. 5, 1897, Hopkins Collection, THL.

69. "A Pretty Idea, and One We Hope to See Duly Encouraged," *Albany (Ga.) Daily Herald*, Apr. 25, 1897, Geiger Family Papers, 1868–1903, GSA.

70. Scott D. Clarke, "Memorial Address," Apr. 26, 1902, Florida Miscellaneous Manuscripts, UFL.

71. Park Trammell, speech, June 3, 1910, Park Trammell Papers, 1876–1935, UFL.

72. Miss B., "Delivered on the night of Feb. 1, 1865, to 57th GA Regt.," news clipping, n.d., Hopkins Collection, TLH.

73. Cummings, *Gleanings from the Southland*, 274, 275.

74. "In Memoriam for Mrs. Emily C. Jones, dated Feb. 1906," UDC Pensacola chapter meeting minutes, Apr. 1899–Nov. 18, 1906, United Daughters of the Confederacy, Pensacola Papers, UWF.

75. Davis, "Dougherty's Women," 367, 271, 273, 275.

76. Annie White, "The First Memorial Day," ca. 1926. UDC John B. Gordon chapter, Thomasville, Ga., Hopkins Collection, THL.

77. Ayers, *The Promise of the New South*, 334; Cox, *Dixie's Daughters*, 73, 94–101; Hale, *Making Whiteness*, 86.

78. "Constitution and By-Laws of the Pensacola Chapter of the Daughters

of the Confederacy, established April 4, 1899," United Daughters of the Confederacy, Pensacola Papers, UWF.

79. Mrs. A. E. McDavid, "United Daughters of the Confederacy," *Pensacola (Fla.) Journal*, Jul. 2, 1907.

80. Mrs. A. E. McDavid, "Two Views of Memorial Exercises," *Pensacola (Fla.) Journal*, Jul. 2, 1907.

81. Susan Bradford Eppes, "'Lest we Forget': Memorial Address Delivered before Anna Dummett Chapter, 1089," Oct. 1, 1907, Susan Bradford Eppes Papers, FSU.

82. Mildred Rutherford, "Monthly Programs, United Daughters of the Confederacy and Children of the Confederacy," 1916, United Daughters of the Confederacy Collection, Mobile Public Library, Mobile, Ala. In response, members would say, "He that walketh uprightly, and worketh righteousness, and speaketh the truth in his heart. He that slandereth not with his tongue, nor doeth evil to his friend, nor taketh up a reproach against his neighbor. In whose eyes a vile person is contemned; but he honoureth them that fear the Lord. He that sweareth to his own hurt and changeth not. He that putteth not his money to usury, nor taketh reward against the innocent."

83. "The Jefferson Davis Chapter, Children of the Confederacy," 279.

84. Mrs. R. P. Holt, "Children of the Confederacy Pledge," in "John Triplett Chapter, Children of the Confederacy, No. 24, Georgia Division, Organized 1906," pamphlet, Hopkins Collection, THL.

85. Blight, *Race and Reunion.*

86. Eppes, "'Lest we Forget': Memorial Address Delivered before Anna Dummett Chapter, 1089," Oct. 1, 1907, Susan Bradford Eppes Papers, FSU.

87. Eppes, *Through Some Eventful Years*, 41–42.

88. Susan Bradford Eppes, "The Real Reason for the Assassination of Abraham Lincoln," manuscript, Mar. 17, 1927, Susan Bradford Eppes Papers, FSU.

89. Donald, *Lincoln*, 605; Barton, *The Paternity of Abraham Lincoln.*

90. Albert M. Smith, "Like the Wail of a Fallen Angel," *Scranton (Pa.) Tribune,* Feb. 10, 1900. For his work with the Grand Army of the Republic, see *Proceedings of the 42nd Annual Encampment.*

CHAPTER FOUR. *Jewish Voices, Gentile Voices*

1. *Macon (Ga.) Telegraph,* Nov. 30, 1882; "The Races Today," *Columbus (Ga.) Daily Enquirer,* Oct. 26, 1892; "Lion Attacks Animal Trainer," *San Jose (Calif.)*

Evening News, Feb. 22, 1909; Peggy Sheppard, "Albany's Farkas Family," *Georgia Magazine*, Oct.–Nov. 1970.

2. Landau, "The Jew in Albany."

3. Jews rarely represented more than 1 percent of the population in the South (Dinnerstein and Palsson, introduction, 3).

4. Leon Schwarz, qtd. in "District Grand Lodge No. 7, IOBB Meets in Its Thirty-Ninth Annual Convention in Galveston, Texas," *New Orleans (La.) Jewish Ledger*, May 17, 1912, Leon Schwarz Scrapbook, MMA.

5. Cash, *The Mind of the South*, 342.

6. Goldstein, "'Now Is the Time'," 143. See also Clive Webb, "A Tangled Web."

7. Sarna, *American Judaism*, 214–15; Melnick, "Jews in the South."

8. Sarna, *American Judaism*, 151, 195, 197. See also Woocher, *Sacred Survival.* Woocher calls philanthropy "a precept of Jewish religion on which all could agree" (19). The resulting "civic Judaism," he explains, "expressed and sustained the unity American Jews felt among themselves, legitimated the endeavors of the community to maintain Jewish group life while promoting maximal involvement in American society, and inspired Jews to contribute to the support of other Jews and the pursuit of social justice" (26).

9. Schmier, *Reflections of Southern Jewry*, 3–26; Schmier, "Jewish Press."

10. Schmier, *Reflections of Southern Jewry*, 53, 52, 64, 32, 68.

11. Ibid., 31, 85 (his emphasis), 53.

12. Grusd, *B'nai B'rith*; Jick, *The Americanization of the Synagogue.*

13. "Lazarus Schwarz," 710. Born in 1846, the German immigrant first came to New Orleans and as a teen lived in Mobile working as a merchant. In 1878, yellow fever struck Mobile; Schwarz became the president of the "Can't Get Away Club" that assisted the sick and dying. Later, Schwarz returned to his mercantile business, opening a men's furnishing store in 1889. In 1912, he became Mobile's mayor.

14. "Corner Stone Laid with Impressive Ceremonies," *Mobile (Ala.) Register*, ca. Dec. 11, 1911, Leon Schwarz Scrapbook, MMA.

15. Tindall, *The Emergence of the New South*, 33–69; Wilson, *Baptized in Blood*, 161–82.

16. Moses (1878–1956) was born in Livingston, Alabama, and came from a family of rabbis. His father, Adolph, left Poland in 1870 and settled first in Montgomery and then in Mobile in 1871, where he served for ten years. He left in 1883 for Louisville and in 1885 participated in developing the Pittsburgh Platform. In 1901, Alfred finished his rabbinic degree at Hebrew Union College

in Cincinnati and moved back to Mobile where he served until 1940 and remained emeritus until 1946. He oversaw the building of the Government Street Temple in 1910, presided over the Jewish Welfare Board from 1915 on, and was an active speaker on the chautauqua circuit. In 1913, he was Mobile's delegate to the Alabama Sociological Congress in Birmingham. Moses served as the chaplain for the Mobile Elks, Masons, Temple of the Mystic Shrine, and Knights of Pythias and was a member of the Fidelia Club and Gulf Fishing and Hunting Club ("Rev. Alfred Geiger Moses," 736; Zietz, *The Gates of Heaven*, 77, 78; Umansky, *From Christian Science to Jewish Science*, 35–62).

17. "Corner Stone Laid with Impressive Ceremonies," *Mobile (Ala.) Register*, ca. Dec. 11, 1911, Leon Schwarz Scrapbook, MMA.

18. Letter from Henry Hanaw to the "Jewish Citizens of Mobile," Nov. 24, 1905, Leon Schwarz Scrapbook, MMA.

19. "250th Anniversary Jews in America," *Mobile (Ala.) Register*, ca. Dec. 1, 1905, Leon Schwarz Scrapbook, MMA.

20. Moses, *A Congregation*, 8.

21. Qtd. in Craighead, *From Mobile's Past*, 216, 217.

22. Qtd. in Sherwin, "Portrait of a Romantic Rebel," 56.

23. Conkin, *American Originals*, 226–75; Porterfield, *The Transformation of American Religion*, 195–98.

24. Umansky, *From Christian Science to Jewish Science*, 8, 23.

25. Qtd. in ibid., 16.

26. Ibid., 35–62; Moses, *Jewish Science: Divine Healing in Judaism*; Moses, *Jewish Science: Psychology of Health, Joy and Success*. Moses could likely identify with the health concerns of those coreligionists attracted to Christian Science. Mental problems plagued the rabbi throughout his adult life and he lived his final years in a mental institution. According to Umansky, Moses made no serious attempt to institute Jewish Science in Mobile. He believed members of his synagogue had no desire to join Christian Science. Christian Science had come to Mobile by 1897, but its membership was small and influence on Jews was minimal. Jewish Science saw its greatest growth in New York City through the efforts of Rabbi Morris Lichtenstein and his wife, Tehilla. While the number of members was never very high, the movement's focus on health and well-being attracted many more Jews than the bare numbers indicate.

27. Moses, *Jewish Science: Psychology of Health, Joy and Success*, 60.

28. Ibid., 60, 4, 16, 74, 79, 108.

29. Carnegie, "Wealth."

30. Moses, *Jewish Science: Psychology of Health, Joy and Success*, 108–9.

31. See chapter 3.

32. Proskauer, *A Segment of My Times*, 12, 13; Hacker and Hirsch, *Proskauer*.

33. George Franklin Thompson Diary, 1865–66, Dec. 6–7, 1865, UFL.

34. Abernethy, *The Jew a Negro*, 11.

35. Rogoff, "Is the Jew White?" 228, 229, 230. It should be noted that Rogoff's argument has historiographical counters. Most notably, Leonard Dinnerstein has posited that the South's "Protestant fundamentalist culture" fed a distinct brand of southern anti-Semitism that resulted in "a pervasive sense of anxiety" among Jews. Jews were able to "survive, thrive, and interact pleasantly" in the South because they acculturated and established "a facile cordiality with Gentiles." While the religious minority contributed to "rebuilding the southern society," they also "did nothing to disturb community tranquility." My evidence leads me to side more with Rogoff, since none of the sources I use outwardly indicate that Jews' relationship with non-Jews was "facile." See Dinnerstein, *Antisemitism in America*, 176.

36. Rockaway and Gutfeld, "Demonic Images," 380.

37. Qtd. in Rosen, *The Jewish Confederates*, 268.

38. Qtd. in Schmier, *Reflections of Southern Jewry*, 5.

39. Ibid., 3–25; Rogers, *Thomas County*, 176–77.

40. Landau, "The Jew in Albany," 203, 206, 205, 208, 209, 213.

41. Clark, "The Post–Civil War Economy," 163; Schmier, "Jews and Gentiles"; Schmier, "Hellooo! Peddlerman! Hellooo!"

42. Qtd. in Schmier, "Jews and Gentiles," 3, 4.

43. Sarna, "Jewish-Christian Hostility," 6. See also Ariel, *Evangelizing the Chosen People*.

44. Stephens Croom, "The Persecution of the Jews," ca. 1856–59, Velma and Stephens G. Croom Collection, USA.

45. Richardson, *The Lights and Shadows*, 265–66, 252.

46. "District Grand Lodge No. 7, IOOB, Assembled in Mobile, Al.," *Atlanta (Ga.) Jewish South*, Apr. 22, 1910, Leon Schwarz Scrapbook, MMA.

47. Craighead, *From Mobile's Past*, 134.

48. "Julius Diamond," n.d., Ruby Diamond Collection, FSU. German-born Julius Diamond came to America after the Civil War at the age of thirteen and lived briefly in Pennsylvania before moving to Florida two years later. Diamond was a successful merchant in Tallahassee, who, as a Democrat, became chair of the Board of Leon County Commissioners.

49. John L. Neeley, W. H. Markham, and W. H. Chancey, "In Memoriam,"

Tallahassee (Fla.) Weekly True Democrat, Jul. 24, 1914, Ruby Diamond Collection, FSU.

50. A. L. Woodward, "Recollections of Some Old Tallahasseeans, No. 7: Julius Diamond," n.d., Woodward Family Collection, FSA.

51. "Sidney H. Diamond for County Judge," *Tallahassee (Fla.) Weekly True Democrat,* Sept. 3, 1915.

52. Letter from Sidney Catts, Tallahassee, Fla., Sept. 13, 1918, Ruby Diamond Collection, FSU.

53. Letter from J. B. Christian, Tallahassee, Fla., Sept. 23, 1918, Ruby Diamond Collection, FSU.

54. Letter from H. Clay Crawford, Tallahassee, Fla., Sept. 14, 1918, Ruby Diamond Collection, FSU.

55. Letter from Van C. Swearingen, Tallahassee, Fla., Sept. 13, 1918, Ruby Diamond Collection, FSU.

56. Woodward, *Tom Watson,* 435–49; Dinnerstein, *The Leo Frank Case.*

57. Letter from Sidney Catts, Tallahassee, Fla., to Thomas E. Watson, Thompson, Ga., Jan. 9, 1917, Sidney J. Catts Papers, UWF; Flynt, *Cracker Messiah,* 132.

58. Vance, "A Karl Marx for Hill Billies."

59. Arsenault, "Charles Jacobson of Arkansas," 73.

60. Resolution of the Mobile Lodge no. 67, Knights of Pythias, Mar. 23, 1909, Leon Schwarz Scrapbook, MMA.

61. *Who's Who in the South and Southwest,* 399–400; Zietz, *The Gates of Heaven,* 138–39; Umansky, *From Christian Science to Jewish Science,* 40. Born in Perry County near Marion on March 28, 1872, Schwarz finished his college degree at the University of Alabama. He married Addie Bloch Herzfeld in December 15, 1909. The couple had no children. Schwarz was a manufacturer and president of the Mobile Mattress Company and worked in insurance. He enlisted in the Alabama State Troopers in 1890 and served in the Spanish-American War. By 1898, Schwarz had earned the rank of lieutenant. When World War I started, he transferred to the U.S. Army and served as a captain. After the war, he became a member of the Paris conference and assisted in founding the American Legion. He became the sheriff of Mobile in 1924. In 1926, voters elected the Democrat Schwarz to the city commission. From 1929 to 1932, he was Mobile's mayor. In 1932, Schwarz became president of Mobile's Reform congregation. He died April 24, 1943, at seventy-one.

62. "Leon Schwarz," 582.

63. *Tuscaloosa (Ala.) Gazette*, ca. Mar. 15, 1892, Leon Schwarz Scrapbook, MMA.

64. Letters of recommendation from Governor Charles Henderson, General Hubbard, and Mayor Pat J. Lyons, ca. Sept. 12, 1918, Leon Schwarz Scrapbook, MMA.

65. Rosen, *The Jewish Confederates*, 372. Rosen indicates that many second-generation Jews were not as committed to the Lost Cause as their southern white counterparts.

66. Leon Schwarz, "A Civil War Memorial Day," *Montgomery (Ala.) Advertiser*, June 4, 1907, Leon Schwarz Scrapbook, MMA.

67. Charles Reagan Wilson, "Confederate Memorial Day."

68. "Flowers Placed on Confederate Graves Sunday," *Mobile (Ala.) Register*, Apr. 26, 1920, Leon Schwarz Scrapbook, MMA.

69. *Mobile (Ala.) Register*, Sept. 27, 1906, Leon Schwarz Scrapbook, MMA.

70. Letter from William W. Brandon, Montgomery, Ala., to Leon Schwarz, Mobile, Ala., Sept. 13, 1906, Leon Schwarz Scrapbook, MMA. Brandon became governor of Alabama in 1922 after losing the race to Thomas Kilby in 1918 (Rogers et al., *Alabama*, 421–23).

71. Letter from William W. Brandon, Montgomery, Ala., to Leon Schwarz, Mobile, Ala., Jul. 22, 1907, Leon Schwarz Scrapbook, MMA.

72. Samuel L. Webb, "The Great Mobile Whiskey War."

73. Qtd. in "Leon Schwarz," 581–82.

74. "250th Anniversary Jews in America," *Mobile (Ala.) Register*, ca. Dec. 1, 1905, Leon Schwarz Scrapbook, MMA.

75. "Corner Stone Laid with Impressive Ceremonies," *Mobile (Ala.) Register*, ca. Dec. 11, 1911, Leon Schwarz Scrapbook, MMA.

76. Schwarz's scrapbooks show that he belonged to an array of civic organizations including B'nai B'rith, Masons, Kiwanis Club, Red Cross, American Legion, Salvation Army, Community Chest, Knights of Pythias, Elks, Odd Fellows, Red Men, United Spanish War Veterans, Forty and Eight Society, Mobile Rifles Honorary Association, Mobile Association for the Blind.

77. Leon Schwarz, speech, ca. October 18, 1910, Leon Schwarz Scrapbook, MMA.

78. "Report of the Committee on Intellectual Culture at the Convention in Memphis," B'nai B'rith convention, Apr. 24, 1907, Memphis, Tenn., Leon Schwarz Scrapbook, MMA.

79. Letter from Leon Schwarz, Mobile, Ala., to the members of Beth Zur Lodge, Mobile Ala., Dec. 1, 1907, Leon Schwarz Scrapbook, MMA.

80. "B'nai B'rith Day Observed," *Mobile (Ala.) Register*, ca. early Dec. 1907, Leon Schwarz Scrapbook, MMA.

81. "B'nai B'rith Day Is Celebrated," *Mobile (Ala.) Register*, ca. Dec. 11, 1907, Leon Schwarz Scrapbook, MMA.

82. "The Stage Jew," *New Orleans (La.) Jewish Ledger*, Oct. 23, 1908, Leon Schwarz Scrapbook, MMA.

83. Letter from Leon Schwarz, Mobile, Ala., to the officers and members of the B'nai B'rith, district 7, Mobile, Ala., Feb. 1, 1913, Leon Schwarz Scrapbook, MMA.

84. On February 14, 1913, President Taft had vetoed a bill requiring a literacy test (Fairchild, "The Literacy Test and Its Making"; Knobel, *"America for the Americans"*, 235–79).

85. Leon Schwarz, "President's Message . . . for the Term May 12, 1912 to April 13, 1913," pamphlet, Leon Schwarz Scrapbook, MMA.

86. "The B'nai B'rith," *New Orleans (La.) Jewish Ledger*, Jul. 17, 1908, Leon Schwarz Scrapbook, MMA.

87. "Leon Schwarz," 582.

88. "District Grand Lodge No. 7, IOBB Meets in Its Thirty-Ninth Annual Convention in Galveston, Texas," *New Orleans (La.) Jewish Ledger*, May 17, 1912, Leon Schwarz Scrapbook, MMA.

89. Letter from Leon Schwarz, Mobile, Ala., to officers and members of the B'nai B'rith, district 7, Mobile, Ala., Mar. 1, 1913, Leon Schwarz Scrapbook, MMA

90. "Jewish Home Greets Fifty-Eighth Year," *New Orleans (La.) Daily Picayune*, Jan. 5, 1913, Leon Schwarz Scrapbook, MMA.

91. Letter from Leon Schwarz, Mobile, Ala., to the B'nai B'rith Lodge, Mobile, Ala., Sept. 7, 1912, Leon Schwarz Scrapbook, MMA.

92. Letter from Leon Schwarz, Mobile, Ala., to Albert Herskowitz, Oklahoma City, Ok., June 1, 1912, Leon Schwarz Scrapbook, MMA.

93. Letter from Leon Schwarz, Mobile, Ala., to an unnamed Orthodox Mobile rabbi, Oct. 1, 1912, Leon Schwarz Scrapbook, MMA.

94. "B'nai B'rith Convention," *New Orleans (La.) Jewish Ledger*, Apr. 11, 1913, Leon Schwarz Scrapbook, MMA. Among the places visited were Donaldson, La.; Nashville, Tenn.; New Orleans, La.; Birmingham, Ala.; Pensacola, Fla.; Memphis, Tenn.; Hot Springs, Ark.; Jackson, Miss.; Laurel, Miss.; Selma, Ala.; Demopolis,

Miss.; Meridian, Miss.; Chattanooga, Tenn.; Huntsville, Tenn.; Gadsden, Fla.; Jacksonville, Fla.; Tampa, Fla.

95. "The B'nai B'rith of District No. 7," *Dallas (Tex.) Jewish Monitor,* Apr. 30, 1920, Leon Schwarz Scrapbook, MMA.

96. *Montgomery (Ala.) Advertiser,* ca. 1906, Leon Schwarz Scrapbook, MMA.

97. "Brotherly Love," *Tallahassee (Fla.) Weekly True Democrat,* Dec. 29, 1905.

CHAPTER FIVE. *Catholic Voices, Nativist Voices*

1. Bresnahan, *Seeing Florida with a Priest,* 17, 79, 75.

2. R. Laurence Moore, *Religious Outsiders,* 203.

3. Knobel, *"America for the Americans",* xvii, xix, xxv, xxviii, 198. See also Bennett, *The Party of Fear;* Michaels, *Our America.*

4. Holmes, "Anti-Catholicism in Georgia"; Gatewood, "Strangers and the Southern Eden."

5. Qtd. in Gatewood, "Strangers and the Southern Eden," 4.

6. Litwack, *Trouble in Mind,* 119; Woodward, *Origins of the New South,* 297–99.

7. Qtd. in Gatewood, "Strangers and the Southern Eden," 9.

8. Qtd. in Gatewood, "Strangers and the Southern Eden," 13–14.

9. Alfred L. Woodward, "How Shall We Boost Tallahassee and Leon," *Tallahassee (Fla.) Weekly True Democrat,* Aug. 20, 1915.

10. Mohl and Pozzetta, "From Migration to Multiculturalism," 393–94.

11. Gatewood, "Strangers and the Southern Eden," 17.

12. Kerber, "Park Trammell," 257. In 1916, there were 24,650 Roman Catholics in Florida, making them the fifth largest denomination in the state. There were 57,732 Baptists organized in 686 churches.

13. "Knights of Columbus Oath, Extract 4th Degree," pamphlet, ca. Feb. 1913, Park Trammell Papers, 1876–1936, UFL. The archive notes indicate that this was a fictitious oath, but there is no clear indication to whether the legislators believed this was true or not.

14. Qtd. in Page, "Bishop Michael J. Curley," 107–8. Curley was something of a southern "Americanist," much like his counterparts to the North, Archbishop John Ireland and Cardinal James Gibbons. Each confirmed that Catholics of all ethnicities could reconcile their American and religious identities. Essentially, the religious leaders carved a new identity for the "Catholic patriot."

15. Page, "Bishop Michael J. Curley," 104. Ironically, in 1878, Bishop John Moore of Saint Augustine procured public funds for this very school.

16. *Laws of Florida*, 311; Rackleff, "Anti-Catholicism," 358; Kerber, "Park Trammell."

17. News clipping, May 8, 1916, Park Trammell Papers, 1876–1936, UFL.

18. "Recent State Law Is to Be Tested in St. Augustine," *Florida Times-Union* (Jacksonville, Fla.), Apr. 25, 1916.

19. Letter from S. S. Dalzell [?], Ft. Lauderdale, Fla., to Park Trammell, Tallahassee, Fla., May 25, 1916, Park Trammell Papers, 1876–1936, UFL.

20. Letter from H. Whitaker, Muscogee, Fla., to Park Trammell, Tallahassee, Fla., May 13, 1916, Park Trammell Papers, 1876–1936, UFL.

21. Letter from J. L. Crews, Okeechobee, Fla., to Park Trammell, Tallahassee, Fla., Apr. 22, 1916, Park Trammell Papers, 1876–1936, UFL.

22. Letter from George F. Ensey, Tropic Indian River, Fla., to Park Trammell, Tallahassee, Fla., May 20, 1916, Park Trammell Papers, 1876–1936, UFL.

23. Letter from J. B. George, Morristo, Fla., to Park Trammell, Tallahassee, Fla., May 19, 1916, Park Trammell Papers, 1876–1936, UFL.

24. Letter from R. C. Hodges, Jennings, Fla., to Park Trammell, Tallahassee, Fla., May 26, 1916, Park Trammell Papers, 1876–1936, UFL.

25. Letter from Y. J. Holder, Georgiana, Fla., to Park Trammell, Tallahassee, Fla., May 24, 1916, Park Trammell Papers, 1876–1936, UFL.

26. Letter from A. C. Pierce, DeLand, Fla., to Park Trammell, Tallahassee, Fla., May 19, 1916, Park Trammell Papers, 1876–1936, UFL.

27. Letter from William Collins, Okeechobee, Fla., to Park Trammell, Tallahassee, Fla., May 15, 1916, Park Trammell Papers, 1876–1936, UFL.

28. Letter from H. P. Carpenter, Montverde, Fla., to Park Trammell, Tallahassee, Fla., May 20, 1916, Park Trammell Papers, 1876–1936, UFL.

29. Letter from R. L. McMullen of Largo, Fla., to Park Trammell, Tallahassee, Fla., May 20, 1916, Park Trammell Papers, 1876–1936, UFL.

30. Letter from D. A. Reid, Perry, Fla., to Park Trammell, Tallahassee, Fla., May 21, 1916, Park Trammell Papers, 1876–1936, UFL.

31. Letter from R. L. Park, Crystal River, Fla., to Park Trammell, Tallahassee, Fla., May 29, 1916, Park Trammell Papers, 1876–1936, UFL.

32. Letter from C. A. Stanford in Minneola, Fla., to Park Trammell, Tallahassee, Fla., May 21, 1916, Park Trammell Papers, 1876–1936, UFL.

33. Letter from F. K. Demmo [?], Ocala, Fla., to Park Trammell, Tallahassee, Fla., May 25, 1916, Park Trammell Papers, 1876–1936, UFL. Education was a significant point of contention between Catholics and Protestants in the North and South after the Civil War. See McGreevy, *Catholicism and American Freedom*, 113–21.

34. Letter from L. M. Drake, Daytona, Fla., to Park Trammell, Tallahassee, Fla., May 22, 1916, Park Trammell Papers, 1876–1936, UFL.

35. "Senator Bryan Scores Secret Political Societies in Opening Address of Campaign," pamphlet, ca. spring 1916, N. P. Bryan Papers, UFL. This "separation of church and state" rhetoric developed in the mid-nineteenth century and served as a rallying call for nativists who tried to alienate and acculturate Catholics. See Hamburger, *Separation of Church and State.*

36. Woodward, *Tom Watson,* 421; Knobel, *"America for the Americans",* 191.

37. Qtd. in Kerber, "Park Trammell," 263.

38. Letter from Herbert Felkel, Tallahassee, Fla., to Bradford Byrd, Atlanta, Ga., ca. March 1916; letter from Byrd to Felkel, Mar. 14, 1916, Park Trammell Papers, 1876–1936, UFL. Byrd forwarded both of these letters accompanied by a note to Trammell on May 15, 1916. The *Recorder's* editor, T. J. Appleyard, discovered that E. J. Long, the editor of a Guardian publication called the *American Citizen,* was black. Appleyard had been sympathetic to Knott (Flynt, *Cracker Messiah,* 50–51).

39. "Negro Membership in Guardians of Liberty," *Florida Recorder* (Orlando, Fla.), March 16, 1916.

40. Kerber, "Park Trammell," 264.

41. Letter from Fred Taylor, DeLeon Springs, Fla., to Park Trammell, Tallahassee, Fla., May 28, 1916, Park Trammell Papers, 1876–1936, UFL.

42. Knobel, *"America for the Americans",* 198. Established in New Haven, Connecticut, in 1881, the Knights of Columbus grew rapidly in an age when many other fraternal organizations developed. The "organizational" acumen of the group, Knobel remarked, irked nativists who believed the Knights were plotting "un-American" activities.

43. Letter from E. R. Ensey [?], Tropic Indian River, Fla., to Park Trammell, Tallahassee, Fla., May 16, 1916, Park Trammell Papers, 1876–1936, UFL.

44. Qtd. in Kerber, "Park Trammell," 269.

45. Letter from W. S. Moore, Hawthorn, Fla., to Park Trammell, Tallahassee, Fla., June 7, 1916, Park Trammell Papers, 1876–1936, UFL.

46. Letter from Warren B. Rush, Lake City, Fla., to Park Trammell, Tallahassee, Fla., June 10, 1916, Park Trammell Papers, 1876–1936, UFL.

47. Letter from T. J. Bunting, Milton, Fla., to Park Trammell, Tallahassee, Fla., Jul. 3, 1916, Park Trammell Papers, 1876–1936, UFL.

48. Letter from W. T. Brantley, Apalachicola, Fla., to Park Trammell, Tallahassee, Fla., June 10, 1916, Park Trammell Papers, 1876–1936, UFL.

49. Letter from Frank E. Patten, Jacksonville, Fla., to Park Trammell, Tallahassee, Fla., June 11, 1916, Park Trammell Papers, 1876–1936, UFL.

50. Letter from A. M. McMillan, Pensacola, Fla., to Park Trammell, Tallahassee, Fla., June 13, 1916, Park Trammell Papers, 1876–1936, UFL.

51. "In the State He Loved," *Pensacola (Fla.) Daily Star,* ca. Oct. 1897, Jones Family Papers, UWF.

52. Page, "Bishop Michael J. Curley," 104. Stephen Mallory served as a U.S senator for two terms, the first beginning in 1897.

53. *Florida Times-Union* (Jacksonville, Fla.), Oct. 8, 1914.

54. Flynt, *Cracker Messiah,* 48. Catts moved from Alabama to DeFuniak Springs in 1911 and preached at a Baptist church. His first political venture came in 1904 when he ran for and lost a congressional seat in Alabama's fifth district.

55. Letter from T. J. Morris, Jacksonville, Fla., to Sidney Catts, DeFuniak Springs, Fla., Oct. 24, 1914, Sidney J. Catts Papers, UWF.

56. Letter from J. P. Sevinstime [?], Jacksonville, Fla., to Sidney Catts, DeFuniak Springs, Fla., Oct. 16, 1914, Sidney J. Catts Papers, UWF.

57. Letter from Irvin Kelsey, Griffin, Fla., to Sidney Catts, DeFuniak Springs, Fla., Nov. 8, 1914, Sidney J. Catts Papers, UWF.

58. Letter from Herbert M. Brockell, Tampa, Fla., to Sidney Catts, DeFuniak Springs, Fla., Nov. 2, 1914, Sidney J. Catts Papers, UWF.

59. Letter From O. N. Williams, Dade City, Fla., to Sidney Catts, DeFuniak Springs, Fla., Oct. 27, 1914, Sidney J. Catts Papers, UWF.

60. Letter from B. M. Phelps, Aurora, Mo., to Sidney Catts, DeFuniak Springs, Fla., Nov. 25, 1914, Sidney J. Catts Papers, UWF.

61. Letter from Springfield Court no. 1, Guardians of Liberty, Jacksonville, Fla., to Sidney Catts, DeFuniak Springs, Fla., Oct. 15, 1914, Sidney J. Catts Papers, UWF.

62. Letter from A. F. Lovelace [?], Jacksonville, Fla., to Sidney Catts, DeFuniak Springs, Fla., ca. Oct. 1914, Sidney J. Catts Papers, UWF.

63. Letter from "A POWERFUL SECRET SOCIETY OPPOSED TO PERVERSION OF AMERICAN RIGHTS," Jacksonville, Fla., to Sidney Catts, DeFuniak Springs, Fla., Oct. 17, 1914, Sidney J. Catts Papers, UWF.

64. Flynt, *Cracker Messiah,* 47, 71–72.

65. Letter from Richard Hargrave, Jacksonville, Fla., to Sidney Catts, DeFuniak Springs, Fla., Oct. 23, 1914, Sidney J. Catts Papers, UWF.

66. Letter from R. G. Kennan [?], Tampa, Fla., to Sidney Catts, DeFuniak Springs, Fla., Nov. 23, 1914, Sidney J. Catts Papers, UWF.

67. Letter from "a Catholic," Lancaster, Pa., to Sidney Catts in DeFuniak Springs, Fla., Oct. 15, 1914, Sidney J. Catts Papers, UWF.

68. Letter from P. H. Callahan, Louisville, Ky., to Sidney Catts, DeFuniak Springs, Fla., Dec. 7, 1914, Sidney J. Catts Papers, UWF.

69. Letter from Richard Hargrave, Jacksonville, Fla., to Sidney Catts, DeFuniak Springs, Fla., Jan. 16, 1915, Sidney J. Catts Papers, UWF.

70. Hearing notes from the Guardians of Liberty, Springfield Court no. 1, Jacksonville, Fla., signed by E. B. Donnell, Ralph Roberts, and J. B. Burke, passed by unanimous vote, Jan. 15, 1915, Sidney J. Catts Papers, UWF.

71. Letter from E. S. Morrison, Jacksonville, Fla., to Sidney Catts, DeFuniak Springs, Fla., Oct. 11, 1914, Sidney J. Catts Papers, UWF.

72. Letter from Richard Hargrave, Jacksonville, Fla., to Sidney Catts, DeFuniak Springs, Fla., Oct. 23, 1914, Sidney J. Catts Papers, UWF.

73. Letter from Richard Hargrave, Jacksonville, Fla., to Sidney Catts, DeFuniak Springs, Fla., Nov. 18, 1914, Sidney J. Catts Papers, UWF.

74. Letter from the Florida State Committee of Civil and Religious Liberty, Jacksonville, Fla., to William Burbridge, location illegible, Nov. 2, 1914, Sidney J. Catts Papers, UWF.

75. Flynt, *Cracker Messiah*, 61. Most of Catts's votes came from the rural panhandle and central Florida region.

76. Sidney Catts, "To the People of Florida," independently published political advertisement, ca. fall 1916, Sidney J. Catts Papers, UWF.

77. Flynt, *Cracker Messiah*, 63–93.

78. Qtd. in ibid., 93.

79. Qtd. in ibid., 92. Like the primary election, Catts received the majority of his votes from rural counties.

80. Letter from Jefferson McClillun, Lisbon, Fla., to Sidney Catts, Tallahassee, Fla., Jan. 8 1917; letter from Catts to McClillun, Jan. 13, 1917, Sidney J. Catts Papers, UWF.

81. Letter from George R. Mauck, Orlando, Fla., to Sidney Catts, Tallahassee, Fla., Jan. 28, 1917, Sidney J. Catts Papers, UWF.

82. Letter from J. A. Minter, Tyler, Ala., to Sidney Catts, Tallahassee, Fla., Jan. 25, 1917, Sidney J. Catts Papers, UWF.

83. Letter from LeGrand W. Jones, Texarkana, Ark./Tex., to Sidney Catts, Tallahassee, Fla., Jan. 7, 1917, Sidney J. Catts Papers, UWF.

84. Letter from G. W. Nance, Refugio, Tex., to Sidney Catts, Tallahassee, Fla., Jan. 13, 1917, Sidney J. Catts Papers, UWF.

85. Letter from J. P. Stephens, Tabor, N.C., to Sidney Catts, Tallahassee, Fla., Jan. 10, 1917, Sidney J. Catts Papers, UWF.

86. Letter from Virgil G. Hinshaw, Chicago, Ill., to Sidney Catts, DeFuniak Springs, Fla., Dec. 4, 1916, Sidney J. Catts Papers, UWF.

87. Letter from [?], Prohibition Party chairman, Drewry's Bluff, Va., to Sidney Catts, DeFuniak Springs, Fla., Dec. 20, 1916, Sidney J. Catts Papers, UWF.

88. Letter from L. J. U. Smay, Laurel, Iowa, to Sidney Catts, Tallahassee, Fla., Jan. 17, 1917, Sidney J. Catts Papers, UWF.

89. Letter from Carl V. Anderson, Prentice, Wis., to Sidney Catts, Tallahassee, Fla., Jan. 3, 1917, Sidney J. Catts Papers, UWF.

90. Letter from Nelson S. Parker, Asbury Park, N.J., to Sidney Catts, Tallahassee, Fla., Dec. 31, 1916, Sidney J. Catts Papers, UWF.

91. Letter from O. F. Garner, Chicago, Ill., to Sidney Catts, Tallahassee, Fla., Jan. 13, 1917, Sidney J. Catts Papers, UWF.

92. *Florida House Journal*, 22–28. See also, Rackleff, "Anti-Catholicism."

93. *Florida Times-Union* (Jacksonville, Fla.), Apr. 26, 1917, quoted in, ibid., 364.

94. Letter from Thomas J. Conger, Statesville, N.C., to Sidney Catts, Tallahassee, Fla., Jan. 6, 1917, Sidney J. Catts Papers, UWF.

95. Letter from T. W. Morgan, San Francisco, Calif., to Sidney Catts, Tallahassee, Fla., Jan. 5, 1917, Sidney J. Catts Papers, UWF.

96. Letter from A. D. Bulman, Portland, Oreg., to Sidney Catts, Tallahassee, Fla., Jan. 13, 1917, Sidney J. Catts Papers, UWF.

97. Qtd. in Flynt, *Cracker Messiah*, 36.

98. Greg Garrison, "The Courage of Father Coyle," *Birmingham (Ala.) News*, May 18, 2001.

99. Qtd. in Flynt, *Cracker Messiah*, 92.

100. Letter from Edward Allen, Mobile, Ala., to James Coyle, Birmingham, Ala., Mar. 26, 1915, Bishop Edward Patrick Allen Collection, CDA. Coyle had served at Saint Paul's since 1904.

101. Letter from James Coyle, Birmingham, Ala. to Edward Allen, Mobile, Ala., Dec. 18, 1916, Edward Patrick Allen Collection, CDA.

102. Letter from James Coyle, Birmingham, Ala., to Edward Allen, Mobile, Ala., Feb. 16, 1917, Edward Patrick Allen Collection, CDA.

103. Garrison, "The Courage of Father Coyle," *Birmingham (Ala.) News*, May 18, 2001.

104. Letter from James Coyle, Birmingham, Ala., to Edward Allen, Mobile, Ala., Sept. 19, 1917, Edward Patrick Allen Collection, CDA.

105. Letter from James Coyle, Birmingham, Ala., to Edward Allen, Mobile, Ala., Jul. 19, 1918, Edward Patrick Allen Collection, CDA.

106. Pruitt, "The Killing of Father Coyle."

107. Information on Coyle's murder and the events surrounding it come from Hamilton, *Hugo Black*, 84–93; Pruitt, "The Killing of Father Coyle"; Davies, *Rising Road.*

108. Qtd. in Hamilton, *Hugo Black*, 86.

109. See Hodes, *White Women, Black Men.*

110. Edward Allen, "Eulogy for Father James Coyle," ca. Aug. 1921, Bishop Edward Patrick Allen Collection, CDA.

111. Letter from Philip Pullen, Pensacola, Fla., to Edward Allen, Mobile, Ala., Aug. 17, 1921, Bishop Edward Patrick Allen Collection, CDA.

112. Letter from [?] Kerrigan, Warren, R.I., to Edward Allen, Mobile, Ala., Aug. 15, 1921, Bishop Edward Patrick Allen Collection, CDA.

113. Letter from M. Aloysia, Pittsburgh, Pa., to Edward Allen, Mobile, Ala., Aug. 15, 1921, Bishop Edward Patrick Allen Collection, CDA.

114. Letter from M. Praxedes [?], Loretto, Ky., to Edward Allen, Mobile, Ala., Aug. 20, 1921, Bishop Edward Patrick Allen Collection, CDA.

115. Hamilton, *Hugo Black*, 84–93.

116. *Birmingham (Ala.) Age-Herald*, Aug. 25, 1921; *Birmingham (Ala.) News*, Oct. 17, 1921; *New York Times*, Sept. 4, 1921.

117. Trial quotes and information come from Charles F. Hill, "Transcript of Father Coyle's Murder Trial," 10th Judicial Circuit, Criminal Investigation, Birmingham, Ala., CDA; *Birmingham (Ala.) Age-Herald*, Oct. 20, 1921; *Birmingham (Ala.) News*, Oct. 20, 1921; *Birmingham (Ala.) Age-Herald*, Oct. 22, 1921; "Free Stephenson of Priest's Murder," *New York Times*, Oct. 22, 1921.

118. "Free Stephenson of Priest's Murder," *New York Times*, Oct. 22, 1921.

119. Ibid.

120. Letter from Joseph M. Sheridan, Albany, Ala., to Edward Allen, Mobile, Ala., Sept. 17, 1921, Bishop Edward Patrick Allen Collection, CDA.

121. Letter from M. E. Kitrick, Ensley, Ala., to Edward Allen in Mobile, Ala., Aug. 20, 1921, Bishop Edward Patrick Allen Collection, CDA.

122. Letter from [illegible], Pratt City, Ala., to Edward Allen, Mobile, Ala., Aug. 23, 1921, Bishop Edward Patrick Allen Collection, CDA.

123. Letter from Joseph A. Malone, Pratt City, Ala., to Edward Allen, Mobile, Ala., Oct. 20, 1921, Bishop Edward Patrick Allen Collection, CDA.

124. Qtd. in Hamilton, *Hugo Black*, 91.

125. Letter from John E. Gunn, Natchez, Miss., to Edward Allen, Mobile, Ala., Oct. 22, 1921, Bishop Edward Patrick Allen Collection, CDA.

126. Letter from W. H. Zinn, New York, N.Y., to Edward Allen, Mobile, Ala., Oct. 25, 1921; letter from Allen to Zinn, Oct. 28, Bishop Edward Patrick Allen Collection, CDA.

127. Helen McGough, "Things I Remember about Father Coyle, His Death, Twenty Years Afterwards," *Catholic Weekly*, Aug. 1, 1941.

128. Fukuyama, "The Contours of Remoralization." Fukuyama explains that remoralization "presumes that there are certain moral values that are good for a given society, values that can be lost during a period of moral decay" (105).

129. Andrew S. Moore, *The South's Tolerable Alien*.

AFTERWORD

Epigraph: Gilderhus, *History and Historians*, 126.

1. Bynum, *Fragmentation and Redemption*, 14 (her emphasis).

2. Samuel S. Hill, *The New Encyclopedia of Southern Culture*; Hill and Lippy, *Encyclopedia of Religion in the South*. Of note, neither resource references free-thinking, agnosticism, or atheism.

3. Charles C. Moore, review of *The Negro a Beast*, by Charles Carroll, *Lexington (Ky.) Blue Grass Blade*, June 12, 1902.

4. Charles C. Moore, "The Negro Question Up Again," *Lexington (Ky.) Blue Grass Blade*, Sept. 30, 1906.

5. Charles C. Moore, "Religious Liberty Threatened," *Lexington (Ky.) Blue Grass Blade*, May 31, 1908. For a biography of Moore, see Sparks, *Kentucky's Most Hated Man*.

6. Fessenden, *Culture and Redemption*, 137–60. Interestingly, Fessenden shows how outside of Dixie, unbelievers like Robert G. Ingersoll and Mark Twain had more success finding favor with the mainstream. She shows how Twain in particular developed a civil religious piety that, while devoid of explicit adherence to Protestant dogma, still spoke to the favored categories of this population's social worldview.

7. Goldfield, *Still Fighting the Civil War*.

8. Andrew S. Moore, *The South's Tolerable Alien*, 27, 64.

9. Koehlinger, *The New Nuns*, 156, 145–175.

10. Qtd. in Heschel, "Theological Affinities," 177, 175.

11. Clive Webb, *Fight against Fear*, 141, 165.

12. Manis, *Southern Civil Religions in Conflict*, 137, 141.

13. Ibid., 5. See also Newman, *Getting Right with God.*

14. "Annexation," *Democratic Review,* Jul. 1845, 5.

15. Beecher, *Autobiography, Correspondence, Etc.,* 224. See also Howe, *What Hath God Wrought,* 702–8.

16. Pasquier, *Fathers on the Frontier.*

17. Smoak, *Ghost Dances and Identity,* 10; Utley, *The Last Days,* 60–83.

18. Marsden, *Religion and American Culture,* 53. See also Glass, "Peace Reform." Commenting on war and peace in the twentieth century, Glass claims that America's civil religion was "quite resistant to the concerns of peace activists" (497).

19. Butler, *War Is a Racket.*

BIBLIOGRAPHY

Abernethy, Arthur T. *The Jew a Negro: Being a Study of the Jewish Ancestry from an Impartial Standpoint.* Moravian Falls, N.C.: Dixie, 1910.

Ariel, Yaakov. *Evangelizing the Chosen People: Missions the Jews in America, 1880–2000.* Chapel Hill: University of North Carolina Press, 2000.

Arsenault, Raymond. "Charles Jacobson of Arkansas: A Jewish Politician in the Land of the Razorbacks, 1891–1915." In *"Turn to the South": Essays on Southern Jewry,* edited by Nathan M. Kaganoff and Melvin I. Urofsky, 55–75. Charlottesville: University Press of Virginia, 1979.

Ayers, Edward L. *The Promise of the New South: Life after Reconstruction.* New York: Oxford University Press, 1992.

Bailey, Thomas. *Race Orthodoxy in the South.* New York: Neale, 1914.

Baker, Ray Stannard. *Following the Color Line: An Account of Negro Citizenship in the American Democracy.* New York: Doubleday, Page, 1908.

Baptist, Edward E. *Creating an Old South: Middle Florida's Plantation Frontier before the Civil War.* Chapel Hill: University of North Carolina Press, 2002.

Barton, William E. *The Paternity of Abraham Lincoln: Was He the Son of Thomas Lincoln?* New York: Doran, 1920.

Beecher, Charles, ed. *Autobiography, Correspondence, Etc., of Lyman Beecher.* Vol. 2. 1864. Reprint, Whitefish, Mont.: Kessinger, 2006.

Beemer, Matthew A. "The Florida Chautauqua as Text: Creating and Satisfying a Disposition to Appropriate Cultural Goods in Northwest Florida." PhD diss., Louisiana State University, 1997.

Bellah, Robert N. *Beyond Belief: Essays on Religion in a Post-Traditional World.* New York: Harper and Row, 1970.

———. "Civil Religion in America." In *Beyond Belief: Essays on Religion in a Post-*

Traditional World, edited by Robert N. Bellah, 168–89. New York: Harper and Row, 1970.

———. "Comment." *Sociological Analysis* 50, no. 2 (1989): 147.

Bellah, Robert N., Richard Madsen, William M. Sullivan, Ann Swidler, and Steven M. Tipton. *The Good Society*. New York: Knopf, 1991.

———. *Habits of the Heart: Individualism and Commitment in American Life.* Berkeley: University of California Press, 1985.

Bennett, David H. *The Party of Fear: The American Far Right from Nativism to the Militia Movement.* 1988. Reprint, New York: Vintage, 1995.

Bennett, James B. *Religion and the Rise of Jim Crow in New Orleans*. Princeton, N.J.: Princeton University Press, 2005.

Berkhofer, Robert F. *Beyond the Great Story: History as Text and Discourse.* Cambridge, Mass.: Harvard University Press, 1995.

Blight, David W. *Race and Reunion: The Civil War in American Memory.* Cambridge, Mass.: Harvard University Press, 2001.

Bordin, Ruth. *Woman and Temperance: The Quest for Power and Liberty, 1873–1900.* New Brunswick, N.J.: Rutgers University Press, 1990.

Bowden, Jesse Earl. "The Colonel from Columbus." In *Iron Horse in the Pinelands: Building West Florida's Railroad, 1881–1883*, edited by Virginia Parks, 17–21. Pensacola, Fla.: Pensacola Historical Society, 1982.

———. "Editors and Other Hell Raisers in West Florida Journalism." In *Threads of Tradition and Culture along the Gulf Coast*, edited by Ronald V. Evans, 1–33. Pensacola, Fla.: Gulf Coast History and Humanities Conference, 1986.

Boylan, Anne M. *Sunday School: The Formation of an American Institution, 1790–1880.* New Haven, Conn.: Yale University Press, 1988.

Bragaw, Donald H. "Status of Negroes in a Southern Port City in the Progressive Era: Pensacola, 1896–1920." *Florida Historical Quarterly* 51, no. 3 (1973): 282–303.

Braude, Ann. "Women's History *Is* American Religious History." In *Retelling U.S. Religious History*, edited by Thomas A. Tweed, 87–107. Berkeley: University of California Press, 1997.

Bresnahan, Patrick J. *Seeing Florida with a Priest.* Zephyrhills, Fla.: Economy Print Shop, 1937.

Brevard, Caroline Mays. *A History of Florida from the Treaty of 1763 to Our Own Times.* Vols. 1–2. Deland, Fla.: Florida State Historical Society, 1924.

Brown, Canter, Jr. "The Civil War, 1861–1865." In *The New Florida History*, edited by Michael Gannon, 231–47. Gainesville: University Press of Florida, 1996.

———. *Florida's Black Public Officials, 1867–1924*. Tuscaloosa: University of Alabama Press, 1998.

Burns, Ken. *Reconstruction: The Second Civil War*. PBS, 2004.

Butler, Smedley D. *War Is a Racket: The Anti-War Classic by America's Most Decorated General*. Los Angeles: Feral House, 2003.

Bynum, Caroline Walker. *Fragmentation and Redemption: Essays on Gender and the Human Body in Medieval Religion*. New York: Zone, 1992.

Callahan, Richard J., Jr., Kathryn Lofton, and Chad E. Seales. "Allegories of Progress: Industrial Religion in the United States." *Journal of the American Academy of Religion* 78, no. 1 (2010): 1–39.

Campbell, Will D. *Brother to a Dragonfly*. New York: Continuum, 1977.

Carnegie, Andrew. "Wealth." *North American Review*, June 1889, 653–64.

Carroll, Austin. *A Catholic History of Alabama and the Floridas*. Vol. 1. New York: P. J. Kennedy and Sons, 1908.

Carroll, Charles. *The Negro a Beast*. St. Louis, Mo.: American Book and Bible House, 1900.

Cash, Wilbur J. *The Mind of the South*. New York: Knopf, 1941.

Champion, Lillian D. *Giant Tracking: William Dudley Chipley and Other Giants of Men*. Columbus, Ga.: Quill, 1985.

Chernus, Ira. Review of *Myths America Lives By*, by Richard T. Hughes. *Journal of the American Academy of Religion* 73, no. 2 (2005): 539–41.

Cherry, Conrad, ed. Introduction. *God's New Israel: Religious Interpretations of American Destiny*. 2nd ed. Chapel Hill: University of North Carolina Press, 1998.

Chidester, David. *Christianity: A Global History*. New York: HarperCollins, 2000.

Clark, Thomas D. "The Post–Civil War Economy in the South." In *Jews in the South*, edited by Leonard Dinnerstein and Mary Dale Palsson, 159–69. Baton Rouge: Louisiana State University Press, 1973.

Cohen, William. *At Freedom's Edge: Black Mobility and the Southern White Quest for Racial Control, 1861–1915*. Baton Rouge: Louisiana State University Press, 1991.

Coker, Joe L. *Liquor in the Land of the Lost Cause: Southern White Evangelicals and the Prohibition Movement*. Lexington: University Press of Kentucky, 2007.

Conkin, Paul K. *American Originals: Homemade Varieties of Christianity*. Chapel Hill: University of North Carolina Press, 1997.

Cox, Karen L. *Dixie's Daughters: The United Daughters of the Confederacy and the Preservation of Confederate Culture*. Gainesville: University Press of Florida, 2003.

Craighead, Erwin. *From Mobile's Past: Sketches of Memorable People and Events.* Mobile, Ala.: Powers, 1925.

Crary, John Williamson. *Reminiscences of the Old South from 1834 to 1866: Things Noted Not Found in History.* 1897. Reprint, Pensacola, Fla.: Perdido Bay Press, 1984.

———. *Sixty Years a Brickmaker.* Indianapolis, Ind.: T. A. Randall, 1890.

Cresswell, Tim. *In Place/Out of Place: Geography, Ideology, and Transgression.* Minneapolis: University of Minnesota Press, 1996.

Cristi, Marcella. *From Civil Religion to Political Religion: The Intersection of Culture, Religion and Politics.* Waterloo, Can.: Wilfrid Laurier University Press, 2001.

Crowley, John G. *Primitive Baptists of the Wiregrass South: 1815 to Present.* Gainesville: University Press of Florida, 1998.

Cummings, Kate. *Gleanings from the Southland: Sketches of Life and Manners of the People of the South before, during and after the War of Secession.* Birmingham, Ala.: Roberts and Son, 1895.

Cummings, Kathleen Sprows. *New Women of the Old Faith: Gender and American Catholicism in the Progressive Era.* Chapel Hill: University of North Carolina Press, 2010.

Davies, Sharon. *Rising Road: A True Tale of Love, Race, and Religion in America.* New York: Oxford University Press, 2009.

Davis, Benjamin J. *Communist Councilman from Harlem: Autobiographical Notes Written in a Federal Penitentiary.* New York: International Publishers, 1969.

Davis, Cyprian, and Jamie Phelps, eds. *"Stamped with the Image of God": African Americans as God's Image in Black.* New York: Orbis, 2003.

Davis, Ella Catherine. "Dougherty's Women during the '60s and After." In *History and Reminiscences of Dougherty County Georgia,* edited by Daughters of the American Revolution, Thronateeska Chapter, 271–78. Albany, Ga.: Herald, 1924.

Davis, William Watson. *The Civil War and Reconstruction in Florida.* 1913. Reprint, Gainesville: University of Florida Press, 1964.

DeBolt, Dean. "The Florida Chautauqua." *FEH Forum* 8, no. 3 (1990): 6–10.

Demerath, N. J., and Rhys Williams. "Civil Religion in an Uncivil Society." *Annals of the American Academy* 480, no. 1 (1985): 154–66.

Dinnerstein, Leonard. *Antisemitism in America.* New York: Oxford University Press, 1994.

———. *The Leo Frank Case.* New York: Columbia University Press, 1969.

Dinnerstein, Leonard, and Mary Dale Palsson. Introduction. In *Jews in the South,* edited by Leonard Dinnerstein and Mary Dale Palsson, 3–23. Baton Rouge: Louisiana State University Press, 1973.

Dittmer, John. *Black Georgia in the Progressive Era, 1900–1920*. Urbana: University of Illinois Press, 1980.

Doherty, Herbert J., Jr. *Richard Keith Call: Southern Unionist*. Gainesville: University of Florida Press, 1961.

Donald, David Herbert. *Lincoln*. New York: Touchstone, 1995.

Dorsey, Allison. *To Build our Lives Together: Community Formation in Black Atlanta, 1875–1906*. Athens: University of Georgia Press, 2004.

Douglas, Davison M. *Jim Crow Moves North: The Battle over Northern School Desegregation, 1865–1954*. New York: Cambridge University Press, 2005.

Dunning, William Archibald. *Essays on the Civil War and Reconstruction and Related Topics*. New York: Macmillan, 1898.

Durkheim, Emile. *The Elementary Forms of Religious Life*. Translated by Karen E. Fields. New York: Free Press, 1995.

Eppes, Susan Bradford. *The Negro of the Old South: A Bit of Period History*. Chicago: Joseph G. Branch, 1925.

———. *Through Some Eventful Years*. 1926. Reprint, Gainesville: University Press of Florida, 1968.

Etemadi, Judy Nicholas. "'A Love-Mad Man': Senator Chares W. Jones of Florida." *Florida Historical Quarterly* 56, no. 2 (1977): 123–37.

Etzioni, Amitai. *The New Golden Rule: Community and Morality in a Democratic Society*. New York: Basic, 1996.

Ewens, Mary. "Women in the Convent." In *American Catholic Women: A Historical Exploration*, edited by Karen Kennelly, 17–47. New York: Macmillan, 1989.

Fairchild, Henry Pratt. "The Literacy Test and Its Making." *Quarterly Journal of Economics* 31, no. 3 (1917): 447–60.

Fessenden, Tracy. *Culture and Redemption: Religion, the Secular, and American Literature*. Princeton, N.J.: Princeton University Press, 2007.

———. "Gendering Religion." *Journal of Women's History* 14, no. 1 (2002): 163–69.

Fialka, John J. *Sisters: Catholic Nuns and the Making of America*. New York: St. Martin's, 2003.

Flynt, J. Wayne. *Cracker Messiah: Governor Sidney J. Catts of Florida*. Baton Rouge: Louisiana State University Press, 1977.

Foner, Eric. *Reconstruction: America's Unfinished Revolution, 1863–1877*. New York: Harper and Row, 1988.

Foster, Gaines M. *Ghosts of the Confederacy: Defeat, the Lost Cause, and the Emergence of the New South 1865–1913.* New York: Oxford University Press, 1987.

Frederickson, George M. *Racism: A Short History.* Princeton, N.J.: Princeton University Press, 2003.

Friedman, Jean E. *The Enclosed Garden: Women and Community in the Evangelical South, 1830–1900.* Chapel Hill: University Press of North Carolina, 1985.

Fukuyama, Francis. "The Contours of Remoralization." In *The Communitarian Reader: Beyond the Essentials,* edited by Amitai Etzioni, Drew Volmert and Elanit Rothschild, 105–10. Lanham, Md.: Rowman and Littlefield, 2004.

Gaston, Paul M. *The New South Creed: A Study in Southern Mythmaking.* New York: Knopf, 1970.

Gatewood, Willard B., Jr. "Strangers and the Southern Eden: The South and Immigration, 1900–1920." In *Ethnic Minorities in the Gulf Coast Society,* edited by Jerrell H. Shofner and Linda V. Ellsworth, 1–24. Pensacola, Fla.: Gulf Coast Historical and Humanities Conference, 1979.

Gilderhus, Mark T. *History and Historians: A Historiographical Introduction.* 4th ed. Upper Saddle River, N.J.: Prentice Hall, 2000.

Ginzburg, Ralph. *100 Years of Lynching.* Baltimore, Md.: Black Classic Press, 1988.

Girard, René. *Violence and the Sacred.* Translated by Patrick Gregory. Baltimore, Md.: Johns Hopkins University Press, 1977.

Glass, Matthew. "Peace Reform." In *The Encyclopedia of American Religious History,* edited by Edward L. Queen II, Stephen R. Prothero, and Gardiner H. Shattuck Jr., 496–97. New York: Facts on File, 1996.

Goldfield, David. *Still Fighting the Civil War: The American South and Southern History.* Baton Rouge: Louisiana State University, 2002.

Goldstein, Eric L. "'Now Is the Time to Show Your True Colors': Southern Jews, Whiteness, and the Rise of Jim Crow." In *Jewish Roots in Southern Soil: A New History,* edited by Marcie Cohen Ferris and Mark I. Greenberg, 134–55. Lebanon, N.H.: University Press of New England, 2006.

Grady, Henry. "The New South." In *The New South: Writings and Speeches of Henry Grady,* edited by Mills Lane, 3–13. Savannah, Ga.: Beehive Press, 1971.

Grantham, Dewey W. *Southern Progressivism: The Reconciliation of Progress and Tradition.* Knoxville: University of Tennessee Press, 1983.

Griffith, Benjamin W. "Chautauqua." In *Encyclopedia of Southern Culture,* edited by Charles Reagan Wilson and William Ferris, 273. Chapel Hill: University of North Carolina Press, 1989.

Grossman, James R. *Land of Hope: Chicago, Black Southerners, and the Great Migration*. Chicago: University of Chicago Press, 1989.

Grusd, Edward E. *B'nai B'rith: The Story of a Covenant*. New York: Appleton-Century, 1966.

Guthrie, John J. *Keepers of the Spirits: The Judicial Response to Prohibition Enforcement in Florida, 1885–1935*. Westport, Conn.: Greenwood, 1998.

Hacker, Louis M., and Mark D. Hirsch. *Proskauer: His Life and Times*. Tuscaloosa: University of Alabama Press, 1978.

Hackney, Sheldon. *Populism and Progressivism in Alabama*. Princeton, N.J.: Princeton University Press, 1969.

Hale, Elizabeth Grace. *Making Whiteness: The Culture of Segregation in the South, 1890–1940*. New York: Pantheon, 1998.

Haller, John S., Jr. *Outcasts from Evolution: Scientific Attitudes of Racial Inferiority, 1859–1900*. Urbana: University of Illinois Press, 1971.

Hamburger, Philip. *Separation of Church and State*. Cambridge, Mass.: Harvard University Press, 2002.

Hamilton, Virginia Van der Veer. *Hugo Black: The Alabama Years*. Louisiana State University Press: Baton Rouge, 1972.

Hammond, Phillip E., Amanda Porterfield, James G. Moseley, and Jonathan D. Sarna. "American Civil Religion Revisited." *Religion and American Culture* 4, no. 1 (1994): 1–23.

Harrison, Jo-Ann. "School Ceremonies for Yitzhak Rabin: Social Constructions of Civil Religion in Israeli Schools." *Israel Studies* 6, no. 3 (2001): 113–34.

Harvey, Paul. *Redeeming the South: Religious Cultures and Racial Identities among Southern Baptists, 1865–1925*. Chapel Hill: University of North Carolina Press, 1997.

———. "Religion in the American South since the Civil War." In *A Companion to the American South*, edited by John B. Boles, 387–406. Malden, Mass.: Blackwell, 2002.

Harwell, Richard B., ed. *Kate: The Journal of a Confederate Nurse*. Baton Rouge: Louisiana State University Press, 1959.

Henry, Josephine. "The New Woman of the New South." *Arena*, Feb. 1894–95, 334–35.

Heraclitus. "Universal Flux." In *The Presocratics*, edited by Philip Wheelwright, 70–71. New York: Odyssey Press, 1966.

Heschel, Susannah. "Theological Affinities in the Writings of Abraham Joshua Heschel and Martin Luther King, Jr." In *Black Zion: African American Religious*

Encounters with Judaism, edited by Yvonne Chireau and Nathanial Deutsch, 168–86. New York: Oxford University Press, 2000.

Hewitt, Nancy A. *Southern Discomfort: Women's Activism in Tampa, Florida 1880s–1920s.* Urbana: University of Illinois Press, 2001.

Hill, Patricia R. *The World Their Household: The American Woman's Foreign Mission Movement and Cultural Transformation, 1870–1920.* Ann Arbor: University of Michigan Press, 1985.

Hill, Samuel S., Jr., ed. *The New Encyclopedia of Southern Culture.* Volume 1: *Religion.* Chapel Hill: University of North Carolina Press, 2006.

———. *Southern Churches in Crisis.* New York: Holt, Rinehart, and Winston, 1966.

Hill, Samuel S., Jr., and Charles H. Lippy, eds. *Encyclopedia of Religion in the South.* 2nd ed. Macon, Ga.: Mercer University Press, 2005.

"History of the Albany Womans Christian Temperance Union." In *History and Reminiscences of Dougherty County Georgia*, edited by Daughters of the American Revolution, Thronateeska Chapter, 306–9. Albany, Ga.: Herald, 1924.

Hodes, Martha. *White Women, Black Men: Illicit Sex in the 19th-Century South.* New Haven, Conn.: Yale University Press, 1997.

Holmes, William F. "Anti-Catholicism in Georgia During the Progressive Era: A Comment." In *Ethnic Minorities in Gulf Coast Society*, edited by Jerrell H. Shofner and Linda V. Ellsworth, 31–37. Pensacola, Fla.: Gulf Coast History and Humanities Conference, 1979.

Howe, Daniel Walker. *What Hath God Wrought: The Transformation of America, 1815–1848.* New York: Oxford University Press, 2007.

"The Jefferson Davis Chapter, Children of the Confederacy." In *History and Reminiscences of Dougherty County Georgia*, edited by Daughters of the American Revolution, Thronateeska Chapter, 279. Albany, Ga.: Herald, 1924.

Jick, Leon. *The Americanization of the Synagogue, 1820–1870.* Hanover, N.H.: Brandeis University Press, 1976.

Johnson, Dudley S. "The Florida Railroad after the Civil War." *Florida Historical Quarterly* 47, no. 3 (1969): 293–310.

Jones, Sam. *Sam Jones' Own Book: A Series of Sermons.* Cincinnati, Ohio: Cranston and Stowe, 1887.

Journal and Yearbook of the Florida Conference Methodist Episcopal Church, South. Lakeland, Fla.: Tribune Printing Company, 1909.

Journal of the Florida House of Representatives. Tallahassee, Fla.: State Printer, 1917.

Kelley, William D. *The Old South and the New: A Series of Letters by Hon. William D. Kelley.* New York: G. P. Putnam's Sons, 1888.

Kerber, Stephen. "Park Trammell and the Florida Democratic Primary of 1916." *Florida Historical Quarterly* 3, no. 3 (1980): 255–72.

Knobel, Dale T. *"America for the Americans": The Nativist Movement in the United States.* New York: Twayne, 1996.

Koehlinger, Amy L. *The New Nuns: Racial Justice and Religious Reform in the 1960s.* Cambridge, Mass.: Harvard University Press, 2007.

Landau, Edmund A. "The Jew in Albany." In *History and Reminiscences of Dougherty County Georgia,* edited by Daughters of the American Revolution, Thronateeska Chapter, 199–213. Albany, Ga., 1924.

Laws of Florida. Tallahassee, Fla.: State Printer, 1913.

"Lazarus Schwarz." In *History of Alabama and Her People,* edited by Albert Burton Moore, 710. New York: American Historical Society, 1927.

Lebsock, Suzanne. "Radical Reconstruction and the Property Rights of Southern Women." *Journal of Southern History* 43, no. 2 (1977): 195–216.

"Leon Schwarz." In *History of Alabama and Her People,* edited by Albert Burton Moore, 581–82. New York: American Historical Society, 1927.

Link, William A. *The Paradox of Southern Progressivism, 1880–1930.* Chapel Hill: University of North Carolina Press, 1992.

Litwack, Leon F. *Trouble in Mind: Black Southerners in the Age of Jim Crow.* New York: Knopf, 1998.

Long, Ellen Call. *Florida Breezes; or, Florida, New and Old.* 1883. Reprint, Gainesville: University of Florida Press, 1962.

Love, E. K. *History of the First African Baptist Church.* Savannah, Ga.: Morning News Print, 1888.

Luker, Ralph E. *The Social Gospel in Black and White: American Racial Reform, 1885–1912.* Chapel Hill: University of North Carolina Press, 1991.

Lyerly, Lynn. "Women and Southern Religion." In *Religion in the American South: Protestants and Others in History and Culture,* edited by Beth Barton Schweiger and Donald G. Mathews, 247–81. Chapel Hill: University of North Carolina Press, 2004.

Manis, Andrew M. *Southern Civil Religions in Conflict: Black and White Baptists and Civil Rights, 1947–1957.* 1987. Reprint, Athens: University of Georgia Press, 2002.

Marsden, George M. *Religion and American Culture.* 2nd ed. New York: Harcourt College, 2001.

Marvin, Carolyn, and David W. Ingle. "Blood Sacrifice and the Nation:

Revisiting Civil Religion." *Journal of the American Academy of Religion* 64, no. 4 (1996): 767–80.

Mathews, Donald G. "Lynching Is Part of the Religion of Our People: Faith in the Christian South." In *Religion in the American South: Protestants and Others in History and Culture*, edited by Beth Barton Schweiger and Donald G. Mathews, 153–94. Chapel Hill: University of North Carolina Press, 2004.

Mathisen, James A. "Twenty Years after Bellah: Whatever Happened to American Civil Religion." *Sociological Analysis* 50, no. 2 (1989): 129–46.

McDowell, John Patrick. *The Social Gospel in the South: The Woman's Home Mission Movement in the Methodist Episcopal Church, South, 1886–1939*. Baton Rouge: Louisiana State University Press, 1982.

McGreevy, John T. *Catholicism and American Freedom: A History*. New York: Norton, 2003.

McGregory, Jerrilyn. *Wiregrass Country*. Jackson: University Press of Mississippi, 1997.

McGuire, Peter S. "The Railroads of Georgia, 1860–1880." *Georgia Historical Quarterly* 16, no. 3 (1932): 179–213.

McPherson, James M. *Battle Cry Freedom: The Civil War Era*. New York: Ballantine, 1988.

Melnick, Ralph. "Jews in the South." In *Encyclopedia of Religion in the South*, edited by Samuel S. Hill Jr., 354–62. Macon, Ga.: Mercer University Press, 1997.

Meyer, Jeffrey F. *Myths in Stone: Religious Dimensions of Washington D.C.* Berkeley: University of California Press, 2001.

Michaels, Walter Benn. *Our America: Nativism, Modernism, and Pluralism*. Durham, N.C.: Duke University Press, 1995.

Mims, Edwin. "The South Realizing Itself: Redeemers of the Soil." *Workers World*, Nov. 1911, 41–54.

Minnix, Kathleen. *Laughter in the Amen Corner: The Life of Evangelist Sam Jones*. Athens: University of Georgia Press, 1993.

Mixon, Gregory. *The Atlanta Riot: Race, Class, and Violence in a New South City*. Gainesville: University Press of Florida, 2005.

Mohl, Raymond A., and George E. Pozzetta. "From Migration to Multiculturalism: A History of Florida Immigration." In *The New Florida History*, edited by Michael Gannon, 391–417. Gainesville: University of Florida Press, 1996.

Montgomery, David. "Radical Republicanism in Pennsylvania, 1866–1873." *Pennsylvania Magazine of History and Biography* 85, no. 4 (1961): 439–57.

Montgomery, William E. *Under Their Own Vine and Fig Tree: The African-American Church in the South, 1865–1900*. Baton Rouge: Louisiana State University Press, 1993.

Moore, Andrew S. *The South's Tolerable Alien: Roman Catholics in Alabama and Georgia, 1945–1970*. Baton Rouge: Louisiana State University Press, 2007.

Moore, R. Laurence. *Religious Outsiders and the Making of Americans*. New York: Oxford University Press, 1986.

Morgan, Henry. "History of Albany." In *History and Reminiscences of Dougherty County Georgia*, edited by Daughters of the American Revolution, Thronateeska Chapter, 14–20. Albany, Ga.: Herald, 1924.

Morris, Vivian Gunn, and Curtis L. Morris. *The Price They Paid: Desegregation in an African American Community*. New York: Teachers College Press, 2002.

Moseley, Charlton, and Frederick Brogdon. "A Lynching in Statesboro: The Story of Paul Reed and Will Cato." *Georgia Historical Quarterly* 65, no. 2 (1981): 104–18.

Moses, Alfred G. *A Congregation in the Name of God*. Mobile, Ala.: Brisk, 1905.

———. *Jewish Science: Divine Healing in Judaism*. Mobile, Ala.: Alfred Moses, 1916.

———. *Jewish Science: Psychology of Health, Joy and Success*. New Orleans, La.: Searcy and Pfaff, 1920.

Muldrey, Mary H. *Abounding in Mercy: Mother Austin Carroll*. New Orleans, La.: Habersham, 1988.

Newman, Mark. *Getting Right with God: Southern Baptists and Desegregation, 1945–1995*. Tuscaloosa: University of Alabama Press, 2001.

Northern, William J., ed. *Men of Mark in Georgia*. Atlanta: A. B. Caldwell, 1911.

O'Brien, Michael. "A Private Passion: W. J. Cash." In *Rethinking the South: Essays in Intellectual History*. Baltimore, Md.: Johns Hopkins University Press, 1988.

Ochs, Stephen J. "The Ordeal of the Black Priest." *U.S. Catholic Historian* 5, no. 1 (1986): 45–66.

Oltman, Adele. *Sacred Mission, Worldly Ambition: Black Christian Nationalism in the Age of Jim Crow*. Athens: University of Georgia Press, 2008.

Ortiz, Paul. *Emancipation Betrayed: The Hidden History of Black Organizing and White Violence in Florida from Reconstruction to the Bloody Election of 1920*. Berkeley: University of California Press, 2005.

Ownby, Ted. *Subduing Satan: Religion, Recreation, and Manhood in the Rural South, 1865–1920*. Chapel Hill: University of North Carolina Press, 1990.

Page, David P. "Bishop Michael J. Curley and Anti-Catholic Nativism in Florida." *Florida Historical Quarterly* 45, no. 2 (1966): 101–17.

Paisley, Clifton. *From Cotton to Quail.* Tallahassee: Florida State University Press, 1968.

Parsons, Talcott. "Durkheim's Contribution to the Theory of Integration of Social Systems." In *Essays on Sociology and Philosophy,* edited by Kurt H. Wolff, 118–53. New York: Harper, 1960.

Pasquier, Michael. *Fathers on the Frontier: French Missionaries and the Roman Catholic Priesthood in the United States, 1789–1870.* New York: Oxford University Press, 2010.

———. "'Though Their Skin Remains Brown, I Hope Their Souls Will Soon Be White': Slavery, French Missionaries, and the Roman Catholic Priesthood in the American South, 1789–1865." *Church History* 77, no. 2 (2008): 337–70.

Pennington, Edgar L. "The Organization of the Protestant Episcopal Church in the Confederate States of America." *Historical Magazine of the Protestant Episcopal Church* 17, no. 4 (1948): 308–38.

Poole, W. Scott. *Never Surrender: Confederate Memory and Conservatism in the South Carolina Upcountry.* Athens: University of Georgia Press, 2004.

Porterfield, Amanda. *The Transformation of American Religion: The Story of a Late Twentieth-Century Awakening.* New York: Oxford University Press, 2001.

Proceedings of the 42nd Annual Encampment of the Grand Army of the Republic, Department of Pennsylvania. Harrisburg, Pa.: Harrisburg Publishing Company, 1908.

Proctor, Samuel. "Prelude to the New Florida, 1877–1919." In *The New Florida History,* edited by Michael Gannon, 265–86. Gainesville: University Press of Florida, 1996.

Proskauer, Joseph M. *A Segment of My Times.* New York: Farrar, Straus and Company, 1950.

Pruitt, Paul M., Jr. "The Killing of Father Coyle: Private Tragedy, Public Shame." *Alabama Heritage,* no. 30 (1993): 24–37.

Pruitt, Paul M., Jr., and David I. Durham, eds. *The Private Life of a New South Lawyer: Stephens Croom's 1875–1876 Journal.* Tuscaloosa: University of Alabama School of Law, 2002.

Raboteau, Albert J. *A Fire in the Bones: Reflections on African-American Religious History.* Boston: Beacon Press, 1995.

———. *Slave Religion: "The Invisible Institution" in the American South.* New York: Oxford University Press, 1978.

Rackleff, Robert B. "Anti-Catholicism and the Florida Legislature, 1911–1919." *Florida Historical Quarterly* 50, no. 4 (1972): 352–65.

Rerick, Rowland H. *Memoirs of Florida.* Atlanta, Ga.: Southern Historical Association, 1902.

"Rev. Alfred Geiger Moses." In *History of Alabama and Her People,* edited by Albert Burton Moore, 736. New York: American Historical Society, 1927.

Richardson, Simon Peter. *The Lights and Shadows of Itinerant Life: An Autobiography of Rev. Simon Peter Richardson, DD, of the North Carolina Conference.* Nashville, Tenn.: Publishing House Methodist Episcopal Church, South, 1900.

Rieser, Andrew C. *The Chautauqua Movement: Protestants, Progressives, and the Culture of Modern Liberalism.* New York: Columbia University Press, 2003.

Rivers, Larry Eugene, and Canter Brown Jr. *Laborers in the Vineyard of the Lord: The Beginnings of the AME Church in Florida, 1865–1895.* Gainesville: University Press of Florida, 2001.

Roberts, Albert Hubbard. "Wilkinson Call, Soldier and Senator." Pt. 1. *Florida Historical Quarterly* 12, no. 14 (1934): 95–113.

———. "Wilkinson Call, Soldier and Senator." Pt. 2. *Florida Historical Quarterly* 12, no. 4 (1934): 179–97.

Rockaway, Robert, and Arnon Gutfeld. "Demonic Images of the Jew in the Nineteenth Century United States." *American Jewish History* 89, no. 4 (2002): 355–81.

Rogers, William Warren. *Thomas County, 1865–1900.* Tallahassee: Florida State University Press, 1973.

———. *Transition to the Twentieth Century: Thomas County, Georgia, 1900–1920.* Tallahassee, Fla.: Sentry Press, 2002.

Rogers, William Warren, Robert David Ward, Leah Rawls Atkins, and Wayne Flynt. *Alabama: The History of a Deep South State.* Tuscaloosa: University of Alabama Press, 1994.

Rogoff, Leonard. "Is the Jew White? The Racial Place of the Southern Jew." *American Jewish History* 85, no. 3 (1997): 195–230.

Rogow, Faith. *"Gone to Another Meeting": The National Council of Jewish Women, 1893–1993.* Tuscaloosa: University of Alabama Press, 1993.

Rosen, Robert N. *The Jewish Confederates.* Columbia: University of South Carolina Press, 2000.

Rousseau, Jean-Jacques. *The Social Contract and Other Later Political Writings.* Translated by Victor Gourevitch. New York: Cambridge University Press, 1997.

Sarna, Jonathan D. *American Judaism: A History.* New Haven, Conn.: Yale University Press, 2004.

———. "Jewish-Christian Hostility in the United States: Perceptions from a Jewish Point of View." In *Uncivil Religion: Interreligious Hostility in America,* edited by Robert N. Bellah and Frederick E. Greenspahn, 5–22. New York: Crossroads, 1987.

Schmier, Louis. "Hellooo! Peddlerman! Hellooo!" In *Ethnic Minorities in the Gulf Coast Society,* edited by Jerrell H. Shofner and Linda V. Ellsworth, 75–88. Pensacola, Fla.: Gulf Coast History and Humanities Conference, 1979.

———. "Jewish Press." In *Encyclopedia of Religion in the South,* edited by Samuel S. Hill Jr., 352–54. Macon, Ga.: Mercer University Press, 1997.

———. "Jews and Gentiles in a South Georgia Town." In *Jews of the South: Selected Essays from the Southern Jewish Historical Society,* edited by Samuel Proctor, Louis Schmier, and Malcolm Stern, 1–16. Macon, Ga.: Mercer University Press, 1984.

———, ed. *Reflections of Southern Jewry: The Letters of Charles Wessolowsky, 1878–1879.* Macon, Ga.: Mercer University Press, 1982.

Schofield, Malcolm. *Saving the City: Philosopher-Kings and Other Classical Paradigms.* New York: Routledge, 1999.

Schweiger, Beth Barton. *The Gospel Working Up: Progress and the Pulpit in Nineteenth-Century Virginia.* New York: Oxford University Press, 2000.

Scott, Anne Firor. *The Southern Lady: From Pedestal to Politics, 1830–1930.* Chicago: University Press of Chicago, 1970.

Semonche, John E. *Keeping the Faith: A Cultural History of the U.S. Supreme Court.* Lanham, Md.: Rowman and Littlefield, 1998.

Shadgett, Olive H. "Charles Jones Jenkins, Jr." In *Georgians in Profile,* edited by Horace Montgomery, 220–44. Athens: University of Georgia Press, 1958.

Shattuck, Gardiner H., Jr. "Lost Cause Myth." In *The Encyclopedia of American Religious History,* edited by Edward L. Queen II, Stephen R. Prothero, and Gardiner H. Shattuck Jr., 368–69. New York: Facts on File, 1996.

Sherwin, Byron L. "Portrait of a Romantic Rebel: Bernard C. Ehrenreich (1876–1955)." In *"Turn to the South": Essays on Southern Jewry,* edited by Nathan M. Kaganoff and Melvin I. Urofsky, 1–12. Charlottesville: University Press of Virginia, 1979.

Sims, Anastatia. *The Power of Femininity in the New South: Women's Organizations and Politics in North Carolina, 1880–1930.* Columbia: University of South Carolina Press, 1997.

Smith, Craig R. *Daniel Webster and the Oratory of Civil Religion.* Columbia: University of Missouri Press, 2004.

Smith, John David. *An Old Creed for the New South: Proslavery Ideology and Historiography, 1865–1918*. Westport, Conn.: Greenwood, 1985.

Smoak, Gregory E. *Ghost Dances and Identity: Prophetic Religion and American Indian*. Berkeley: University of California Press, 2006.

Sommerville, Diane Miller. *Rape and Race in the Nineteenth-Century South*. Chapel Hill, N.C.: University of North Carolina Press, 2004.

Sparks, John. *Kentucky's Most Hated Man: Charles Chilton Moore and the "Blue Grass Blade."* Nicholasville, Ky.: Wind Publications, 2009.

Standiford, Les. *Last Train to Paradise: Henry Flagler and the Building of the Railroad That Crossed the Ocean*. New York: Crown, 2002.

Stout, Harry S. *Upon the Altar of the Nation: A Moral History of the American Civil War*. New York: Viking, 2006.

Stowell, Daniel W. *Rebuilding Zion: The Religious Reconstruction of the South, 1863–1877*. New York: Oxford University Press, 1998.

———. "Why 'Redemption'? Religion and the End of Reconstruction, 1869–1877." In *Vale of Tears: New Essays on Religion and Reconstruction*, edited by Edward J. Blum and W. Scott Poole, 133–46. Macon, Ga.: Mercer University Press, 2005.

Summers, Mark W. "Railroads." In *Encyclopedia of Southern Culture*, edited by Charles Reagan Wilson and William Ferris, 656–58. Chapel Hill: University of North Carolina Press, 1989.

Tetzlaff, Monica Maria. *Cultivating a New South: Abbie Holmes Christensen and the Politics of Race and Gender*. Columbia: University of South Carolina Press, 2002.

Tindall, George B. *The Emergence of the New South*. Baton Rouge: Louisiana State University Press, 1967.

Tindall, George B., and David E. Shi. *America: A Narrative History*. 5th ed. Vol. 2. New York: Norton, 1999.

Tolonay, Steward E., and E. M. Beck. *A Festival of Violence: An Analysis of Southern Lynching, 1882–1930*. Chicago: University of Illinois Press, 1995.

Umansky, Ellen M. *From Christian Science to Jewish Science: Spiritual Healing and American Jews*. New York: Oxford University Press, 2005.

Utley, Robert Marshall. *The Last Days of the Sioux Nation*. New Haven, Conn.: Yale University Press, 2004.

Vance, Rupert B. "A Karl Marx for Hill Billies: Portrait of a Southern Leader." *Social Forces*, Dec. 1930, 180–90.

Walker, Randi Jones. "Liberators for Colonial Anahuac: A Rumination on

North American Civil Religions." *Religion and American Culture* 9, no. 2
(1999): 183–203.

Ward, Geoffrey C. *Unforgivable Blackness: The Rise and Fall of Jack Johnson.* New
York: Knopf, 2004.

Washington, Booker T. *The Negro in Business.* New York: AMS Press, 1907.

Washington, James Melvin. *Frustrated Fellowship: The Black Baptist Quest for Social
Power.* Macon, Ga.: Mercer University Press, 1986.

Webb, Clive. *Fight against Fear: Southern Jews and Black Civil Rights.* Athens:
University of Georgia Press, 2001.

———. "A Tangled Web: Black-Jewish Relations in the Twentieth-Century
South." In *Jewish Roots in Southern Soil: A New History*, edited by Marcie Cohen
Ferris and Mark I. Greenberg, 192–209. Lebanon, N.H.: University Press of
New England, 2006.

Webb, Samuel L. "The Great Mobile Whiskey War." *Alabama Heritage*, Winter
2005, 30–44.

———. "Southern Politics in the Age of Populism and Progressivism: A
Historiographical Essay." In *A Companion to the American South*, edited by
John B. Boles, 321–35. Malden, Mass.: Blackwell, 2002.

Welter, Barbara. "The Cult of True Womanhood, 1820–1960." *American
Quarterly* 18, no. 2 (1966): 151–74.

———. "The Feminization of American Religion: 1800–1860." In *Clio's
Consciousness Raised*, edited by Mary Hartman and Lois Banner, 137–57. New
York: Harper, 1973.

Wheeler, Marjorie Spruill. *New Women of the New South: The Leaders of the Woman
Suffrage Movement in the Southern States.* New York: Oxford University Press,
1993.

Whillock, Rita Kirk. "Dream Believers: The Unifying Visions and Competing
Values of Adherents to American Civil Religion." *Presidential Studies Quarterly*
24, no. 2 (1994): 375–88.

Whites, LeeAnn. *The Civil War as a Crisis in Gender: Augusta, Georgia, 1860–1890.*
Athens: University of Georgia Press, 1995.

Who's Who in the South and Southwest. Vol. 1. Chicago: Larkin, Roosevelt, and
Larkin, 1947.

Wiggins, Sarah Woolfolk. "The 'Pig Iron' Kelley Riot in Mobile, May 14, 1867."
Alabama Review 23, no. 1 (1970): 45–55.

Williams, Rhys H. "Constructing the Public Good: Social Movements and
Cultural Resources." *Social Problems* 42, no. 1 (1995): 124–44.

————. "Religion as Political Resource: Culture or Ideology?" *Journal for the Scientific Study of Religion* 35, no. 4 (1996): 368–78.

————. "Visions of the Good Society and the Religious Roots of American Political Culture." *Sociology of Religion* 60, no. 1 (1999): 1–34.

Williamson, Edmund C. *Florida Politics in the Gilded Age, 1877–1893*. Gainesville: University Presses of Florida, 1976.

————. "W. D. Chipley, West Florida's Mr. Railroad." *Florida Historical Quarterly* 25, no. 4 (1947): 335–63.

Wilmer, Richard H. *The Recent Past from a Southern Standpoint: Reminiscences of a Grandfather*. New York: Thomas Whittaker, 1887.

Wilson, Charles Reagan. *Baptized in Blood: The Religion of the Lost Cause, 1865–1920*. Athens: University of Georgia Press, 1980.

————. "Confederate Memorial Day." In *Encyclopedia of Southern Culture*, edited by Charles Reagan Wilson and William Ferris, 681. Chapel Hill: University of North Carolina Press, 1989.

Wilson, Richard L. "Sam Jones: An Apostle of the New South." *Georgia Historical Quarterly* 57, no. 4 (1973): 459–74.

Woocher, Jonathan S. *Sacred Survival: The Civil Religion of American Jews*. Bloomington: Indiana University Press, 1986.

Woodward, C. Vann. *Origins of the New South, 1877–1913*. Baton Rouge: Louisiana State University Press, 1951.

————. *Tom Watson: Agrarian Rebel*. New York: Macmillan, 1938.

Yrigoyen, Charles, Jr. "Haygood, Laura Askew." In *American National Biography*, edited by John A. Garraty and Mark C. Carnes, 407–8. New York: Oxford University Press, 1999.

Zietz, Robert J. *The Gates of Heaven: Congregation Sha'arai Shomayim the First 150 Years Mobile, Alabama 1844–1994*. Mobile, Ala.: Congregation Sha'arai Shomayim, 1994.

INDEX

Abernethy, Arthur T., 116
Adams, Henry Austin, 88–89
agriculture, 23–24
Alabama: Birmingham, 89–90,
   154–62; and Catholicism, 56–58,
   87–91, 154–62; and Judaism, 115,
   122–32, 166; and race, 56–58,
   166; and Wiregrass Gulf South,
   6–7. *See also* Mobile, Ala.
Albany, Ga.: and Catholicism, 160;
   and gender, 82–83, 94, 96, 98,
   101–2; and Judaism, 106–8, 117;
   and progress and redemption, 32;
   and race, 58; and Wiregrass Gulf
   South, 7, 9. *See also* Georgia
Allen, Edward, 12, 56–57, 87–91,
   154–55, 157–58
American Protective Association, 136
Anderson, Carl V., 152
anti-Catholicism, 29, 89–91, 121,
   134–38, 140–41, 144–54, 168;
   and Coyle affair, 154–62; *Menace*,
   141, 146, 152; and nativism, 12,
   135–38; and prohibition, 151; and
   race, 137–38. *See also* Catholicism

anti-Semitism, 107, 115–17, 121,
   129–30, 133; and nativism, 12,
   135–38; southern white Protestant
   responses to, 118, 121, 125. *See
   also* Judaism
Appleyard, T. J., 200n38
Arsenault, Raymond, 122
Ashburn, George W., 30–31
Atlanta, Ga., 1906 riots, 75–76, 93
Atlantic and Gulf Railroad, 9
Ayers, Edward, 19, 99, 176n5

Bacon, Milton E., 84–85
Bailey, Thomas P., 47–48
Baker, Ray Stannard, 68
Barrett, Nathanial, 155
Barton, Clara, 129
Beecher, Lyman, 168
Before Day clubs, 11, 67; in
   Milledgeville, Ga., 69–70;
   in Statesboro, Ga., 68–69;
   in Talbotton, Ga., 70–71; in
   Tallahassee, Fla., 71–75; in
   Thomasville, Ga., 71
Bellah, Robert, 3, 4–5, 6, 174n8

northerners: as assistants in rebuilding South, 21, 23, 43; perceptions
by, of South and race, 52–55. *See
also* carpetbagger; redemption
narrative

Oberdorfer, A. Leo, 129
Oklahoma Jewish Review, 131
O'Neal, Emmet, 161

Paine, Anna, 74
Palms, Clothilde, 27
Park, R. L., 139
Parker, Nelson, 152
Parsons, Talcott, 6
Partridge, Henry, 80
Pasco, Samuel, 27
Patriotic League of America, 131
Patten, Frank E., 144
Pensacola, Fla.: and Catholicism, 156;
and gender, 78, 93–94, 98–99;
and progress and redemption,
11, 22–23, 26–27, 29–33, 38; and
race, 50–52, 54–55, 59–60, 62–63,
68; and Wiregrass Gulf South, 7, 9.
See also Florida
Pensacola and Atlantic Railroad,
35
Pensacola Commercial, 33
Pensacola Daily Times, 28
Perry, Edward, 27
Persons, Henry, 70
Phagan, Mary, 121
Phelps, B. M., 146
Phelps, Wilbur, 141
Pierce, A. C., 139
Pius IX, 87

place problem, 11, 46, 60, 66; and
Catholicism, 55–58. *See also* blacks;
civil religion
Plant, Henry, 8
Plantevigne, John, 57
Pollard, Edward A., 15
Poole, W. Scott, 174n7
progressivism: and Catholicism, 88–
89; and Judaism, 106–7, 110–22,
133; and northern whites, 25–26;
and southern blacks, 58–62; and
southern whites, 15–17, 30–33, 40,
136–37; and "true womanhood,"
84, 85–86
prohibition and temperance, 11, 79,
93–95, 188n30; and anti-Catholicism, 150–53; and race, 51, 93–94;
and WCTU, 85–87, 93–94
Prohibition Party, 150
Proskauer, Adolph, 111, 115
Proskauer, Joseph, 115
Prosser, Gabriel, 67
public schools, 23
Pullen, Philip, 157

Quimby, Phineas P., 112

race, 11, 45–46; and Catholicism
11, 46, 55–58, 165–66; and civil
religious violence, 63–64; and civil
rights, 162, 165–67; and immigration, 136–37; and Judaism, 107,
166–67; and prohibition, 51, 93.
See also blacks; place problem;
white supremacy
railroads, 8–10, 31–33
Rawls, John, 38–39

Stewart, W. G., 64–66, 183n67, 184n70
Stockbridge, H. E., 6
Stone, Barton W., 164
Stout, Harry S., 14
Stowe, Harriet Beecher, 102
Swearingen, Van C., 121, 147
Sweeney, Charles, 156

Tallahassee, Fla.: and Catholicism, 134–35; and gender, 83, 86–87, 94; and Judaism, 119–20; and progress and redemption, 20, 22, 49, 52; and race, 55, 64–66, 71–75; and Wiregrass Gulf South, 7–8. *See also* Florida
Tate, Joseph, 159
Taylor, Fred, 142–43
Tepper, Sol, 166
Thomasville, Ga.: and gender, 83–84, 96–98, 102; and Judaism, 116–17; and progress and redemption, 19, 22, 24; and race, 47, 52–53, 60; and Wiregrass Gulf South, 7, 9. *See also* Georgia
Thompson, George F., 115
tourism, 33, 52
Trader, Ella K., 98
Trammell, Park, 97; and anti-Catholicism, 138, 140–41, 144; and Saint Augustine affair, 138–40; senatorial campaign of, 140–44
True Americans, 154, 155, 158. *See also* anti-Catholicism
Turnbull, Mary A., 92
Turner, Nat, 67–68

Umansky, Ellen M., 113
United Daughters of the Confederacy (UDC), 96–103

values, 6, 10; anti-Catholicism, 12–13, 135–38, 155; black freedom, 11, 46, 58–62; Catholics and religious liberty, 12–13, 134–35, 158; female devotion to family and society, 11–12, 79–95; female devotion to Lost Cause, 11–12, 95–103; Jewish unity and citizenship, 12, 108–12, 133; progress, 10–11, 16–18, 42–43; tradition, 10–11, 17–18; white supremacy, 47–58. *See also* civil religion
Vesey, Denmark, 67
Vincent, John H., 33, 34

Walker, David S., 19
Walker, Randi Jones, 4
Ward, George, 155
Washington, Booker T., 58, 59–60
Washington, F. E., 59
Watson, Tom, 121, 133, 141
Webb, Clive, 166
Welter, Barbara, 79
Wessolowsky, Charles, 108–10, 116
White, Annie, 98
White, Frank W., 58
White, Isaac, 75
white supremacy, 11, 45–48, 52–53, 68, 138, 165
Willard, Frances, 85
Williams, O. N., 146
Williams, Rhys, 3–4, 5, 174–75n17

Williams, Robert, 73
Wilmer, Richard H., 18, 20–21, 82, 176n7
Wilson, Charles Reagan, 2, 3, 82, 95–96, 176n7
Wilson, Woodrow, 110
Winthrop, John, 5
Wiregrass Gulf South, 6–10, 175n26; and Catholicism, 135, 141, 153, 163; and gender, 78–79, 91, 95–96; and Judaism, 107, 115, 117, 132–33; and progress and redemption, 26, 30, 42–44; and race, 46, 48, 55, 62, 65–66. *See also individual cities and states*
Witaker, H., 138
Woman's Christian Temperance Union (WCTU), 85–87, 93–94

women: and devotion as civil religious value, 79–81; and education, 84–85; and mission work, 92–93; during New South era, 80–81; and prohibition, 93–95; and purity, 81–83; and responses to woman's rights, 85, 104
Women's Missionary Society (WMS), 92
Woocher, Jonathan S., 192n8
Woodward, Alfred L., 86–87, 119–20, 136–37
Wright, T. T., 35

Young, Elijah Remer, 176n12
Young Female College, 176n12

Zimmerman, G. B., 52–53
Zinn, W. H., 161

THE NEW SOUTHERN STUDIES

*The Nation's Region: Southern Modernism,
Segregation, and U.S. Nationalism*
by Leigh Anne Duck

*Black Masculinity and the U.S. South:
From Uncle Tom to Gangsta*
by Riché Richardson

*Grounded Globalism: How the U.S. South
Embraces the World*
by James L. Peacock

*Disturbing Calculations: The Economics of Identity in
Postcolonial Southern Literature, 1912–2002*
by Melanie R. Benson

American Cinema and the Southern Imaginary
edited by Deborah E. Barker and Kathryn McKee

*Southern Civil Religions: Imagining the Good Society
in the Post-Reconstruction Era*
by Arthur J. Remillard

*Reconstructing the Native South: American Indian Literature
and the Lost Cause*
by Melanie Benson Taylor

CPSIA information can be obtained at www.ICGtesting.com
Printed in the USA
LVOW040945230712

291164LV00004B/20/P